Soul on Earth

a guide to

Living and Loving Your Human Life

Ruth L. Schwartz, Ph.D.

Soul on Earth

a guide to
Living and Loving
Your Human Life

Ruth L. Schwartz, Ph.D.

Six Directions Press

Six Directions Press
Oakland, California
ISBN: 978-0-61563-126-4
Copyright 2012 by Ruth L. Schwartz

Names of clients and identifying details have been changed.

Book design by Lisa DeSpain

Manufactured in the United States of America.

Library of Congress Cataloging-in-Publication Data
Schwartz, Ruth L.
Soul on Earth: A Guide to Living and Loving Your Human Life /
by Ruth L. Schwartz

TABLE OF CONTENTS

Section II

The Big Picture

Section III

Challenges on the Path

Section IV

Prayers and Intentions

With thanks to all of my teachers, in every form—
and with special gratitude to Isa,
who helped me open the door to transformation,
and to Michelle, soul kin and co-adventurer,
who keeps walking through it with me.

Introduction

There is happiness in the divine soul-temple within you. There is good-ness there, and loyalty, hope, courage, peace and joy.

— Paramahansa Yogananda

When I was a small child, each night I said a silent thank-you to everything I could see from my window—the lampposts and their shining lights, the trees with their solid bodies and moonlit shimmer of leaves, even the bicycles locked to their sturdy posts. When I blew out the candles on my birthday cakes, my wish was always the same: *Whatever is supposed to happen.* Although I grew up in a secular household and no one had ever talked to me about such things, somehow I sensed my place in the larger fabric of the world. In ways I couldn't speak of, I *knew* I was connected and held.

Yet that connection and holding didn't stop my father from molesting me; it didn't prevent my sister from cutting her arms with razor blades, starving herself, or becoming an addict; it didn't keep my mother out of a second abusive marriage. Nor did it teach me how to heal their pain, or my own. It only left me with a burning desire to understand. What was I—what were any of us—doing here? Why did people hurt so much? And what, if anything, could I do about it?

That drive to understand turned me into an observer and a listener. Wherever I went, people seemed to tell me their stories. "You should be a therapist," they often said, but I shuddered at the thought; I already felt burdened by hearing, seeing and sensing too much. Besides, I had no idea how to help. So I became a poet instead, using poetry to tap into the larger field of wisdom that seemed to me to hover just beyond, yet also somehow within, the forms and shapes of my life. In the words of poet Audre Lorde, I wrote to find out "what I didn't know I knew."

And it did often feel as if my poems knew more than I did. As I moved into adulthood, poetry helped me glimpse the beauty in what might otherwise have seemed wholly unbeautiful: the playful, vibrant young men I worked with who were dying of AIDS; the armless woman in the locker room, tugging her shirt on with her teeth; the frequent sounds of gunshots in the city streets; the intricate damage my lovers and I seemed to inflict on each other, despite our best intentions.

Yet as mental illness and addiction ravaged my family, and as my intimate relationships grew increasingly painful, the questions that had driven me since childhood became more urgent. Although poetry had taken me far, it was no longer enough; my heart was too broken. To heal it, I needed more direct access to that larger fabric I had sensed as a child.

My search led me in directions I would never have anticipated. Although I had always thought of myself as a fairly left-brain person, my skepticism gave way to awe during what turned out to be a four-year apprenticeship to a brilliant shamanic teacher and healer. As I became able to contact and trust my own sources of inner guidance, I learned how to heal damaging patterns that had plagued me all my life. I also developed an entirely new understanding of myself and my place in the universe. These changes made my life more purposeful and more free, more focused and more joyful than I could ever have imagined.

Eventually, compelled to share what I'd learned, I finally did become a therapist myself. I have spent the last decade working with individuals and couples in a transformational healing method I call *HeartMind Integration,* and have been overjoyed to witness and facilitate deep healing in hundreds of clients and students. I wrote this book in the hope of reaching many more people with the tools that have made such a difference to me, and to so many others I've known.

This is not a book about shamanism *per se,* although shamanic methods helped me to arrive at the understandings in these pages. Rather, it's about accessing the larger wisdom, compassion and guidance available to all of us, however we may experience and perceive it—and also about how to work with that larger part of ourselves in ways that help us change, heal and love our human lives. In addition to shamanism, this book draws on psychology, neuroscience, energetic and somatic healing, Buddhism, 12-step recovery, and other bodies of knowledge. The words and work of theologians, philosophers, healers, monks, scientists, nuns, spiritual teachers, poets and mystics are all included here. My own deepest influences have included mystical Christianity and Buddhism, with a bass note of 12-step program folk wisdom. In the spirit of the Zen Buddhist saying that cautions us not to confuse the finger pointing at the moon with the moon itself, I have intentionally tried to point with many different fingers. Within these pages I hope to create a conversation that is flexible and elastic enough to include you in it, whoever you are.

This book is both conceptual and pragmatic. It will teach you how to heal emotional wounds you might have believed you would have to live with forever; it will also offer you new understandings about the causes, nature and purpose of such wounds. I have also included a lot of deeply personal stories in these pages. I hope that reading about my errors and confusions will help you to better understand and forgive your own—and I also hope that this intimate glimpse of my process of transformation will help you see and feel more of what is possible for you. Whoever you are and whatever the shape of your struggles, you **do** have the capacity to turn your life toward joy.

When you understand that old hurts are encoded into us in the form of energy—and that energy, unlike matter, is infinitely changeable—it becomes easier to understand why we can transform whatever needs transforming *right now*, in the present moment. Healing doesn't require us to change the past, only the way we hold that past within ourselves. There are a great many ways to do that; I've tried to describe a range of approaches here in the hope that, no matter who you are, you will find some that fit for you.

All of my work is based on the understanding that the human self—the unique mix of physical traits, personality characteristics, gifts, fears and wounds that most of us think of as "us"—is only one part of who and what we are. Each of us is also a much larger being, an eternal self that exists beyond the boundaries of time and space. That larger self is radiant, whole and intact, unscarred by whatever damage our human selves have endured. When we partner with that wiser aspect of self, our human lives gain dimensionality, meaning and richness. We also become able to dissolve destructive patterns, connect more fully with ourselves and with life, and feel more joy. This book will show you how.

I encourage you first and foremost to use the material here to improve your own life. Inevitably, as you do so, the impact of that "personal healing" will radiate outward. Consciousness is contagious! Every step you take toward inner freedom and joy is also a contribution to a larger evolutionary process that benefits the human collective. As spiritual author Marianne Williamson says, "Personal transformation can and does have global effects. As we go, so goes the world, for the world is us. The revolution that will save the world is ultimately a personal one."

If we do not find ways to heal ourselves—if we "soldier on" in pain, alienation, anger and confusion—we not only cause harm to ourselves, but also to our species. If we allow internal "business as usual" to continue, we condemn ourselves and each other to the cycles of violence, confusion and destruction that human beings have enacted for millennia. These cycles have been with us for so long that some of us even believe that this kind of devastation is "the human condition." *It doesn't have to be this way.* This book will give you a path out of these cycles of suffering, and into a life lived in deep harmony with yourself, others, and the planet.

"Harmony" is a word my inner teachers use often. From their perspective, nothing is ever "good" or "bad," "right" or "wrong;" all things simply are as they are. Yet some things are more *harmonious,* more in concert with and supportive to the larger movement of love within us and beyond us, than others. Working with the principle of harmony helps us avoid the trap of judging ourselves when we realize we have done, said, thought or felt something that has created suffering. We can restore internal harmony instantly by accepting whatever *is*—which also means accepting ourselves, exactly as we are. Acceptance of what *is* is not resignation; it does not preclude the possibility of working with our whole beings toward inner and outer change. In fact, accepting what *is* actually *creates* the conditions for change.

In the much-quoted words of scientist Alfred Korzybski, "The map is not the territory." Although the territory of human life is far too vast to chart, my inner teachers have given me many useful maps. One such map takes the form of ten principles which can help us create and sustain inner and outer harmony. These are not "commandments" imposed by external authorities; nothing except our own well-being commands us to follow them. However, like all true divine rules, they become self-evident when we pay close attention.

⊙ Soul on Earth Principles

1. Our purpose on earth is to fulfill our inner design.

2. Joy is our best navigational aid.

3. Support from higher levels of consciousness is always available.

4. *What* we do matters much less than *why and how we do it.*

5. The "individual self" is a portal into the world.

6. Self-responsibility gives us power; blaming ourselves or others robs us of power.

7. The locus of power is always within us. We have the capacity to heal, shift or transform all that we feel and experience.

8. *Now* is the point of power. The past is never really past; if something affects us now, we can heal it now.

9. Saying Yes to life as it is creates the conditions for joy and change.

10. Love and compassion are the strongest forces in the universe.

Later chapters will explain each of these principles in much more detail, and also provide analogies, examples and context to help you integrate and make use of these principles in your daily life.

Section One, *The Why and How of Personal Transformation,* describes the current structure of human consciousness, explains why and how we have come to feel so separate from one another and from ourselves, and then shows you how to leave this painful illusion behind. This section is packed with tools to facilitate personal healing and transformation. You'll learn how to form relationships with compassionate inner teachers; engage the technologies of intention and prayer; access archetypal wisdom and healing through the tool of the shamanic journey; restore inner wholeness through the art of soul retrieval; identify and release destructive patterns of thought and emotion; open to the transformational medicine of compassion; connect with other human beings in ways that truly support your growth and evolution, and more. In the process, you'll also learn why self-responsibility is crucial to your healing—even as you connect and receive support from forces far larger than your personal self.

Section Two, *The Big Picture,* tackles some of the most far-reaching questions people have ever asked about our lives on earth. It will teach you about your soul's purpose, the relationship between your human self and your soul, the evolutionary mandate of choice, the true nature and role of service, and the spiritual significance of joy. It also explains why our lives contain hardship and pain, and how to mine the gifts and lessons available from such difficult experiences. This section will help you understand your individual place in the larger tapestry of reality, an understanding which can bring about a deep soul-level ease even as you recognize the inevitability of ongoing challenge in your human life.

Section Three, *Challenges on the Path,* explores the deeper purpose of many challenging aspects of life, including intimate relationships, sexuality, physical pain, illness, doubt, fear, power and crisis. The material in this section will help you clarify your relationship to romantic partnership, heal the distortions at the root of physical illness, and navigate states of doubt and fear with greater ease. You'll also learn how to harmoniously embrace your own power, how to allow crises to do their real work in your life, and how and why everything matters, even though nothing matters in the ways we tend to think.

Section Four, *Intentions and Prayers*, contains powerful energetic medicine in the form of twenty-one prayers and statements of intention. Regular work with intention and prayer is a gentle yet highly effective way to engender change. This section can help you deepen your appreciation for life, free yourself from energetic enmeshments, cultivate transformational states like receptivity, forgiveness, compassion and gratitude—and also offers a jumping-off point for composing your own statements of intention and prayers, a powerful healing practice in its own right.

As you read through the book, you may notice that it contains a number of voices and tones. In some chapters I speak as one human being to another; in others, the wiser, more detached voice of my inner teachers takes center stage. Because all of us operate on many frequencies at once, from the rational and cognitive to the intuitive and mystical, I hope that this approach will open more doorways of understanding within you. As you pass through those doorways, you may feel a sense of recognition, as if you're re-encountering information that some part of you already knew—because, in fact, you are! Any knowledge that comes to me from inner sources is also available to you.

Yet parts of this book may feel difficult for you to accept or to believe; that's okay, too. There are many ways to describe certain truths, and many different things that are true at the same time. I hope you'll read these pages with an openness to being provoked, surprised, challenged and stretched. At the same time, I encourage you to heed the invitation offered by 12-step recovery programs: "Take what you like, and leave the rest." As the Tao Te Ching tells us, "The Tao that can be spoken is not the true Tao." Although words are the necessary building-blocks of books, the fullness of truth can never be captured in words. Therefore, my hope is that the words in this book will serve as signposts, arrows, maps and trailheads, helping you to move beyond these pages and into personal contact with your own deepest sources of guidance.

Ruth L. Schwartz, Ph.D.
Oakland, California, June 2012

I

The Why and How of Personal Transformation

1

How Our Consciousness is Changing, and Why it Must

When faced with a radical crisis, when the old way of being in the world, of interacting with each other and the realm of nature, doesn't work any more, when survival is threatened by seemingly insurmountable problems, an individual life-form—or a species—will either die or become extinct, or rise above the limitation of its condition through an evolutionary leap.

- Eckhart Tolle

During our time on planet earth, human beings have proven ourselves to be a smart, resourceful and creative species—yet our emotional and spiritual development has lagged far behind our intellectual and technological prowess. Over two thousand years have passed since Jesus told us to love our neighbors and enemies as ourselves, and as a group, we've made little headway. In fact, we seem instead to have added ourselves to the list of those we struggle to love. This way of being—and its myriad ramifications—have brought us to the crisis point to which Tolle refers.

Both as individuals and as societies, we have repeatedly done terrible things to ourselves, each other, and the earth. As Tolle points out in *A New Earth*, if the history of humanity were the history of a single individual, that person would be diagnosed criminally insane. And since this insanity has recurred, albeit in different forms, in every human time, place and culture, it's safe to say that it won't end without a major shift in consciousness.

Now, many inner and outer signs indicate that we may be on the brink of that shift. As economies falter, climate change grows more extreme, and our individual lives offer up their endless array of challenges, many of us

19

are finding that our old ways of being are no longer available, effective or sustainable. Crisis is a difficult but effective portal to transformation. When systems and beliefs we had relied on fail us, we feel disoriented, angry or terrified. Yet at the same time, increasing numbers of people are accessing deep levels of consciousness, wisdom and healing. These are the conditions that can prepare us for an evolutionary leap.

If we are to avoid destroying ourselves and the planet, we must shift from a consciousness of separation into a profound awareness of our connection to all of life. Yet, although many of us intellectually understand the importance of this shift, it continues to elude us. To understand why this change in consciousness is both possible and difficult, we must look at the way human consciousness is currently configured, how that affects us, and what possibilities it offers us for transformation.

The objective reality is that, like all other species on earth, human beings are part of a vast, interconnected web of support. Life works constantly and synergistically on our behalf, aiding us in myriad seen and unseen ways; each second of our existence is made possible by vast numbers of other life forms, and supports other life forms in turn. Even the bodies we think of as our own provide homes for billions of mitochondria and bacteria, and in turn these living organisms help keep us metabolically balanced. Every one of us is able to live the lives we live because of the past and present labor of millions of other people, as well as many thousands of products created or extracted from animals, plants, earth and sea.

So why do we so often feel isolated, lost or disconnected? We have this experience—we experience this illusion—because of the individuated structure of our consciousness, the psychic apparatus through which we perceive ourselves and our world. Albert Einstein explained it this way: "A human being is a part of the whole... [yet] experiences himself (sic), his thoughts and feelings as something separated from the rest, a kind of optical delusion of his consciousness. This delusion is a kind of prison for us, restricting us to our personal desires and to affection for a few persons nearest to us. Our task must be to free ourselves from this prison by widening our circle of compassion to embrace all living creatures and the whole of nature in its beauty."

Depending on how we look at it, individuated consciousness is a blessing or a curse, a devastating punishment or an amazing opportunity. Because we experience ourselves as separate from others and from life, we suffer and cause harm. Yet because we experience ourselves as separate from others and from life, we also have the ability—in fact, the mandate—to make individual choices. *Used wisely, this process of choice-making can eradicate our suffering.* If you include our thoughts and our words, as well as our actions, each of us makes thousands of choices each day. And with every one of those choices, we either align ourselves more fully with the energies of love and compassion—or energize within ourselves the forces of fear, separation and hatred.

Is this starting to sound a bit like Star Wars? There's a good reason for that! The Star Wars movies, like so many of the tales we tell as a species, center on this archetypal conflict and opportunity. The battle between "light" and "dark" that is so often dramatized on our screens is also alive within each of us, in each moment.

If we could viscerally *feel* the truth of our connection to other human beings, other species, and the earth, we would automatically think, act and speak with love and compassion. If we experienced everyone and everything around us as part of "self" rather than as "other"—and if we had not been warped in ways that turned us against ourselves—then adherence to the "Golden Rule," treating others as we wish to be treated, would not be a lofty goal, but an obvious and logical way to live. After all, when you have a blister on your foot, your hands automatically make themselves available to tend to it, because both feet and hands know themselves to be part of the same body. Yet this palpable experience of oneness remains difficult for human beings to access, due to the "optical delusion" Einstein described—and since we do not consistently *feel* that connection, few of us regularly affirm it with our choices .

Whether true or apocryphal, an unattributed story recently circulated on Facebook offers a great example of what human life might look like if we freed ourselves from the prison of individuated consciousness:

An anthropologist proposed a game to the kids in an African tribe. He put a basket full of fruit near a tree and told the kids that whoever got there first would get to eat the fruit. When he told them to run, they all took each other's hands and ran together, then sat together enjoying their treats. When he asked them why they had run like that rather than competing for the fruits so that one of them could eat them all, they said, "Ubuntu—how can one of us be happy if all the other ones are sad?"

Even within our current consciousness, most of us have briefly tasted the joy of this kind of connection. When we "fall in love," we often experience such an upwelling of generosity that we genuinely care as much for our lover's well-being as for our own. Inevitably, however, our love object disappoints us, and the walls of separation crash back down.

Becoming a parent may affect us similarly; in fact, many people long to have children in order to be lifted beyond the confines of the narrow, separate self. Yet the thinning of the boundary of self that can occur between parents and children—or, in some cases, between other family, tribe or group members—usually remains highly specific. Social psychologists call this phenomenon "parochial altruism." Rather than helping us to connect more deeply to all other things and beings, our devotion to any specific "us" often leads us to define some other group even more firmly as *other*, "not us," and whatever or whomever we identify as "not us" becomes a potential enemy. As human consciousness has grown more complex, we have fractured internally, increasingly leading us to experience an "us" and a "not us" *even inside ourselves.*

Most human suffering is caused by these patterns of disconnection, all of which are based on the illusion that we are wholly separate from one another. Caught in this illusion, we cannot possibly see life accurately. We form damaging, distorted beliefs, and these beliefs in turn create an energetic matrix within us and around us, a kind of magnetic field which determines what we are able to see and experience. Because of this, *whatever we believe appears to us to be proven true.*

There are many ways to understand how and why this occurs. The psychological term *projective identification* describes one part of this phenomenon, explaining that we unconsciously act in ways that ensure that those around us will behave as we expect them to. Neuroscientists have found that our brains are programmed to register and amplify only stimuli that *support what we already believe*, while failing to perceive or record evidence to the contrary. Our habitual thoughts actually carve physiological tracks in our brains, predisposing us to continue to think and experience life along those tracks.

Neurological research also indicates that the oldest component of our brain, often called the "reptilian" brain, is specifically designed to keep us from harm by responding to potential threats, while ignoring all other input. In the words of psychologist Robert Weisz, "This hypersensitivity to threat amounts to what I call 'the imprisonment of the mind'—a state in which the mind is primed to perceive threat, is continually assaulted by and frozen in the past, and cannot conceive of a self that is free of physical and emotional pain."

Although other parts of our brains do have access to different perceptions, our individuated consciousness often leads us to identify with this primitive response rather than override it. As a result, many of us live much of our lives in defensive or offensive postures, alternately or simultaneously judging and fighting against ourselves, others, God or life.

This is a bleak way to live. It leads to despair, depression and anxiety, which we as a species now frequently medicate with myriad legal and illegal substances and addictive behaviors. These addictions and compulsions further separate us from ourselves and each other, causing even greater suffering. Our suffering and alienation produce suicide, homicide, and every imaginable form of oppression and abuse, which we perpetrate against ourselves, those we experience as "other," and even those whom we believe we love.

And yet there is an entirely different option available to us as a species—not only available, in fact, but increasingly accessible. All of this devastation stems from a single basic error in perception, the delusion that leads us to perceive ourselves as separate from one another and from life. *As we correct this error in perception and begin to viscerally experience the truth of our connection to one another and to all other life forms, everything changes.* We become able to live in joy rather than despair, and to care for ourselves, each other, other species and the planet in ways that both reflect and deepen our sense of connection and love. The very same individuated consciousness that has nearly destroyed us as a species also offers each one of us a way out—or rather, a way *in* to a more accurate understanding of who and what we really are. And all of us have the opportunity to choose this shift in perception, moment by moment, thought by thought, action by action, in every sphere and aspect of our lives.

This shift in consciousness is not "enlightenment" in the traditional sense; it doesn't require us to catapult completely and permanently out of identification with our individual human selves. It's more like what neo-enlightenment teacher Craig Hamilton calls *integral enlightenment,* a state in which we retain our identity as individuals, yet also consciously connect and identify with the larger aspects of ourselves. Rather than giving up our human personalities and merging into the All, we become able to experience the individual self as a sphere of influence, a tool or vessel we can live both within and beyond. Because we viscerally feel our connection to each other and to life, we need never suffer from a sense of isolation and separation. Yet because we still experience ourselves as "individuals," we can continue to make our own unique contributions to the unfolding of human consciousness.

This consciousness shift is not merely a cognitive process. Because the intellect is only a small part of who and what we are, intellectual understanding alone does very little to change our lives. We are complex, multifaceted beings, made up of many layers of energetic, emotional and somatic experience. Each of us contains strata of personal, familial, ancestral and collective wounding, marbled through us like minerals through rock. In order to make deep change possible, we have to heal, clear or release that residue of trauma.

Life is synergistic; as we heal, it becomes easier for us to connect with higher consciousness, and as we connect more fully with higher consciousness, we become more able to heal. In the process, we build transformational momentum, not only for ourselves but for our species. Each instance of "personal" healing carves new pathways in the collective field of human consciousness, making it easier for others to access the same shifts.

Life on the earth plane, life in a physical body, will always be challenging. My inner teachers tell me that from the soul's perspective, life is actually *designed* to be challenging. These challenges offer us vast numbers of choices and creative opportunities, each of which can help us explore, grow and learn. And when we understand the purpose of these challenges and access the abundance of tools and support available to us, we can dwell in peace and gratitude, even as we confront inner and outer tumult.

That may sound far-fetched, I know. If you're trapped in a small, dim corner of consciousness right now, it may be very hard to imagine the light and connection that are available to you. Or perhaps you've sometimes glimpsed that expanded perspective, and then lost touch with it again. The pain of feeling lost, found, and then lost again is a human experience so common, so archetypal, that it may even be a necessary part of our developmental arc. Nonetheless, as we grow in awareness we can get *less* lost, less of the time, and emerge more fully and more frequently into clarity and light.

So whoever you are, and wherever you are on your evolutionary journey, I hope you'll keep reading. It's fine if you feel doubtful or skeptical. Wherever you are, I've been there, too. And I'm quite certain that somewhere, sometime, some part of you has also experienced the much more radiant inner landscape I'm describing. How can I be so sure? Because we're separate, on one level of reality, but we're also not separate at all.

Here is a story—one of many I could tell—about a time when I felt caught in one such dim corner of my own psyche.

Years ago, before I had consciously embarked on any sort of healing or spiritual journey, I took a cross-country trip with Jim, my boyfriend of a few months. I was madly in love with Jim, and felt thrilled at the thought of all those days in the car together.

Our first few days were sweet and intimate. Then, halfway across the country, we spent Thanksgiving with Jim's family. When we got back on the road, Jim was moody, withdrawn and silent—and his silence and energetic absence precipitated truly awful feelings in me, feelings I had no idea what to do with.

Intellectually, I recognized that Jim's silence most likely had nothing to do with me. The witnessing part of me couldn't understand why I felt so devastated. Yet the feelings wouldn't shift, and my efforts to draw him out only pushed him further away. The worse I felt, the more he distanced himself. I grew panicky; my need for contact and reassurance felt truly desperate.

With a bit of time alone, I might have regained my equilibrium. Spending time in nature, walking and journaling were tools I had already used to help me through hard times. When all else failed, I had also used Valium or alcohol to numb difficult feelings. But now I couldn't do any of that. Instead, I was trapped with Jim in the small space of a car, with days of driving still ahead of us.

Having no other escape, my devastation began to shift to anger. Why couldn't Jim just make eye contact, hug me and connect with me, even for a few minutes? What would be so hard about that? My desires were perfectly reasonable, I told myself—and him. Naturally, this caused him to pull even further into himself. As we drove on, with the silence between us growing increasingly embittered and hostile, I wanted to be anywhere in the world but in that car. Sitting beside someone so unreachable made me feel as if I shouldn't exist.

The next few days passed largely in painful silence, interrupted only by the times when I tried to connect with Jim, and he pushed me away. The worst moment was when I tried to kiss him, and he turned his face from me. "I can't," he said. I didn't understand what he meant. What had happened to our love?

When I look back now on those two young people, trapped not only in a car but in an emotional dynamic they couldn't understand or work through, my heart aches for both of them. At the same time, I see that that experience was part of what spurred my quest for consciousness and healing. I knew that something felt very, very wrong—though at the time, I had no idea what it was.

Clearly, my pain was caused by a feeling of disconnection. But during that trip, I believed that the problem was my disconnection from Jim. I saw him as the one causing my distress, and believed he was the only one who could alleviate it.

I didn't understand the wounds playing themselves out between us, or within me; I had no idea how to compassionately connect with the part of me that felt so terrified and alone. I had never heard of the healing technique shamans call "soul retrieval," which could restore my sense of wholeness and help me to feel intact, no matter what happened with Jim or with anyone else. I didn't know that it was possible to energetically release damaging beliefs (like the belief that I shouldn't exist) from my body and psyche. I also didn't realize that if I took responsibility for my own wounds and began to heal them, I would be able to form relationships with people with similar levels of self-responsibility and healing, making possible an entirely different level of intimacy.

In short, I had no idea that the lasting solution to my pain had nothing to do with anyone else's actions or inactions. The locus of power lay within me.

The young woman in that car didn't know how to take responsibility for her own emotions. She didn't understand that the man beside her was merely triggering pain that had lodged in her a very long time before—or that, even beyond her own specific history, the real source of pain was her experience of individuated consciousness. She had no idea, then, how to connect with compassionate forces larger than her small, wounded human self—forces that could help her heal that small self, while also giving her a much broader, deeper understanding of human existence. And because she didn't know these things, she caused herself a great deal of pain—and also deeply hurt the people who tried to love her, and those she tried to love.

It took me years, and a lot of false starts, to find my way through these and other painful thickets. My hope is that this book will help speed up that process for you.

After I wrote these words, I left the rental cabin where I've been staying for the week and took a walk on a country road at dusk. A flock of wild turkeys flared up in front of me, and I stopped to enjoy the small wind their wings had made. Frogs were singing their frog-songs from the ditches in every direction. Such small beings, such loud voices! I love hearing so many of them, but seeing so few. I spied a patch of blooming narcissus across the road, walked over to it, and squatted down to smell its fragrant blossoms. Then I picked one flower to carry with me. Someone must have planted these bulbs long ago, or perhaps they spread on their own from a patch planted somewhere else; life has a way of doing that. Quail startled before me as I walked; trees leaned over me, rustling. When I reached the pond, I noticed that a bufflehead duck had arrived to keep company with the American Coot already in residence. My host had told me that the coot had been alone for weeks, so I was glad he would be alone no longer. I don't know if those two types of water-birds share a common language, but at least to my human eyes they looked at home together, paddling around the pond.

The world is still alive all around us and within us, still vibrant, blooming and beautiful in spite of all of the terrible damage we have suffered and caused. And each of us still has the capacity to sense and respond to this beauty and aliveness. In the words of psychologist James Hillman, "Soul is born in beauty, and feeds on beauty, and requires beauty for its life." We can draw from it strength and inspiration for the journey ahead.

2

Understanding the Physical and Non-Physical Worlds

No journey carries one far unless, as it extends into the world around us, it goes an equal distance into the world within.

– Lillian Smith

As we have already seen, the physical world is a vast network of synergy, interdependence and connection. For instance, I am typing these words on a laptop computer, a device invented by people using tools and knowledge amassed by millions of other people who came before them. After it was invented and designed, my laptop was assembled by people in a factory somewhere—a factory built by other people, using materials extracted and refined by other people, using machinery created by other people, which was made of materials that had been extracted and refined by other people before being assembled… and so on. And that's just the *making* of my laptop! If I think about how this laptop came to be in my hands—packaged, transported, and sold to me by other people—or how the chair I'm sitting on came to be, and to be in my house—or how the cup of tea I'm sipping from was created, how the tea itself was planted and harvested and packaged and shipped, how I boiled the water for the tea in a teapot which was… Well, you get the picture.

We are physically connected to other human beings, and in fact, to all of human history, in every instant and in every aspect of our lives. And of course, we are also connected to the larger physical world, the earth and the sea, the plants, animals and minerals, the sun, sky, rain and wind, and everything else which surrounds us. Each of those natural elements contributes to our lives in myriad daily ways, seen and unseen.

Yet the physical world is only a reflection of, or a window into, a much larger non-physical realm to which we are also inextricably connected. We might understand the physical as a hologram of the non-physical, a tiny, tangible representation of the vast, multidimensional universe we inhabit and are supported by.

Human beings in every time, place and culture have been aware of this unseen realm, which shamans call "non-ordinary reality" or "non-physical reality." Every spiritual and religious tradition acknowledges the existence of non-physical phenomena. In fact, spiritual traditions exist for the express purpose of guiding and supporting the non-physical aspect of our being we call *the spirit*.

Yet contemporary Western culture has a rather confusing relationship to the physical and non-physical aspects of self. On the one hand, we tend to believe that we *are* our bodies, or are completely contained within our bodies—since our bodies are the only parts of us that we can physically see, hear, smell, taste and touch. On the other hand, we experience our internal non-physical matter—our memories, longings, hopes, dreams and fears—as quintessentially "us," yet we lack tools for working with this aspect of our being.

From the time we were very young, we were taught to manage, manipulate and impact our physical lives—for instance, to dress ourselves, clean our rooms, and move physical objects around. Yet few of us were ever taught how to move around, shift, transform or clean our desires, beliefs and emotions. Although much of our actual lived experience takes place within the non-physical self, we are largely ignorant about how to cultivate and maintain non-physical well-being.

For instance, when we are in non-physical pain—perhaps sad, lonely, angry or emotionally hurt—most of us have only physical means at our disposal for working with that pain. Anyone who has ever taken a tranquilizer or an alcoholic drink knows that physical interventions can impact non-physical states. Yet these interventions can't resolve our non-physical pain at its source; in fact, most often they simply create new problems.

You've probably already discovered that the old maxim, "Time heals all wounds," isn't really true. Although non-physical wounds may grow the emotional equivalent of scabs, life inevitably brings circumstances that rip off those scabs, often leaving us with pain or anger even more intense than before. As individuals and as a species, we urgently need more understanding about how to work with our non-physical wounds.

Fortunately, there are tremendous non-physical resources available to us. And despite the fact that contemporary mainstream Western culture doesn't acknowledge their existence, most of us have already experienced at least some of them. For instance, as children, many of us had "imaginary friends." When we understand non-physical reality, we realize that these friends were *real,* though not physical. Because children have not yet been fully socialized to disbelieve in non-physical phenomena, they tend to have many experiences and perceptions of non-physical reality, and are more likely than adults to see, hear or sense angels, spirits, ghosts and inner teachers.

And despite our socialization, people of all ages feel the presence of God, angels, spirit guides, or other divine or discarnate beings. In fact, many well-known artists, writers, musicians, technological innovators and scientists have experienced their creations or ideas being given to them by unseen forces or teachers. The legendary psychologist Carl Jung developed many of his theories through conversations with a non-physical guide he called Philemon. Novelist and memoirist Isabel Allende describes her writing process by saying, "I feel that there's a dark space, and I go into that dark space where the story is… it's like going into another world." And singer-songwriter Joan Baez admits, "It seems to me that those songs that have been any good, I have nothing much to do with the writing of them. The words have just crawled down my sleeve and come out on the page."

In addition to creative inspiration, contact with the non-physical realm can take many forms. Some people get messages from dreams, have psychic visions, or feel guided by "gut feelings" or intuition. Some sense the presence of dead loved ones. Some find themselves able to tune into the different qualities of energy in physical places or things. Some practice Reiki or other forms of energy medicine, using their hands and the power of their intention to bring healing energies from the non-physical realm into the physical. Some have had near-death or out-of-body experiences which have given them glimpses of the realities beyond physical life. Some have experienced moments of divine intervention, or glimpses of the larger tapestry of reality—even in the most seemingly unlikely circumstances. For instance, psychologist and researcher Richard Tedeschi recounts the experience of a patient of his, a former military pilot whose helicopter had been shot down in Vietnam. "As he fell from the sky in the midst of gunfire and explosions, a peace came over him. He saw the jungle around him, and it was beautiful. He felt connected to everyone, even enemy soldiers."

Every one of these experiences involves an interaction with non-physical reality. Yet due to the cultural bias against acknowledging these realms, much less working with them, many of us have shut down—or resisted developing—our capacity to perceive and interact with non-physical phenomena. We may fear "going crazy," or being seen as crazy, if we acknowledge perceptions and experiences that fall outside the narrow confines of what shamans call "consensus reality." If we grew up in a religious context, we may even have been told that such perceptions were "the work of the devil." Tragically, these fears and social proscriptions keep us from fully accessing the most powerful sources of support, love, wisdom, compassion and healing available to us.

Yet this is changing. Many people who never imagined that they would be able to contact non-physical guides and teachers are discovering that they can do so; I am one such person. Brief or sustained "awakening" experiences—in which, like Tedeschi's patient, we viscerally feel our connection to all of life—are becoming more common. For some people, like spiritual teachers Eckhart Tolle and Byron Katie, both of whom "awakened" to enlightenment out of states of profound depression, these openings in consciousness create unlikely new vocations. Edgar Mitchell, one of the original Apollo astronauts, experienced such an awakening on his way back to Earth; it led him to found the Institute of Noetic Sciences, an organization that aims to "bring objective scientific tools and techniques together with subjective inner knowing to study the full range of human experiences." And in less dramatic yet equally profound ways, increasing numbers of people are using tools like meditation, yoga, Tai Chi and Qi Gong—all of which acknowledge and work with non-physical aspects of the being—to access states of peace, inner balance and harmony, as well as other kinds of healing.

Whoever you are, you, too, can access the support of wise, loving and compassionate non-physical teachers and energies. If one method, approach or paradigm doesn't work for you, another will. Skepticism is no barrier; I have helped many people who "weren't sure what they believed" or "didn't believe" connect with inner guidance, or with their larger selves, in one form or another. Although this book will describe some of the specific practices I have found helpful, there are hundreds of other books, courses and methods available, as well. The most important thing for you to know is this: whoever you are and wherever you find yourself on your life's trajectory, there *are* trust-worthy, compassionate, wise and benevolent non-physical beings, forces and energies who can help you shift your consciousness, grow and heal.

My first conscious contact with non-physical teachers took place when I was four years old, lying awake on my nursery school cot one afternoon. I was visited by three beings who told or showed me what I was here to do with my life—but afterward, although I never forgot the visit, I was unable to remember exactly what they had shown me.

This experience affected me profoundly. Even as a small child, I understood that it had taken place on a level of reality different from the reality the people around me were talking about, so I told no one about it until I was in my twenties. Keeping this secret was difficult, and it left me with many conflicting emotions. On the one hand, it was exciting and comforting to know that my life had a larger purpose; on the other hand it filled me with confusion and dread. I didn't know whether I wanted to do whatever it was that I was supposed to do, much less whether I would be able to do it—especially since I didn't even remember what it was!

Decades later, it was the memory of that early visit that led me to study hyp-notherapy and shamanic journeying. Through journeying, I re-established con-tact with those beings, and also developed relationships with other non-physical teachers. Yet I was still very surprised when, several years later, I found myself hearing an inner voice which told me very matter-of-factly where I was on-target and what I needed to do in a difficult life situation.

I knew immediately that this voice was distinct from my ordinary levels of thought. It was more certain than I was, but its certainty wasn't narrow; it re-sponded with good humor, even when I argued with it. And I did argue, because what it was saying was not what I had wanted to hear! It took several weeks before I realized that rather than argue, I should investigate who or what this voice was, and what else it might be able to tell me. I soon realized that I was speaking with a very wise guide, what some would call an "ascended master."

Although I had heard of channeling and had read some channeled books, I would never, ever have imagined that I would become a channel myself. At first, I wondered if I was crazy. Next, I wondered if other people would think I was crazy. Finally, I remembered that during my many years of writing poetry, I had often felt that my poems "knew more than I did." I suddenly wondered just where I had thought that wisdom was coming from!

Once I finally opened to the experience of speaking to this new guide, I asked "him" (he sounded male to me, though of course, without a body there is no gender) many questions about how to understand and work with our contact. Here is a transcript of part of that conversation.

Me: *Tell me about who you are, in relation to Seth, or the Pathwork Guide, or the other beings that people are channeling in public these days.*

Guide: [Amused.] Are you asking for my curriculum vitae? ... There are many of us who can speak from our plane to yours. We sound similar in tone because we share a frequency. In your terms, I am not the "same" being as Seth or the Pathwork Guide. You might call them my colleagues or even [amused] my "elders." Those classifications are not important to us here. We do not conceive of ourselves as "separate" in the way you conceive of yourselves and us. We are more like funnels which bring down the contents of the heavens; one funnel does not compare itself to another and say, *I am wider, thinner, older, younger.* We are each transmitting our portion of the heavens downward (in a manner of speaking. This is not literal, of course. It would be just as accurate to say inward, or outward, or upward), whenever, however and wherever we can. We are always—not looking for, exactly, but responsive to openings. Where there is an opening, one of us finds it and begins to come through. Some openings are, of course, wider, more developed, more sustainable than others.

Me: *Why do you seem "male" to me?*

Guide: The energetic quality of the vibration we are able to send is most often read as "male" on your plane. On our plane, gender as you know it does not exist. On yours, you are unable to refrain from categorizing beings in these terms.

Beyond all of these specifics, you are asking whether you can trust this phenomenon, and trust "me"—whether this is "real." Yet there is much that cannot be explained in this way, in words, to the satisfaction of your mind. As a poet you learned that everything you ever wrote was a translation, a more or less crude approximation. Words are a very imperfect medium. Sometimes they carry energy almost in spite of themselves (of course they do not have "selves," that is a figure of speech—do you see what I mean?) This kind of contact is also terribly inexact.

You might wonder whether we on our level enjoy the challenge of that in some way, as you have enjoyed the challenge of poetry. It is not exactly like that. It is more like water flowing wherever it can, even into the tiniest crevices. It does not discriminate and prefer places into which it can flow more easily, nor does it seek out the challenges of tightly closed places. It simply flows. That is a better image for how we function on this plane.

Me: *Do you have a name? Or, how should I talk about you or describe you to other people?*

Guide: If you must give me a name, you can say I am a voice of the six directions. It must be "a" voice, not "the" voice. There are many others who speak from this vantage point. Some have chosen to give themselves other names. Yet there is a way in which a name constricts the energy flow. A name sets up expectations, associations. It is unavoidable. Humans use names to codify, categorize, compartmentalize. "A voice of the six directions" is not a name; it is a description of my location and orientation. That will have to do.

Me: *Are there limits to the kind of information or knowledge I can receive through you?*

Guide: [Amused.] Are you asking whether *I* have limits, or whether *you* have limits? Theoretically, any knowledge in existence could be passed through a channel such as this one. In practical terms, though, we are limited by your vocabulary, your conceptual framework, and your interests. There are only certain types of knowledge that truly excite you, that feel valuable and relevant to you. Because a *love of knowing* is one of the conditions which keeps the channel open, it would be difficult for you to bring through material of little interest to you. Of course, it would also be unnecessarily cumbersome, like slurping tea from the surface of the table rather than sipping from your cup.

Me: *Where will it lead, this talking to you?*

Guide: You seek to know. This will lead to deeper knowing.

Me: *I am afraid that this talking to you will take me away from life.*

Guide: That fear is based on a misperception of what "life" is. As you know, life is not the outer shell. That would be like saying that your skin is you, and that spending time with your inner organs would take you away from your "self." Just as you have a physical and a nonphysical "body," so too does life. By talking to me you are *in* the nonphysical body of life. You are more deeply in life than you are the rest of the time, when you live on the crust—except sometimes during deep work with clients or life-changing conversations with friends. In those experiences there is contact with both the physical and nonphysical bodies of life. Your life is not that thing that happens on the outside, any more than your clothes are you. They are of you, you chose them, they hold your energy,

Me: *Could everyone do this? What allows or prevents it?*

Guide: One must be comfortable with stillness. Most in your culture are completely unaccustomed to the receptive inner posture. However, many people could receive much more information in this way than they currently do. One must have time in one's life. This process can be slow at first, and tiring. One must be willing to let judgments and doubts slide to the side—they do not need to be absent, but if they take up too much space the contact will not be possible. One must sincerely want to know. It cannot be a "party trick." One must be filled with joy by the knowing. At the same time, one must be willing to dwell in not-knowing. Too much certainty interferes just as surely as too much doubt. Those are the conditions.

As my guide says, I have always "sought to know"—yet until I studied shamanism, which gave me a sense of comfort with non-physical reality, I was unable or unwilling to hear my guide. Fear has led many of my students and clients to shut down their own ability to contact inner guidance, rather than developing it. For that reason, a big part of my work involves helping people learn to recognize, trust and work with the higher-consciousness contact they already have.

3

Accessing Higher Consciousness

You can't solve a problem from the same level of thinking with which you created it.

– Albert Einstein

When we wish to transform our own psyches and consciousness, we encounter the truth of Einstein's words. The wounded, distorted, limited parts of us cannot, by themselves, heal our wounds, correct our distortions, or dissolve our limits. Fortunately, all of us, like Einstein, have access to higher levels of being and thinking, resources that can help us heal and transform.

Actually, shifting non-physical patterns is not difficult, and doesn't have to take a long time. What usually takes much longer is the process of becoming *emotionally ready and willing* to experience this level of change. Life helps us get there, of course, by bringing us the same pain again and again, until, as they say in 12-step programs, "we get sick and tired of being sick and tired." Crises help us by increasing the pressure, forcing us to internal tipping-points. But if we wish to move more quickly and less painfully toward growth and healing, it is essential to call on higher consciousness for assistance.

What is "higher consciousness"? There are many ways to define or describe it, but its essence cannot really be captured in words. It is *us,* on a larger level; it knows us as intimately as we know ourselves. (Actually, it knows us much better than we know ourselves.) It is also larger than us, in the sense that it is not limited or scarred by the wounds and distortions that scar and limit us. It is the timeless, essential aspect of us, which is always whole. It is an aspect of the non-physical world that contains such radiant light, such deep wisdom, such profound compassion and such vast creativity that it truly does not fit into the narrow confines offered by language. People have called it by many names, including the name God.

Here is the explanation my guide has offered.

Understanding Higher Consciousness

The place of higher consciousness is a place where all is held. Each of the six directions, the primal energy fields which together comprise the universe, brings itself to this place and contributes its own particular essence, qualities, characteristics and gifts.

Everything and everyone is always held within this place. Wherever you are, you're always at the center of six directions. But when you know that you are there—when you allow yourself to be conscious of how you are held—then you can make full and conscious use of all the offerings and perspectives available to you. And when you are resisting none of them, when you can welcome each one with its particular brilliance, then you are at the heart of life itself.

All of you have already experienced this place; all of you carry the memory and knowledge of it somewhere within you. That is why you are so easily able to recognize words that come to you from this place, why such words ring true and even feel familiar to you—because they pluck some resonant chord in your soul which already sits in the place of higher consciousness, and already knows what can be known there. This of course exists at a level below, or above, or beyond, or apart from what you know as your humanness, and your humanness often serves to obscure this knowing. Yet it cannot block it out completely; if it could, you would literally not remain alive. All who are alive, even in your limited terms—all whose hearts beat, whose lungs breathe in and breathe out—hold a life force within them, and every iota of that life force, wherever it may be found, carries within it this knowing.

Would it be accurate to call this knowing "God"? Yes, if you understand that God is not just one thing—if you understand that God, in fact, is everything. Of course, with that understanding it would also be accurate to say that you are God. You are God currently manifesting in a human physical form on a plane of matter, of fairly dense vibration. The higher consciousness aspect of self is God manifesting on a different plane, absent of form, made of finer or higher vibrational substance. Of course, speaking in this way strips meaning from the term "God"—or perhaps it adds meaning, so much so as to render the term irrelevant.

Humans are always looking for God, even though God is everywhere. It's as if you keep going from place to place—say, from the kitchen to the bathroom to the car to the forest to the jungle to the city, sniffing and breathing and saying, "Is this air? Is this air, here?" Of course it is all air, though it is also true that the air in the forest or jungle might be clearer or purer, might smell sweeter, than the air in the city or in your bathroom. That which you seek is everywhere, though it is easier for you to recognize it and to contact it in some places, ways, forms, than in others.

As this description makes clear, higher consciousness is as deeply embedded in us, as integral to our non-physical being, as our beating hearts and our breathing lungs are to our physical bodies. So from one perspective, it is only a tiny step—although to our human selves, it may seem like a giant leap—to become able to make deliberate, conscious, regular contact with this aspect of our being. In fact, once you've developed the necessary muscles, it is possible to contact higher levels of consciousness as quickly and easily as you might text or call a friend.

There are many ways to understand our personal "friends," or points of contact, within the field of higher consciousness. Some of us perceive these beings as aspects of ourselves; others experience them as external to us. Of course, this kind of binary distinction—"us" or "not-us"—is always an over-simplification. The Buddhist phrase "both and" is more applicable; higher consciousness is both us *and* not-us.

It's no wonder, then, that this aspect of reality is so difficult to name! Some people resonate with traditional religious terms like *God, angels,* or *archangels.* Some prefer non-religious language like *the universe, Source, All-That-Is.* Some feel at home with the language of shamanism: *spirit guides, helping spirits, power animals.* Some coin their own terms, like *Wisdom Beings* or *Wise One.* Some use terms like *Higher Self, inner teacher, guide,* or *guidance.* Some feel most comfortable with the simple phrase *larger self.* Personally, I like all of these terms, although none of them feels exactly right or complete to me. Language is shorthand; it cannot fully encompass reality, but gives us ways of pointing toward it. So, to keep things simple, I most often use the terms "guide" and "inner teacher" in this book.

However you understand and experience this level of guidance, it is available to support and help you. The most important ingredients for establishing a connection are your *willingness* and your *intention.* If you are willing to make contact with a wise, completely compassionate aspect of yourself or of consciousness, and set an intention to do so, it will happen.

No particular process or ritual is required; our guides are available 24/7, and they not only make house calls, but office calls, highway calls, airplane calls and mountaintop calls. Wherever we are, they're there too. However, since most of us have the habit of paying much more attention to physical reality than to the non-physical, a ritual may help *us* make the transition from what shamans call "ordinary reality"—the regular human level of consciousness—to the state of consciousness in which we are able to hear, sense, see or perceive the non-physical realm. The more often you connect with your guides, the easier and faster this process will become.

Tips for Connecting with Higher Consciousness Guidance

1. First, choose a particular spot where you will physically sit (or stand, or lie down, or dance) each time you want to initiate conversation with inner teachers. If your spot is indoors, you may want to clear up any clutter in that space, and then intentionally decide what to put there. A cloth of some kind, either on a table or the floor, can help define the space; on it you can place any objects that have meaning to you, or feel sacred or beautiful to you. Many people like to use a candle, incense, sage, or perhaps a small vase with a flower or two cut from their garden. Some like to create more formal altars, on which they place many objects that have personal and spiritual significance to them; others prefer to keep it simple.

2. Next, take time to just be in this spot—with your lit candle or with your objects, if you have chosen to put any there—for at least a few minutes a day. It may take a week or even several weeks of daily returning to this inner space of quietness before you are able to sense the presence of an inner teacher. In the meantime, you can take the opportunity to deepen your sense of contact with yourself—which is, of course, part of the same process.

3. Remember that this is not a chore or obligation, nor a task at which you might succeed or fail. No one will be grading or evaluating your efforts or experiences—with the possible exception of you! If it feels like your critical mind might inhibit you, see if you can enlist its cooperation instead. It can be helpful to develop a statement of intention for yourself, and repeat

it to yourself often; you can even incorporate the critical part of your mind into that statement. Here is an example:

"I intend to connect with my larger self, or with sources of wise, compassionate guidance, and I invite all the parts of my being to participate in this process. If any parts of me are not familiar with the energies of openness and compassion, I invite them to learn about those energies through this process, and ask that they lay aside any fears or judgments that might get in the way. Since I know that I have guides already, even if I have not yet met them, I also ask my guides for help in creating a smooth, clear inner pathway to making contact with them."

4. If, in the process of trying to connect to guidance, you encounter an inner voice that seems determined to keep you from making the connection, see if you can dialogue with it or sense into it to find out more about it. Is it scared? If so, what frightens it about the idea of connecting with higher consciousness? You may be able to help allay its fears. But if its fear is too strong, or if it is hostile—for instance, if it asserts that you do not have guides, or do not deserve to connect with them—then you may need to seek help from a human practitioner. (See Chapter 17, "The Role of Human Support.") There are many people who can assist you with this, so don't worry, and don't give up! *Everyone* can access higher consciousness. You may just need some healing or clearing work to get you ready.

5. Remember that you are seeking to connect with inner teachers or guides who hold a "higher consciousness" field of energy—in other words, beings who are completely wise and compassionate, and who have no requirements, needs or agendas. You are *not* issuing a general invitation for any and all non-physical beings! This isn't like playing with a Ouija board— which, by the way, is not a good idea at all. You'd be unlikely to seek deep healing or guidance from any random stranger in the physical world, and it makes no more sense to do that in the non-physical world. The way to ensure that any beings you contact *have only your highest good as their sole intent* is simply by clearly intending that, and being very specific in your invitation. Intention is an extremely powerful tool.

6. It's helpful to remember that guidance can come in many forms. Some people like to start by quieting their minds, writing a question down, then writing whatever comes into their minds as a response. The book *Writing Down Your Soul: How to Activate and Listen to the Extraordinary Voice*

Within, by Janet Conner, offers a detailed and inspirational description of the author's work with this method.

Yet some people prefer to simply listen within, rather than write. Some like complete quiet; other prefer to have music playing. Some like to sit; some prefer to lie down, stand up, dance, or use yoga postures. Some like to connect with their guides while lying in bed or sitting at their kitchen table; others prefer to be outside, perhaps under a tree or next to a flowing stream. If it's cold outside or if you live in a city, you can simply imagine yourself next to a tree or stream.

7. It's generally best to connect to guidance with a specific question or intention in mind. This helps to focus your mind, and also lets your guides know how they can best help you. If you haven't yet met your guides, your intention might be something like this:

> *"I intend, desire, choose and decide to meet my guides now. I invite them to take any form which allows me to perceive them, and I ask for their help in allowing me to recognize and interact with them."*

8. Remember that as a human being, you have free will—and you will continue to have it, even after developing relationships with inner teachers. A higher consciousness guide will never insist that you do anything, prevent you from doing anything, or get angry or offended if you don't follow his/her/their advice. If you sense a presence or hear a voice that is demanding, harsh or judgmental, it isn't a higher consciousness guide. Reaffirm your intention to contact only being(s) who are completely compassionate, who *have only your highest good as their sole intent.*

Remember: we are surrounded by and filled with a field of higher consciousness which is pure love, wisdom and compassion. You have the absolute right and the inherent ability to connect with beings in this field of consciousness, since, in fact, they are *you* at another level of being. They will welcome the opportunity to guide and support you. They have no agenda of their own, and will require nothing from you.

This might be starting to sound like an infomercial. "Wise inner guides are waiting for you! Call now!" But in fact, it's really true—they are, and you can.

My own process for connecting with guidance begins with lighting a candle, then passing a burning leaf of dried sage around my body. As I sage myself, a

process often called "smudging," I use a modified version of a prayer developed by Kristen Madden: "I ask the smoke of the sacred herb to purify my energy, to clear me of my limitations, and to help me serve as a clear and protected channel for contact with the divine."

Next, I use a practice given to me many years ago during a shamanic journey. As I drum or rattle in each of the six directions, I honor and call in the qualities and gifts of that direction as I have come to understand them. Across many time periods and cultures, people have honored the directions—sometimes six, sometimes four, five, seven or ten—as a way of honoring all that is. Different cultures and traditions have different understandings of the particular medicine of each direction; what follows is the wording that came to me from my guides.

Six Directions Invocation

I honor and call in the spirit of the North, which I perceive as the spirit that teaches me and gives to me through the experience of Winter, through cold and darkness and night, through suffering, difficulty, hardship and pain—and all of the lessons and gifts that come to me through those channels. I honor and accept what you give me, North, and I also honor and accept what you take away.

I honor and call in the spirit of the East, which I perceive as the spirit that teaches me and gives to me through the experience of Spring, through sunrise, morning, new beginnings, hope, potential and possibility, the tenderness of new green shoots unfurling—and all of the lessons and gifts that come to me through those channels. I honor and accept what you give me, East, and I also honor and accept what you take away.

I honor and call in the spirit of the South, which I perceive as the spirit that teaches me and gives to me through the experience of Summer, through ease and plenty, joy and abundance, warm mid-day sunshine, fullness and blossoming, the times when everything happens so much more smoothly and easily than I could even have imagined— and all of the lessons and gifts that come to me through those channels. I honor and accept what you give me, South, and I also honor and accept what you take away.

I honor and call in the spirit of the West, which I perceive as the spirit that teaches me and gives to me through the experience of Autumn, through late afternoon, through sunset, through times of closure and completion, the natural termination of cycles, the times of harvest, maturation, ripening and decay—and all of the lessons and gifts that come to me through those channels. I honor and accept what you give me, West, and I also honor and accept what you take away.

I honor and call in the spirit of Below, which I perceive as the spirit that teaches me and gives to me through the experience of physical life on the physical earth—the gifts of time and space, limits and form, physical embodiment, hunger and fullness, sickness and well-being, vitality and mortality—and all of the lessons and gifts that come to me through those channels. I honor and accept what you give me, direction of Below, and I also honor and accept what you take away.

I honor and call in the spirit of Above, which I perceive as the spirit that teaches me and gives to me through the experience of the timeless, eternal part of my being—the gifts of formlessness and vastness, mystery and wonder, the absence of limits—and all of the lessons and gifts that come to me through those channels. I honor and accept what you give me, direction of Above, and I also honor and accept what you take away.

And lastly, I honor myself as the perceiver of the six directions, and I remember that no matter where I go, no matter what is happening inside me or outside of me, I am always at the center of the six directions, always being held and supported by North, East, South, West, Below and Above.

This prayer leaves me feeling both more grounded, and more expansive. Because it reminds me of my commitment to honoring and accepting all of the gifts and lessons that come to me, no matter what forms they may take, it helps me release resistance and open myself to all of the many ways the divine can work in my life.

The version above is the "long form," which I use before teaching, working with clients, speaking to my guide, or engaging in a healing process of my own. When the long form isn't practical, I can do a brief version in my head, simply touching in with each direction and feeling myself at the center of all six. This has proven very helpful when I'm in the midst of a difficult conversation or emotion! In just a few seconds it reconnects me with vast resources of strength, wisdom and clarity.

There are many different versions of prayers to invoke and honor the directions; if you look online or in books, you may find one that particularly resonates with you. Or, of course, you may use mine. However, in my experience it's even more effective to create your own prayers and invocations based on your own needs, experiences and perceptions.

As you get to know your inner teachers—or as you get to better know yourself—you can sense the wording that fits best for your process and intentions, and create a ritual which is both effective and individual.

4

An Overview of Non-Physical Healing

For me therapy is basically the evocation of imagination; it's training, working, struggling with imagination. If I were to say that it has to do with healing, I'd have to say [it's] healing the imagination, or healing the relationship to the imagination.

— James Hillman

To understand the principles of non-physical healing, it helps to start with a refresher about its counterpart, physical healing. We're all familiar with the steps involved in healing common physical wounds and illnesses; if you get a minor cut or scrape, you probably clean the wound, put antibiotic ointment and a Band-Aid on it, and trust in your body's own healing processes to take over from there. If you have a cold, you may dose up on Vitamin C or natural remedies, drink lots of liquids, eat hot soup or other nourishing foods—and trust in your body's own healing processes to take over from there. With more serious illnesses or injuries, you may see a doctor or other health care practitioner, who might prescribe medication or do other healing practices—and then let your body's own healing processes take over from there.

In other words, healing never truly comes from outside of us. Although people, substances and practices can support our healing, the actual healing is always an inside job. Even severe physical wounds will eventually heal on their own, if conditions allow them to. The same is true of non-physical wounds. Just as your body works automatically to heal physical imbalance, there is a part of you that is unerringly oriented toward the non-physical healing you need.

Yet, although healing is a natural process, it's still possible for us to interfere with or prevent healing on the physical *or* non-physical levels. For instance, if instead of disinfecting and bandaging a physical wound, you continually stabbed it and rubbed mud into it, it wouldn't heal. In fact, it would get worse. Many of us do just that with our non-physical wounds. If you encounter a non-physical place of pain inside yourself and respond with love and compassion, you put a psychic bandage over the wound and help it to heal. But if, instead, you criticize yourself—"Why aren't you over this yet? What's wrong with you?" or, "You're so fucked-up, how could anyone ever love you?"—you block yourself from healing, and deepen the wound. Therefore, if your emotional wounds make it difficult or impossible for you to direct love and compassion toward yourself, addressing that pattern may need to be the first step in your non-physical healing. Chapter 8, "Releasing Shame and Self-Hatred," offers some tools to help.

Depression, anxiety, fear, grief, despair and rage are all common symptoms of non-physical wounds. These emotions emerge from circumstance in which we perceive that we did not receive what we wanted, needed or deserved—or *did* receive things we didn't want, need or deserve. At its base, the remedy for all of these non-physical wounds is the same: we must learn to self-administer what we truly need in all circumstances, the ultimate adaptogenic medicine for what ails us: contact, understanding, love, and compassion. As the Dalai Lama says, "Love and compassion are necessities, not luxuries."

"Love and compassion for myself? You've got to be kidding. I'm my own worst enemy," many people tell me. Self-hatred and self-rejection are widespread in contemporary Western culture. Yet this is a relatively recent and localized phenomenon. For many thousands of years, individuated consciousness led people to turn against those they perceived as "other," not against themselves—which is why Christ advised us to "Love thy neighbor as thyself." If self-hatred had been as rampant in Christ's time as it is now, he might just as well have told us, "Love thyself as thy neighbor," as I find myself having to do with many of my clients. Of course, hating oneself *or* hating one's neighbor are simply two sides of a single coin, the coin of the illusion of separation.

I have heard that on one of the Dalai Lama's first Western speaking tours, someone in the audience asked about how to work with self-hatred. Apparently, the translator struggled mightily to communicate the question. Even once he understood the words, the Dalai Lama was baffled. "How can the self hate the self?" he finally asked. It *is* unnatural for the self to hate the self, yet many of us are currently trapped in this unnatural state. Fortunately, it *is* possible to transform this pattern and shift from a posture of self-rejection and negation into one of self-acceptance, affirmation and love. The tools and practices in this book will show you how. Our individuated consciousness has turned on us, creating a poisonous inner climate in which non-physical healing cannot occur.

The truth is, non-physical wounds like depression, anxiety and self-hatred are every bit as real as any physical injury. Just as a broken leg or a metastasized cancer have physical structures, painful emotional states have non-physical structures—forms that exist within non-physical reality, that can be altered when we work with them non-physically. Most of us are very familiar with our ability to impact physical matter, yet few of us know that non-physical matter is just as amenable to change.

Let's compare two types of structures: a kitchen table, which is physical, and a state of depression, which is non-physical. We know that we could change either the physical form of the table or our relationship to it, if we choose. We could alter the table in various ways—clean it, paint it, strip and refinish it, put it up on coasters to make it higher, or chop off a portion of its legs to make it lower. If we don't want the table in our kitchen, we could move it into a different room. If we no longer want it at all, we could chop it into pieces and use it as firewood, take it to the dump, sell it, or give it away. Since we have been taught all our lives to interact with physical matter, we know that these and many other options are available to us; we're not likely to say, "It's my table, it's in my kitchen, so I'm stuck with it. I'll just have to live with it for the rest of my life." Yet this is exactly what many of us believe about our depression.

In fact, we have essentially the same options available to us with our depression—or with our other non-physical matter—as with our table. There are many non-physical means by which we can alter, dismantle, shift, transmute or release our emotional states, and these processes are just as "real," just as effective, as any action we could take with physical matter in the physical world.

We navigate in the non-physical realm primarily through the use of a very powerful yet vastly underestimated tool: *the imagination*. Our culture's over-emphasis on physical reality has led to a profound misunderstanding of the nature and power of the imagination. We are told that when we imagine things, they are "all in our heads." Yes—exactly! That's just another way of describing non-physical reality. The things that happen "inside our heads," including our emotions, are very real, even though they do not have physical substance. The imagination is our inner creator; it is literally the part of us that *makes images*—and can therefore also unmake them, or transform them.

Creating profound, lasting energetic change is much easier than most people realize. We are energetic beings; like everything else that appears solid on this earth, we are literally made of energy, and energy is capable of nearly infinite shapeshifting. In fact, working on the non-physical or energetic level is much easier and faster than working on the physical plane. For instance, it would take a crew of people several weeks to build the average house, yet we could create every detail of that house in our minds in just a few minutes.

Most of us have been taught to disparage our process of internal creation, to believe that what occurs in our imaginations isn't real. But science is amassing substantial evidence that what we imagine or envision *is* powerfully real. Studies have documented the efficacy of visualization in physically measureable arenas as diverse as golf, weight training, boxing, chess, reducing pain, and raising white blood cell counts. In fact, research shows that *what we visualize is processed by the brain in a manner very similar to what we physically do.* For instance, one exercise psychologist compared people who actually went to the gym with people who stayed home and carried out virtual workouts in their heads, and found that the participants who simply sat on their couches and imagined lifting weights increased muscle strength by nearly half as much as the participants who physically lifted those weights! Clearly, then, the imagination is a powerful tool for bringing about change, even on the physical level—and it's even more effective for shifting non-physical states of being.

Since they do not have physical matter, our emotional wounds cannot be physically tended the way we would tend a stab wound or a broken leg. We cannot take our emotional hearts to the gym and teach them to bench-press, but we can increase their "muscle strength"—and transform and heal them in many other ways—using non-physical tools. *What we imagine actually shifts structures in non-physical reality, both "inside" and "outside" of ourselves.* If a non-physical belief, memory or emotion causes us problems, we can "imagine" transforming or releasing it—and thereby make it happen.

Why, then, is it so hard for most of us to change our emotional states? A major reason is simply that we don't know we can; we live in a culture in which this crucial knowledge has been discounted and lost. But even more significantly, we are hindered in changing our non-physical matter because *we tend to confuse it with ourselves*. It's far easier for us to get rid of or alter our kitchen tables, because we are so much less likely to confuse them with ourselves!

There are a number of steps involved in becoming able to work effectively with our non-physical or internal matter. First, we must *acknowledge that it exists*. Again, the comparison with physical reality is useful. For instance, I'm currently resting my elbows on a table. If I tried to pretend that the table didn't exist, I couldn't use it—nor could I move, break, burn, paint it or give it away. In the same way, pretending that our emotional pain or depression does not exist or is not "real" renders us unable to work with it. In order to be able to impact our internal states, we must acknowledge their realness, while also remembering that they are mutable and impermanent.

Next, *we must be able to distinguish our non-physical matter from ourselves*. Meditation and other practices that involve the development of an "inner witness" are useful in large part because they help us realize that *we are not our emotional states*—a crucial step in becoming able to transform or release those states. Seth, the guide channeled by Jane Roberts, had some very funny things to say on this point. "You don't confuse the bacon and eggs you ate this morning with yourself," he quipped once, "even though it's currently passing through you. So why would you confuse your state of sadness with yourself?"

Once we understand that our emotional states and non-physical structures are both *real* and *not us*, we can inquire into them with interest and curiosity, exploring them without identifying with them. It's possible to walk through the "rooms" of our psyche just as we might walk through the rooms of a physical dwelling, noticing what's there and what changes we might wish to make. Many of the emotional states we experience, and the beliefs and imprints we carry, can be shifted with surprising ease. Other aspects of what we experience as "self" are more foundational—in other words, because we have built a great deal of what we believe to be ourselves on top of them, they are more difficult to change. Still, although it is expensive and time-consuming to replace the foundation of a physical house, it can be done, and the most foundational structures of our psyches and personalities be changed, too. They can be changed because in truth, they are *not* us—though it can take time, effort and courage to shift our sense of identity to our deeper selves.

The Pathwork, a body of over two hundred and fifty psychospiritual lectures, offers many insights and tools to help with the process of inner change. Here is an excerpt I've found helpful:

Understanding and Initiating Non-Physical Change

No real growth and happiness can exist unless a change in the personality takes place. Do not say change does not exist. The universe, and everything in it, changes constantly, is constantly in flux. Even your body is not the same as it was several years ago. Everything changes, even in physical matter, though you may not be aware of it. When you are always together with a living, growing being, you do not see the growth taking place. You notice it only retrospectively. But the very essence of life is change. If there is no change, there is no life. If you remain static, you are in a predicament. You are unhappy. You are not alive. To a large degree, the human struggle exists because a part of you grows organically and healthily according to the laws of nature, while another part remains static.

So do not say change is impossible. It is the only thing that is possible, I might say. Change is the only organic, natural process of creation, and therefore it is also within you...

The freeing new thought process might be to begin with: "I do not want to stay in this position. There are powers within me that make it possible for me to change, and to feel good and secure about the change. I do deserve it. This change is my birth-right, which I claim. I decide, wish, request, desire and intend to make the following change_____, and I ask for the assistance of all of the compassionate and loving forces in the universe in doing so."

Even if some part of you still resists while you say these words, if your innermost will pronounces these words strongly and decisively, without covering up or denying the negative will, but meeting it head on, a new power will be created by the force of the intent within your thought. Only too often you wait for change to take place, without your deciding on a new thought process about the issue in question. It is the thought that must change first. In thought lies the intent. This intent can then seep deeper and deeper into the still-resisting layers of your consciousness. In that way the process takes place on the outermost and the innermost levels: on the outermost, by the volitional thoughts you issue forth; on the innermost, by the divine power you mobilize when you meditate for this specific help. In this way, you cannot fail to inactivate the power of the old negative force field, and create a new force field that will bring you into ever increasing fulfillment, meaningful life, joy, peace, and love.

This Pathwork excerpt covers a lot of bases. It affirms our power to change our internal states, explains that such change is both natural and necessary, and provides some specific wording useful for initiating deep change. Throughout this book we'll explore many more ways to shift, transform or release our internal states.

In Chapter 1, I described the painful cross-country journey with Jim during which I first became aware of a voice or belief inside me told me that, "I should not exist." I don't know exactly how this belief got lodged in me, but I suspect it may have something to do with the circumstances of my conception and birth. My mother became pregnant with me accidentally, when she was only seventeen; my father was nineteen and a pre-med student in college. His parents were horrified at the thought of him marrying and having a child so young, and pressured my mother to get an abortion. Although my teenaged parents defied their parents' wishes, married, and chose to bring me into the world, I imagine that they too must have felt some conflict and fear about my existence.

When I was born, my mother was terribly unprepared to care for me; neither she nor my father even realized that babies needed to be burped, so I got colic and cried constantly. Not knowing what to do, my mother sat beside my crib and cried, too. Because infants and fetuses are highly psychically permeable, completely aware of their parents' feelings, and prone to experiencing those feelings as their own, it's easy to see how these circumstances could have led me to believe that I should not exist.

Although for many years I wasn't conscious of holding this belief, I believe it wreaked a subtle kind of havoc in my intimate life. I repeatedly found myself in relationships with people who couldn't fully be there for me, even though they loved me. Once I understood that our internal matter creates our outer experience, I realized that this pattern both emerged from and perpetuated the idea that I should not exist. So, early in my shamanic study, I was very excited when I realized that I could change or release this belief.

Sometimes it's most effective to move a negative belief out of our inner being the same way we might move an object out of our houses. At other times, particularly when the energetic substance of the belief is diffuse, more like a metastasized cancer as opposed to a discrete tumor, it works best to force it out by creating conditions under which it can no longer survive—something like sterilizing liquid by heating it to a temperature so high that any pathogens will be killed. That's the approach my healer helped me take with this belief.

First, she encouraged me to try on various statements of affirmation, searching for those that created the strongest sense of internal discord. "I love my life," for instance, was easy to say, and "I belong on earth" wasn't much harder. However, when I tried on, "It is right for me to exist," I felt an inner push-back, almost as if something or someone internal was shoving me. When I tried saying "It is profoundly right for me to exist," the shove grew even stronger. That's how my healer knew I had found a good statement to work with.

Her instructions were simple: for the rest of that day I was simply to repeat internally, "It is profoundly right for me to exist," as often as I could. The point was not to use this affirmation to deny, drown out or cover up the belief that I shouldn't exist; it was simply to change my inner climate by supporting the part of me that did, in fact, believe and agree with the affirmation.

After several hours of internally repeating "It is profoundly right for me to exist," a very strange thing happened: I had a coughing fit. Although there was no apparent physical cause—I wasn't sick, and have no allergies—I coughed pretty much non-stop for about ten minutes. Then I spent the rest of the evening drinking tea with honey, and forgot about my affirmations until the next day.

The next morning, when I tried saying "It is profoundly right that I exist," I felt no push-back at all. When I tried saying "I shouldn't exist," it rang hollow. The belief was gone.

In this case, it was relatively easy for me to release the belief that *I shouldn't exist*, because most of me didn't subscribe to it. I was able to recognize it as an error, a false conclusion based on a misunderstanding. However, if a large part of me had believed it, more in-depth healing work would have been necessary before I could relinquish the belief. The next few chapters describe that kind of work.

5

Intention and Prayer:
Inner Technologies of Change

If you don't know where you're going, you're not likely to get there.

– Yogi Berra

Nothing in life is static; our bodies, psyches, relationships and circumstances are subject to constant change. Yet without intentional work to shift our underlying internal structures, we are likely to find that our new inner and outer forms replicate existing patterns. "I remember the day I first realized I had married my father," one client told me ruefully. Since her father had been sadistic and abusive, it was a very unhappy day.

Setting a clear intention is the first step in bringing about any desired change, whether physical or non-physical. Asking for help from larger sources—a practice traditionally called "prayer"—is a way of exponentially increasing our power to bring about that change. (If you don't resonate with the word "prayer," feel free to substitute your own word for requesting the help of your larger self or guides.) Together, intention and prayer are a super-technology, our most effective resource for change, healing and transformation.

"Intention" is the process by which we purposefully internally orient ourselves in a given direction. For instance, when we get into our cars in the morning to drive to work, our *intention* to drive to work plays a huge part in our getting there. If we got into our cars with no particular intention, we might not go anywhere at all—or we might find ourselves randomly driving until we ran out of gas. Many of us do exactly this in our lives.

Setting an intention helps us use our personal power more efficiently. Yet no matter how efficient we are, no human being can, on her own, lift a ton, scale a sheer cliff-face, or turn water into wine. That's where our guides' help comes in.

Our inner teachers are always willing to assist us—since they *are* us, on another level of being. However, their ability to help is limited by their respect for our free will. This means that until we specifically request and open ourselves to their assistance, they will most often stand back, watching us compassionately, but not interfering. Prayer is a way of consciously requesting their assistance, signaling that we are open to their help.

Some of us are stubborn, proud do-it-yourselfers. (I know something about that; family lore has it that the first two phrases I uttered were "Let Ruthie do it" and "Let me do it by my *sef*.") However, there is no good reason for us to refuse the assistance of higher forces, and no spiritual merit that accrues to us from doing so. We do not benefit from making things harder for ourselves, any more than a person dragging heavy objects around her back yard would benefit from refusing to use a wheelbarrow. In fact, working with intention gives us access to the non-physical equivalent of that wheelbarrow, while prayer can call to our sides an invisible team of winged horses. If you stop and listen, you may almost be able to hear them now, snorting, pawing and neighing just outside your door…

Yet the quality of the energy we put into our intentions and prayers is also key in determining whether or not they will manifest. When we pray and intend from a deep experience of connection, we are using these power tools according to their design, making them maximally effective. But if we intend and pray out of a place of fear and despair, or attempt to control or manipulate ourselves, others or our lives, we are working against our own strength—like trying to drag a wheelbarrow uphill by the wrong end. Therefore, we sometimes need to begin our work by intending and praying for a greater sense of connection to ourselves, our lives and our guides. That will serve as a sturdy foundation for all other intentions and prayers. Here are some more tips for using this inner technology effectively.

Guidelines for Effective Use of Intention and Prayer

1. Your intentions and prayers must be consonant with your higher self, and with the fulfillment of your inner design.

2. Your intentions and prayers must be *as specific as possible* in essence, yet *as flexible as possible* in form. They must focus on the core of what is most important to you, rather than on specific ways of achieving it. For instance, it will be more effective to pray, "Please help me attract, receive and feel more love in my life," rather than, "Please make so-and-so love me."

3. You must give your intentions and prayers concentrated *daily* attention. Think about the other things you do daily—for instance, perhaps you make coffee every morning, or put on clean clothes. Isn't whatever you are intending at least as important as those activities?

4. Your intentions and prayers must remain dynamic—i.e., they must acknowledge and emerge from what you're feeling in the moment, rather than becoming static or rote.

5. Your intentions and prayers must address your desires from various angles: e.g., "Please help me to attract and experience more of X in my life," *and* "Please help be become willing and able to dissolve my blocks to receiving more of X in my life," *and* "Please help me recognize and appreciate all the ways and places I already have X in my life," *and* "Please help me heal whatever internal factors prevent me from attracting, receiving or retaining X in my life."

6. As you work with your intentions and prayers, it's important to invite awareness of all of the parts of yourself which are not currently in agreement with those intentions, and consciously work (and intend and pray) to heal or shift those parts of yourself.

7. When you fully affirm your commitment to being here on earth, at this time, in this body, in this life, you turbo-charge your intentions. (See Chapter 27, "Saying Yes to Life.") If you haven't completely said *Yes* to life, your wheelbarrow will have a flat tire and the wings on your winged horses will be clipped.

8. Self-criticism or a harsh inner environment also nullifies the effect of your intentions and prayers. There's an inherent contradiction in asking the

universe for support, while disparaging rather than supporting yourself. If you find yourself in this bind, simply make your self-criticism itself a focus of your work with intention and prayer. For example:

"Please help me shift my habit of internal harshness. Help me cultivate an internal atmosphere of gentleness and respect. Help me release whatever keeps me in the contraction of self criticism. Help me see myself with eyes of compassion. Help me to love myself the way the compassionate universe loves me."

Or:

"I decide, desire, wish and intend to become able to hold, view and address myself with love, gentleness and compassion. I choose and decide to release the harsh energies I am presently carrying. I ask for the help of my guides in releasing these energies and cultivating a loving, supportive environment throughout my inner being."

There are many different ways to pray; each carries its own particular energy, and offers its own kind of medicine. You may find that one style resonates more with you at a certain period in your life, or when you're working with a certain issue; at another point, even a few minutes later, a different style might feel more medicinal. You can experience the different energies of each style simply by trying them out.

Since prayer is a dynamic conversation, there is no "right" or "wrong" way to do it. You can choose which kind of conversation to engage in, just as you choose the way you speak with your human friends. Your guides won't judge you, and they're willing to help no matter what. But some communication styles may feel more powerful and opening for *you* in a given moment than others.

For the sake of this example, let's imagine that you're asking your guides to help you embrace the truth that **the locus of power lies within you,** and assume a posture of full self-responsibility. Here are some ways you might pray.

Styles of Prayer

Declaration: *I decide, I choose, I declare my willingness and readiness, I affirm my plan and intention, to take on full and complete self-responsibility. I consciously and deliberately harness and make use of the unseen forces to assist me...*

Blessing: *May I become more and more able to be fully self-responsible. May all the powers of the universe assist me in making this change, and in opening all the levels of my being to this change...*

Request: *Please help me become able to become fully self-responsible. Please help me to open all the levels of my being to this change; help me to heal and release what must be healed and released...*

Affirmation: *I am becoming more and more fully self-responsible. I sense and feel and affirm my own power to make this change, and acknowledge the support I am receiving from larger forces in readying me to make this change...*

Assuming that you have aligned your inner being with your prayer in the ways already described, all prayer styles are equally effective. Throughout this book, and particularly in Section IV, you'll find examples of prayers and statements of intention that I've written for my own use, and for use by my clients and students. At different times I use different prayer styles. "Requesting" is one of my favorite approaches, as it keeps me connected to the act of asking for help, but "declaring" allows me to acknowledge the critical role of my own agency and will. The "Blessing" style has a lovely, gentle feel to it, and the "Affirmation" style works well when I need to galvanize myself into inner change.

Personally, I've found that beginning the day with prayer is a great way to set my internal compass. When we awaken each morning, there is a little window of time in which we are still close to the power of the dream world and all of its guidance; praying at this time of day seems to impact me even more deeply than at other times of day. Here is a morning prayer I like to use.

Daily Prayer

I ask for help in embracing this day, and remaining close to myself and my highest intentions during each moment of the day. I ask for help in appreciating my body, my beating heart, my breathing lungs, my seeing eyes, my hearing ears, my functioning limbs. If any parts of my body are not functioning well, I ask for help in respecting their limitations, and treating them and myself with tenderness and compassion. I also ask and intend to honor and celebrate all of the parts of my body that *are* working well, allowing myself to remember and hold close the intricate workings of my cells, bones, muscles and organs, the beauty and complexity of the ways in which they are supporting me in every moment, and I affirm my intention to support them in return.

I also ask that the community of working parts within my physical form help me remember, celebrate and appreciate the larger communities of which I am a part—the communities of my household, family, circle of friends, town, city, ethnic group, species, nation, planet, or any other communities to which I may be connected. Although each of these communities has its frailties and imperfections, just as my body does, I ask for help in seeing their beauty and strength as clearly as I see those aspects in need of healing or development; I ask for the vision that can enable me to feel joy and wholeness within my-self, within my body, and within the world, even as I know that I and all other aspects of my world are continually changing and evolving, and being sup-ported to evolve.

If I sit or stand or walk outside, I ask for help in being present to the beauty of the world, opening my senses to all of the life forms and consciousness around me. If there are birds in the sky or the trees, I intend to acknowledge them, to greet and salute them in their essential nature—in their life form which is so different from my own, and yet, at its core, so similar. I pray that this recognition of both our difference and our similarity fill me with apprecia-tion and tenderness. If there are squirrels running through the grass or in the trees, I ask for help in truly taking in marvel of these creatures, too. If I live with or encounter cats or dogs, may I also salute those creatures who have chosen to transition from wildness to what we call "domestication," so that they can live more closely with us, and teach and comfort and heal us, and exchange with us.

When I see trees, may I remember that these magnificent life-forms are constantly helping me by producing the oxygen I need to breathe; I affirm my intent to thank them, appreciating their support.

When I drink water, I ask for help in remembering the miracle of that wa-ter—where it has come from, how it has traveled to me, and how it nourishes and hydrates my tissues and cells, entering my body to rejoin the waters al-ready living within me, purifying and cleansing me. I also thank my mouth, my lips, my tongue, my throat, and all the inner chambers and filters and organs of my body. May I remain grateful for their ability to welcome this water, to receive and make use of it for their own good and for mine.

When I eat, I thank the earth and every human being, known or unknown, through whose labor this food has come to me. I thank my nose, my mouth, my teeth, my taste buds, my stomach and all my organs of digestion and elimination for their role in helping this food enter me, nourish me, and leave me as part of the natural cycle of life. I declare my intention to make honorable use of the life force which is increased in me by way of this food. May I return this energy to the world in the form of love.

I ask for help in acknowledging, remembering and recognizing the humanity of every person with whom I interact today, even briefly: the man or woman at the gas station, the grocery store, the fellow passengers on the bus or train, the people with whom I share a household or building or neighborhood or workplace, and those with whom I speak on the phone or exchange emails or text messages. In all of my small encounters with strangers, may I recognize the full humanity of each person; may I remember that each person was once a tiny, helpless baby, who may or may not have been adequately welcomed into the world, who may or may not have received all the care he or she needed. I ask for help in silently sending compassion to her heart or his, to whatever wounds may remain there.

And in all of my encounters with people I know, friends, family members, spouse, children, co-workers or others, I ask for the same. May I be helped to see the essential beauty of each person. May I remember that at the core, each of us shares the same needs. May I allow my own humanness to radiate from me, so that others may more easily see my essential beauty, too.

And when I use the bathroom, I ask for help in looking in the mirror and greeting the person I see there as a friend. If I am tempted at any point during the day to criticize myself, I ask that life shower me with love, and help me remember that love is with me at all times, in all places, in all ways. May the memory, the knowledge, the visceral awareness of that love, reach me and soften me, move me and help me to release any harshness I may have been directing against myself.

If I am tempted to criticize another person today, or find myself doing so, I ask that that same love hold me just as palpably, comforting and nourishing me. May it remind me of that place within me in which all is right with the world; may it help me to soften, to relax into the experience of being held, and to relinquish the sharp edge I have been holding against another.

I ask for help in remembering my intention to care both for myself and for others, to love myself as much as I love others in my best moments, and to love others as much as I love myself in my best moments; and to allow this love that flows from me and to me to carry me like a stream, throughout my day.

If, today, I have a difficult thing to say to another person, I ask that this stream of love help me to remain conscious and present in my own vulnerable humanity as I speak, and that it keep me able to sense and acknowledge and touch the vulnerable humanity of the other. May I speak necessary truths with clarity and kindness.

And when I make a mistake, I ask for help in acknowledging it forthrightly and quickly while also remembering my vulnerable humanness. I affirm that all human beings make mistakes, that I am allowed to make a mistake, and that even with all of my mistakes, I am still held within the loving stream of my larger self.

I ask for help in being a beacon of light today, a light that radiates equally outward, toward everyone and everything I encounter outside of myself, and inward, toward each aspect and facet of my own being. May I feel the love that is within me and around me. May I know myself as part of that love, part of the body that love inhabits in this world.

6

The Shamanic Journey:
A Path to Archetypal Power

The center that I cannot find is known to my unconscious mind.

— W. H. Auden

There is a language that lives more deeply within us than words, a language we speak without ever needing to consciously learn it. This is the language used by our dreams, the language of metaphor, symbol and archetype. Even when we can't easily translate symbolic communications into words, we often understand them viscerally and immediately.

Many of us have already experienced the ways in which nighttime dreams can provide information crucial to our healing. Shamanic teacher Isa Gucciardi calls dreams "emails from the higher self." It's not surprising that our higher selves would find it easier to reach us at night, since we're all processing so much stimulation (and many of us are getting so many actual emails!) during our waking lives. When we're asleep and our rational guard is down, non-ordinary communication can reach us more easily.

Still, some of us have trouble remembering our dreams, or connecting their messages with our waking lives—and few of us have developed the ability to formally consult with our higher selves in our dreams. Can you imagine how helpful it would be if you could request a dream on a particular topic, dream it in just a few minutes' time without even having to go to sleep, and remember it perfectly? Further, can you imagine being able to use these waking dreams to request specific kinds of healing from your guides, and get more insight on any topic you choose? You can do all this and more with the tool of the shamanic journey.

Although the term *shamanic journey* refers to a specific practice which I'll soon describe, many people have intuitively discovered some form of "journeying" on their own. Just as you may already be in contact with your guides even without having thought of it that way, you may also have found yourself able to access healing visions. Human beings seem to come equipped with structures in consciousness that make it easy for us to receive support, insight and healing from the symbolic realm. While such experiences come more readily to most of us during meditation or with the aid of consciousness-altering plant or pharmacologic substances, some of us access them simply by intending to—or sometimes even without intending to. (My own experience being visited by guides at age four is obviously an example of a "journey" I had no conscious intention of making.)

Yet people whose guides appear to them spontaneously often lack both a framework for understanding what is happening, and tools to help them take the contact further. In this case, the shamanic journey can help you better comprehend, trust, organize and make use of the non-physical support you're already receiving. And if you haven't previously found yourself able to access non-ordinary guidance, the shamanic journey can provide you with a safe, structured way to do so.

The type of shamanic journeying that I practice and teach is based on the work of anthropologist Michael Harner, who spent many years studying indigenous healing traditions in various parts of the world. (Although the word *shaman* comes originally from the indigenous healing tradition of Siberia, *shamanism* is now used as a general term for the spirit-based, non-physical forms of healing that have been practiced for milennia all over the globe.) Harner discovered that across many different times, places and cultures, very similar understandings of non-physical reality had emerged. From these diverse sources, he developed what he called *core shamanism.*

Because core shamanism is drawn from the elements held in common by shamanic practitioners from all over the globe, it is likely that at some point in your ancestral history, your relatives practiced healing methods similar to these. Therefore, no matter what your race, ethnicity or nationality, these powerful tools are your birthright.

Taking a Shamanic Journey

Shamanic journeys are usually done with the accompaniment of a regular, rhythmic drum beat, which helps to induce a very slightly altered state of consciousness similar to the state of daydreaming. While listening to the drum beat, either live or recorded, you internally, imaginally "journey" to another world where you can meet with your guides and receive their help.

Core shamanism describes three distinct realms, the upper world, lower world, and middle worlds. Journeyers seeking their own healing should journey only to the upper or lower worlds, since those two realms consist exclusively of trustworthy, compassionate beings and energies. (Experienced shamans also work in the middle world, but that's a more advanced practice.)

To travel to the upper or lower world with more ease, it helps to choose a departure point that you've actually visited in the physical world, ideally a place where you have felt comfortable and safe. Departure points for the upper world are usually a hill, mountain, tree or rooftop; for the lower world, the most common departure points are a cave, hollowed-out tree trunk, or body of water. Generally, you will use the same departure points each time you journey. Once you are a seasoned journeyer, the process of getting to the upper or lower world may become streamlined or instantaneous, but as a beginner, it's advisable to go step by step.

If you are journeying without a friend, teacher or therapist to drum for you, you can use one of the many recordings of shamanic journey drumming available online. While listening to the drumming, simply close your eyes and bring yourself to your departure point in your mind, while holding and re-stating to yourself a clear intention for the journey. For instance, if this is your first journey, your intention might be, "I'm going to the upper [or lower] world to meet a higher-consciousness guide, a compassionate being who has only my highest good as their sole intent." You can journey to the upper and lower worlds in separate journeys, in order to make contact with guides in each world; or, you can simply pick departure points for each world, and then see which world you feel more strongly drawn to in any given journey. The upper and lower worlds are both completely compassionate, trustworthy non-physical realms, although they are dimensionally different in ways each journeyer must discover for herself.

As you wait at your departure point and reaffirm your intention, a way will generally emerge for you to travel into the upper or lower world. For instance, you might find yourself flying, swimming, crawling, running, walking, float-ing, or being carried. When you arrive in either world for the first time, simply continue to hold your intention: "I'm here to meet a higher-consciousness guide." Your guide can take any form in the universe; he or she might appear to you as a tree, rock, plant, animal, or other aspect of the natural world, or might take a human form, the form of an angelic or mythical being, or the form of a voice, light or sound.

Your journey will not necessarily be strongly visual; people can experience journeys with any of our five (or more) senses. Although some people do "see" their journeys in clairvoyant fashion, many people tend to have journeys that are more kinesthetic (clairsentient), auditory (clairaudient), or that simply in-duce a state of knowing (claircognizance) in the journeyer.

However you are perceiving your journey, when you encounter a being you sense might be your guide, it's important to ask, "Are you a guide for me?" You may get a straight Yes or No, but more often, you will simply receive an intuitive sense of the answer. Or, the being may answer with a gesture or action. If the answer seems to be No, simply continue to hold your intention and wait or look for another being. When you do encounter someone who in-dicates that they are your guide, you can use the rest of the journey to get to know them, or ask whether they have any messages or teachings for you right now. In subsequent journeys, you can return to that same guide with specific questions or requests. You can also ask to meet guides who will work with you in specific areas of your life, or will help you with specific healing processes.

Time passes differently in journeys, just as it does in a dream. Often, things happen very quickly. I generally keep each journey to ten minutes or less, so that I'll be more likely to remember every detail when I emerge. As with dreams, journeys tend to fade more quickly from memory than things we've experienced in waking life, so I highly recommend writing down each journey as soon as you've finished it. Messages or symbols that are not imme-diately clear may become clearer when you reread your notes; if not, you can always do another journey to ask your guides for clarification.

Although there are many ways to access information and healing from our guides, the shamanic journey is one of the fastest and most effective tools I have ever used. Later in this book you'll find descriptions of a num-ber of my own shamanic journeys. For now, here's a story of a client's jour-ney, a journey I will never forget.

Laura contacted me in a state of extreme distress. Her girlfriend had broken up with her suddenly, with no explanation, and Laura later found out that she'd been having an affair with a friend of theirs. "I want to move away, but I can't afford to," Laura told me bitterly. She no longer trusted her friends; it seemed to her that any one of them might betray her. She had been through a lot of therapy and done a lot of spiritual work already, but felt as if none of it had helped. She had come to see me only because she felt so desperate—and because at the time I offered a free initial session.

At the time I had only been in private practice for a few months, and as Laura's pain filled the room, I wondered how I could possibly help her. Then, to my relief, I remembered that I didn't have to. Laura had learned shamanic journeying many years before, and vaguely remembered a guide who had taken the form of a dragon. I suggested that she visit with the dragon now, and simply ask for help. Then I picked up my drum.

Ten minutes later, when I stopped drumming, Laura looked transformed. Tears ran down her face as she told me that her dragon guide had scooped her up with his enormous claws and tenderly carried her to a warm pool of water, where he gently washed her from head to toe. Then he blew on her very lightly to dry her off with his warm breath. After that, he held her to his chest—which Laura described as "kind of scaly, kind of feathery, but very soft"—and let her listen to his beating heart.

That was all that happened—but in ten minutes Laura had gone from feeling angry, hostile and betrayed by life, to feeling soothed, comforted, safe and loved.

Of course, this journey was only the beginning of what would clearly be a much longer healing process. I don't know whether or not Laura continued with that process; a few days later she emailed me that she had found a way to move out of town, and was leaving immediately. But even though I never heard from Laura again, this session was a watershed for me as a new healing practitioner. It showed me just how available—and how profoundly gentle, wise, strong and compassionate—our inner teachers are.

Although Laura's journey seems deceptively simple, I believe that her dragon guide was not only comforting her, but also providing her with some very specific types of energetic healing. The "washing" she experienced seems to have been a clearing process, and the warm breath and "heartbeat therapy" helped her experience her vulnerability as safe, rather than life-threatening. In this way, the journey was both helpful on its own, and also set the stage for further work.

It also seems to me that this journey embodies the force that theologian Paul Tillich called "grace." Tillich writes, "Grace strikes us when we are in deep pain and restlessness. It strikes us when we walk through the dark valley of a meaningless and empty life... when our disgust for our own being, our indifference, our weakness, our hostility, and our lack of direction and composure have become intolerable to us. It strikes us when, year after year, the longed-for perfection of life does not appear, when the old compulsions reign within us as they have for decades, when despair destroys all joy and courage. Sometimes at that moment a wave of light breaks into our darkness, and it is as though a voice were saying: *You are accepted. You are accepted... Simply accept the fact that you are accepted!*"

And Tillich adds, "After such an experience we may not be better than before, and we may not believe more than before. But everything is transformed."

7

The Healing Art of Soul Retrieval

Right now we face a crucial struggle on this planet. How do we grow up and use our powers of judgment and insight to be responsible for all forms of life? How can we contact and integrate the child that lives inside each of us—that child who has the power of creative imagination, to envision what we can create?

– Sandra Ingerman

No matter how much we've grown up on the outside, everyone we've ever been, at every stage of our development, is still alive and well—or, more often, *unwell*—inside our psyches. Inevitably, each of us contains many aspects of self that are young, wounded, scared, isolated or angry. Because these different parts of us have radically different needs, perspectives, beliefs and priorities, they pull us in different directions, often interfering with our conscious intentions and recreating the same kinds of painful situations again and again. One very effective way to help these split-off parts of ourselves heal and re-integrate is through the art of *soul retrieval.*

Shamans in many traditions believe that in moments of trauma, pieces of our soul separate from us and become frozen in time. This "soul loss" serves us in the short term by helping us to bear traumatic situations, because there is actually less of us present to endure the trauma. (Western psychology calls this process "dissociation.") But over the long term we are weakened and distorted by the disconnection from parts of ourselves. Even more importantly, because these lost soul parts are cut off from the passage of time, they remain trapped in the experience of their trauma forever—unless and until we heal and reintegrate them. Soul retrieval is a direct and efficient way to bring these pieces of ourselves into present time and restore their—and our—wholeness.

Wikipedia defines psychological trauma as "emotional or psychological injury, usually resulting from an extremely stressful or life-threatening situation." Isa Gucciardi's definition of trauma is "anything that takes you out of your center, disconnects you from your life source." Obviously, major events like serious illnesses, surgeries or other painful medical procedures, car accidents, physical violence, sexual abuse, verbal abuse, the loss of a friend, the dissolution of a relationship, a move, or the death or disappearance of a parent are traumatic. Yet incidents that appear more minor can also lead to the non-physical equivalent of what athletic trainers call "cumulative microtrauma." For instance, a child whose mother is often too busy to listen to him may experience a series of small disappointments that, over time, create beliefs like these: *I'm worthless. I'm not worth listening to. No one will ever listen to me.* Although he may not even be consciously aware that he holds such beliefs, they will deeply impact his sense of himself, as well as his ability to connect with others.

This understanding of trauma helps explain why even people who believe they had "perfectly happy childhoods" may be carrying very damaging internal imprints. Our souls are made of different kinds of fiber; some of us are deeply scarred by circumstances that might not have caused as much harm to another person. Yet the same kinds of sensitivity which render us easily wounded may give us great gifts in other areas of our lives.

There are many ways that soul loss can show up in our lives. Common emotional patterns like depression, anxiety, self-hatred, and addictive or compulsive behaviors usually have soul loss at their core. When we get triggered or "freeze," experiencing emotional reactions that seem out of proportion to what is happening in the present—as I did on my cross-country trip with Jim—it's also a sign that part of us is emotionally caught in the past. Renowned soul retrieval teacher and practitioner Sandra Ingerman points out that many people indicate their soul loss through common statements like "I haven't been the same since the accident," or "My lover took part of my soul with him when he left." Fortunately, soul retrieval is a powerful, highly effective means of getting our lost soul parts back, restoring our vitality and wholeness.

To perform a soul retrieval, we must revisit the place in our beings where the soul part became disconnected, bolstered by the support, love and wisdom of our non-physical guides. This place is always accessible to us in non-ordinary reality, even if the events that caused the soul loss occurred decades or even lifetimes ago; if we are experiencing symptoms from it now, it means that healing is needed—and available—now, too. Soul retrieval allows us to *shift the psychic and physical encoding of the trauma* by removing our soul parts from the traumatic situation, helping them access whatever healing they need, and then reintegrating them.

Sometimes the soul retrieval process can be as simple as finding a young, scared part of yourself, bringing her to a safe place, reassuring her that the trauma is over, and reconnecting her to your heart. At other times, the process can be considerably more challenging. Sometimes soul parts are so confused, scared or mistrustful that they are unwilling to leave the scene of trauma; sometimes they need extensive healing before it's possible or safe to reintegrate them; sometimes your present-day self may feel judgmental or frightened of the disconnected parts; sometimes another person has stolen parts of your soul, and needs to be convinced to let them go. For all of these reasons, you should never attempt a soul retrieval without the support of trustworthy, compassionate inner teachers.

Before attempting to retrieve a specific soul part, it's wise to explore whether you are actually ready to reintegrate that part. For instance, if the soul part left because your parents were verbally abusive and you are currently in a relationship with a verbally abusive partner, the conditions may not yet be right for you to do that piece of healing.

Here are some questions that can serve as guidelines to help you determine your readiness for a soul retrieval.

Questions to Ask Before a Soul Retrieval

- When, and under what circumstances, do you believe the soul part became disconnected?

- How is the absence of this soul part affecting your present-day life?

- Why do you wish to retrieve this soul part?

- How do you anticipate that your present-day life will change, once you have retrieved this soul part?

- How ready and willing are you to experience these changes?

- What changes do you anticipate that this soul part might need from you, and/or in your present-day life, in order to be willing to come back, and to stay?

- How ready and willing are you to make these changes?

Don't worry if you discover while working with these questions that you're not yet ready to bring a particular soul part back. Healing is a multi-step process. There is always *something* you can do now, some healing action or actions you can take, from exactly where you are. For instance, there may be another soul part you can retrieve first, which will help you become strong enough to retrieve this one. There may be some energetic clearing that needs to happen first (see Chapter 12). You may simply need to spend more time with your guides, being nourished and strengthened by their love, compassion and support. Or you might find it helpful to do some focused work with the tools of intention and prayer (see Chapter 5), asking for help in becoming ready to retrieve soul parts.

If you have already done a lot of inner work, have strong relationships with your guides, and are consistently able to hold a posture of love and compassion toward yourself, you may be able to perform soul retrievals without the help of a human practitioner. Otherwise, it's best to get human guidance and help, so you don't risk causing more damage to already-wounded parts of yourself. (See Chapter 17, "The Role of Human Support.")

The Soul Retrieval Process

If you are familiar with the practice of shamanic journeying, you can perform your soul retrieval in a journey while someone else drums; you can also drum or rattle for yourself, or listen to a recording of drumming. Or you may be drawn to work in a more meditative fashion—in silence, or with quiet instrumental music, or in a peaceful, safe natural setting.

To begin, call in your non-physical guides and teachers, reaffirm your connection to them, and let yourself feel their love and support. Then check with them, and with yourself, to see if the time feels right to do more. Remember, there's no rush. You may be working to heal the accumulated traumatic residue of lifetimes. It's okay if you need to wait another hour, day, week or year to be ready.

When you do have an inner sense of readiness, clearly express your intention to your guides and ask for their help as specifically as possible—for instance, "Please help me retrieve any soul parts that left when my mother died," or, "Please help me retrieve any soul parts I need in order to resolve my panic attacks." There are many doorways into soul retrieval. For instance, you can ask your guides to help you return to a specific traumatic event you're already aware of, or you can work backwards from a trigger, phobia, frozen place or other symptom in your present life. If you're not sure where to start, you can simply ask your guides to help you retrieve any part(s) of your soul that are ready to come back to you at this time.

In your journey through non-ordinary reality, your guides may take you to scenes from your earlier adulthood, adolescence, childhood, infancy, the prenatal period, symbolic or apparently past life experiences—or to times and places you don't recognize, or that don't appear "real." Try to trust whatever your guides show you, even if it doesn't make sense to your rational mind. Soul retrievals often take place in the realm of symbolic or emotional truth, as opposed to literal truth. As in nighttime dreams, your guides may present you with scenarios that are not factually accurate, yet help you access the energetic configurations that need attention and healing.

Once you encounter your missing soul part, your guides will help you see and do whatever is necessary for that part to heal, and for you to heal your relationship to that part. Simpler soul retrievals can be completed in one journey, but many soul retrievals take longer.

For my first soul retrieval, I decided to explore my long-standing discomfort about the backrubs I had given to my father as a small child.

My healer gently encouraged me to close my eyes, come more fully into my body, and connect with my guide. Then she verbally guided me to a time when I was rubbing my father's back. "Describe it in the present tense," she encouraged me. "Just as if it's happening right now."

I wasn't sure whether or not I was "making it up," but I hazily saw or imagined the blue carpet in my father's study, and the pine bookshelves he had assembled in every place we lived. "I'm on my father's back," I said hesitantly. "He's moaning."

"How old are you?"

"I don't know—maybe three or four?"

"And what is your little girl self feeling, as her father moans?"

"She feels uncomfortable. She doesn't like it."

"Why doesn't she stop?"

"He doesn't want her to."

"Where is her mother?"

"I don't know. Maybe in the kitchen."

As I felt into the scene more, I realized that my child self actually felt more comfortable with her father than with her mother. Her mother was young, needy and scared in a way that frightened her. Her father navigated the world with more confidence, so she felt safer with him, even though he demanded these back-rubs. That was why she had to please him.

"What's happening?" my healer prodded gently.

"There's all this... feeling, in her body. It's not hers, it's his feeling. It's too big for her body. It's kind of roaring inside of her." I started to cry.

"What happens if she stops rubbing his back?"

"She can't stop. He doesn't want her to stop."

"Why can't she stop?"

The answer seemed obvious. "He doesn't want her to stop. He wouldn't love her if she stopped."

At this point, my healer encouraged me to bring my adult self and my guide into the room, to see what we wanted to do for the little girl.

"I want to get her out of there," I said.

"And how does she feel about that?"

"She wants to know what I'm going to want from her. What she's going to have to do for me."

I was shocked when I heard myself say these words. I had touched into a level of emotional truth that felt profoundly disturbing, yet also explained a great deal about my lifelong relational patterns.

With my healer's encouragement, I helped the little girl connect with my guide. Because she could sense that he didn't need anything from her, she felt safe with him in a way she didn't yet feel with me. My guide took her to the castle where he lived in non-ordinary reality, and explained that I could visit them there. It would take a while before I could establish enough trust with the little girl to be able to reintegrate her, but the process had begun.

In the days following this soul retrieval, I was shocked to find that sexual fantasies I'd had for many years had completely lost their charge. Although

I had never consciously connected those fantasies with the back rubs, this proved to me that an energetic shift had taken place.

The soul retrieval I did with my client José took place in an entirely different context, yet followed the same basic pattern: journeying back to the wounded younger self, discovering what that self needs, and making help available.

José came to me because he had trouble accessing and sharing his feelings. In fact, his last two relationships had ended because his partners complained that he never really let them get close. "I cared about them," José told me, baffled. "But I couldn't give them what they wanted. Maybe I'm just not capable of love."

José quickly made contact with two guides, who took the forms of a wizard and a butterfly. When I suggested that he ask these guides to take him wherever we needed to go in order to resolve this issue, José saw himself in two different places: in his middle school cafeteria, where he'd always felt like an outsider, and in the dorm room where he'd lived during his freshman year at college. The young man in the dorm room was curled in a fetal position, heartbroken after the ending of his first relationship. I asked José to sense which scene had more energy—which was more important for us to work with first—and he chose the dorm room.

"Find the right distance to stand from your younger self, so you can observe him without becoming *him," I suggested. "Remember that you, the present-day self, have the support of your guides. Then get just close enough so you can sense what's going on for the younger José."*

"He feels rejected. Love just isn't worth it, it's pointless. It hurts too much. He's never going to put himself in this position again. He's just going to take extra classes and work overtime. No more love."

"How do you feel toward that 18-year-old as you see him in so much pain?" I asked.

"I feel bad for him. He's really hurting. I wish I could help."

Since I knew that José's present-day self wasn't much more comfortable with pain than his younger self, I sensed that his guides would be an essential resource. "See if you can bring your guides into that dorm room to be with him," I suggested. "What do they want to do for him? What does he need, in order to be able to bear his pain?"

"There's no way he can bear it," José answered automatically. Then he stopped. "No, wait. He could. He could, if… he needs to feel surrounded by love."

"And how can your guides help him experience that?"

The wizard wrapped the younger José in a magical cloak, and the butterfly flew all around the cloak, beating its wings. "He's starting to melt," José reported with surprise. "It's like he's unclenching in there. It's getting brighter and brighter, like the butterfly's wings are generating light."

"And how is your present-day self doing? Does he need access to that bright space, too?"

"Not so much that," José said thoughtfully. "He just needs to know he has somewhere to go when he's hurting. The wizard can listen to him if he feels like talking, and the butterfly can be with him when he doesn't have words."

After a little while, José reported that his younger self had completely dissolved in the light, and gotten absorbed back into his body. Then the wizard shrank the cloak into the size of a wool scarf, and handed it to José. "He says I can wear it any time, as a reminder." José was crying. "The butterfly can ride on my shoulder. They said they'll stay with me from now on."

José's soul retrieval turned out to be an easy one because the present-day José felt compassion toward his younger self. If, instead, José had responded negatively to his younger self's pain—"What a baby, why doesn't he just grow up and be a man?" or "What a stupid kid. It was just infatuation anyway. He's got nothing to be so upset about"—more work would have been needed to dismantle his self-rejection, before he could complete the soul retrieval. For more information about shifting patterns of self-rejection and self-hatred, keep reading.

8

Releasing Shame and Self-Hatred

If I am not for myself, who will be for me?

— Hillel

The work of healing grows more complicated when we have compounded our original pain with inner structures of self-hatred and shame. These are particularly problematic states because their essence, self-rejection, both emerges from, and perpetuates, a feeling of separation from the self, and from all of life—so in addition to causing suffering on their own, they block us from connecting with the resources that can heal that suffering. For instance, if you have a lot of shame and self-hatred, you are probably in need of numerous soul retrievals; however, your shame and self-hatred create an unsafe environment for hurt soul parts to come back to.

Viewed energetically, the posture of self-rejection looks like a kind of doubling-over in response to perceived external pain or attack. Although this posture begins as a way to try to protect ourselves, it blocks us from light; in that cut-off state, we are very likely to form a belief that says, "There is something wrong with me." This self-blame is nothing like the wholesome state of self-responsibility, in which we recognize our own contribution to our suffering and are able to initiate whatever change is needed. Instead, self-blame and shame shift the energetic burden onto the self in a distorted way, leaving us incapacitated and paralyzed.

Shame and self-hatred work like an internal electric fence, corralling us into certain behavioral and energetic patterns and away from others, thus creating an inner state of rigidity. Since they are contracting rather than expansive (i.e., they close us down rather than opening us up), they also narrow the energetic pathways through which whatever we need or desire can potentially come. In this way, they create the non-physical equivalent of hardened arteries, predisposing us to non-physical "heart attacks"—painful states of increasing intensity—just as physical angina predisposes us to physical heart attacks. When we are in trapped in these states, there are too many blocked internal roads for the healing energies of love and compassion to penetrate. Yet just as the physical heart cannot operate properly without the blood and oxygen it needs, the non-physical heart and spirit cannot function without love and compassion. How can we shift this logjam?

Arguing with shame or self-hatred is no more effective than arguing with a piece of furniture you don't want in your house any longer. Trying to talk yourself out of your internal structures won't do any good. Rather, you must acknowledge the existence of the erroneous beliefs you are holding; see that they are not *truth,* even if they still "feel true" to some parts of you; see that they are *not you;* and see that they are not necessary to you. In this way you can become able to transmute or release your self-rejection.

Practice for Releasing Self-Hatred or Shame

1. **See that it is there.** Observe the form or forms that your self-hatred or shame take. In other words, how do these feelings or beliefs present within you? Do you hear inner voices telling you "You're stupid, you're worthless, you'll never amount to anything," or "You're rotten to the core"? Do you feel a generalized physical heaviness, a sick feeling, a stabbing pain between your eyes, an image of wanting to cause yourself physical harm? (These are some ways my clients have described the energetic presence of self-hatred, or self-hating voices, within them.) Do you see a visual image of the self-hatred or shame—a judge pounding a gavel, a black blob in your chest, a dark, sticky mass of tar behind your forehead? Or does it make itself apparent in some other way?

2. **See that it is not truth.** Remind yourself that life itself does not reject any part of itself, nor any part of us. Therefore, since you are a part of life, it is obvious that the rejecting posture of shame and self-hatred cannot be "true," or truth. This emotional posture emerges from a misunderstanding, usually a childhood feeling that "something is wrong." Undoubtedly, something *was* wrong in your childhood, but the shame mistakenly translated that feeling into the idea that something was wrong with *you.* In

fact, there could not possibly be anything "wrong" with you, just as there cannot be anything "wrong" with a tree, bush or flower. It's true, of course, that some trees are healthier than others; some are taller, shorter, greener or less green. Some may even be stunted or diseased. But even a tree in a state of sickliness would clearly be valid and worthy, deserving of compassion and care, not blame. Life does not hate a sickly or malformed tree; life is incapable of hating anything. Life energy is, quite simply, composed of love. Nor would the stunted tree ever hate itself, or feel shame over its condition. It is only because of your individuated consciousness— your ability to perceive yourself as separate—that you have incorrectly translated the general sense, "Something is wrong," into the specific and incorrect conclusion, "Something is wrong with *me.*"

3. **See that it is not you.** As you observe the shame or self-hatred, notice yourself observing it. Just being able to observe it can help you begin to separate "yourself" from "it." To make this distinction even more clear, deliberately direct your memory to a moment in your life, or an aspect of your life, in which the shame or self-hatred was not present. Allow yourself to remember and re-experience this moment or aspect as vividly as possible; tune into how it looks, feels, tastes, sounds, smells. Then, realize clearly that since you can experience life so fully in the absence of shame or self-hatred, those emotions cannot possibly be *you.* No matter how infrequent or brief such instants may have been, they show you that what *you* are is separate and distinct from the shame or self-hatred. No matter how frequently you experience those beliefs, or how "real" they feel, you exist apart from them.

    Even if you cannot remember a single instant when you were free of shame or self-hatred, the very fact that you can search for such a memory—that you have a consciousness capable of even *imagining* a "you" separate from the feeling of shame or self-hatred—indicates that you are larger than those feelings, and therefore distinct from them.

4. **See that it is not necessary to you.** There are many reasons why unpleasant inner states like self-hatred or shame can come to feel necessary to us. They may, for example, serve to block out even more distressing emotional states like terror, loss, grief or rage. If this is the case for you, you'll need to work closely with higher-consciousness sources of love in order to weather the emotional storms that may result when the shame or self-hatred lifts. Such storms generally last only a short time, but they can be very intense.

It's a good idea to seek help from a human healing practitioner if you feel nervous about going through the storm on your own.

Shame or self-hatred may also feel necessary to us simply because they are so familiar. You may find it hard to imagine who you'd be without them, or what your friendships or relationships would be like. A client once said to me, "I don't think my friends would like me any more if I were happy. It's my neurosis that makes me interesting." If shame and self-hatred have been major players in your inner landscape, it's true that releasing them will probably precipitate big shifts in your life. Again, higher-consciousness support will help you become ready for these shifts.

5. **Believe in your ability to release it.** Removing non-physical matter from your being is a process that is both energetic and symbolic. If you start to doubt the process, thinking, "It's all in my head," remember, the shame and self-hatred are "all in your head," too! Non-physical techniques are the most effective way to shift non-physical phenomena.

You can also use Pathwork-style phrasing: *"I decide, choose and wish to release this self-hatred. I declare my readiness to experience this change, and ask all the forces of truth, love and compassion to assist me..."*

6. **Release it.** There are many ways to sense or imagine yourself releasing the shame or self-hatred, according to how you see or perceive it. Your guides can help you find a way that works for you. For instance, you might pick up a non-physical broom or vacuum cleaner and sweep or vacuum the self-hatred away. Or you could pass a powerful non-physical magnet over your being, collecting the bits of shame like iron filings, and then bury them deep in the earth. Your guides could give you a bag or box especially designed to hold the shame or self-hatred, and then take it far away to a place where it could be composted or recycled into positive life energy once again. Or guides that take the form of animals might devour the shame or self-hatred—and perhaps even devour you in the process—and then spit you back out again, cleansed.

However you picture the releasing process, you may find that you can energetically see or sense the shame or self-hatred moving upward, out of your body and energy field, and into the light around you. If you can't see or feel it, allow yourself to imagine that you can. Or, you might sense the shame or self-hatred moving downward into the earth—the earth which is, of course, also a master transformer, capable of transmuting all manner of toxic or decaying matter into new forms. Or, you might envision the powerful light of love surrounding the self-hatred, illuminating and penetrating it so deeply that it ceases to be hatred at all. Since the imagination is the most powerful tool available for working with non-physical reality, any of these visualizations can create real shifts.

7. **Give it back.** If you are aware that the energy of shame or self-hatred came to you from another person—either because she actively shamed you, or because you "caught" the contagious self-hatred he carried—you can also energetically give or send it back to them. If your shame or self-hatred came from someone else, she or he needs to work with it in order to evolve—so you are actually helping them, as well as helping yourself, by giving it back. If the source of the shame refuses to take it back, you can give it to her or his higher self for safekeeping.

8. **Remember your power.** However you see or experience the release of your shame or self-hatred, remember that *the locus of power is within you.* Shame and self-hatred are based on a misunderstanding. They are not true or truth. They also are not you. You do not need them. You *can* release them.

This is just one way to work with shame, self-hatred, and other difficult emotional states. Focused work with prayer and intention can be equally effective. Shamanic journeys offer a useful vehicle for most kinds of healing, including the transformation and release of self-hatred. Shamanic drum healing uses the power and vibration of the drum to help move difficult internal matter out of our bodies and beings; I often drum for my clients when we engage in this kind of process.

All of these approaches give us access to the part of the self in which non-physical structures are held. Since each of us contains a unique inner landscape, with our own particular configuration of non-physical structures, different approaches may be more beneficial or resonant for different people. What's most important to remember is that our internal matter, including our self-rejection, shame and self-hatred, *can* be completely transformed or released.

For a long time I had been aware that whenever I made major changes in my life, a part of me felt terrified and started internally screaming "No!" I had always

prided myself on my ability to ignore this inner voice and just forge ahead. This enabled me to act swiftly, impulsively and decisively. The down side was that I would often get blindsided by fear or grief later, after the move, job change or breakup.

In a healing session, I saw a vision of the part of me I identified as "me" with its back against a closet door. Inside the closet was a monstrous deformed limbless blob which I had starved and imprisoned. In this vision, "I" felt there was nothing more important than keeping that door shut. Letting the monster out would ruin everything.

Of course, my healer had told me to call in my guides at the beginning of the session. Now, she asked how my guides felt about the "monster." Naturally, they didn't perceive it as monstrous at all. Slowly, "I" backed away from the closet door so that my guides could retrieve and hold the infant—and as they held it, I actually watched its monstrous, deformed features turn into the features of a normal infant. "Fear is deforming. Love is undeforming," one guide told me.

At first my vision flipped back and forth between the view of the normal infant and the horribly deformed one. Then it began to stabilize as the normal infant, but I was still scared of integrating the infant, afraid that it would render me helpless and paralyzed. Again, my healer asked me how my guides felt about the baby. Of course, I could tell they weren't afraid that picking up and loving this infant would leave them helpless. "Take a clue," my healer suggested with good humor.

In the light of my guides' love, I could see that the "monster" I had fought so hard to keep locked up was only a young, vulnerable part of me in need of compassion and contact. If I could hold and comfort that part of myself, it wouldn't have to interfere with my life choices. Reconnecting with it would enable me to move through whatever fear or grief I held in an organic way, rather than barricading myself against it and then getting blindsided.

Like many seemingly strong, self-confident people, I had created a persona of strength by internally disowning the part of me that didn't feel or look strong. Although this served me in some ways, it made me energetically lopsided and unsteady, while also stunting the growth of the disowned part. Over time, through this soul retrieval and many others, I have become more able to move through the world as someone who is both strong and weak, both confident and frightened. Increasingly, this authenticity has let me experience true strength—flexible, elastic and resilient—rather than its rigid, defended facsimile.

9

Transforming Victim Consciousness

The only relationship that matters is the relationship to the self.

– Isa Gucciardi

When we feel abused or victimized by others, our gaze is focused outside of ourselves. This outer focus takes us away from the real issue—our relationship to ourselves—and also from the only sphere in which we actually have power.

We may believe that we are angry or in pain because other people judge or dislike us, use us, are cruel to us, or fail to treat us fairly. Of course, in any given instance, we may be correct about other peoples' attitudes or actions; although we might be overreacting, misinterpreting or projecting, it's also possible that other people *may* dislike us, judge us, or treat us cruelly. Yet no matter what other people may feel or do, the focus on feelings and actions that originate outside of ourselves is a trap.

The pattern of being or feeling victimized always begins inside us. It invariably emerges from a lack of self-love, a sense of doubt about our own intrinsic value and worth. When we cannot hold onto a sense of our own power and value—when we cannot dwell internally in a posture of self-love—we naturally look to others for reassurance and validation. Yet when we cannot value ourselves, we often draw to us others who also fail to value us. Even if some people in our lives actually *do* appreciate and affirm us, we may mistrust them, fail to take in their appreciation, find fault with them, or otherwise manage to block out the healing currents of love we so badly want and need.

The real issue—the real source of pain—is never what other people do to us. Our deepest pain comes from the ways in which we mistreat *ourselves,* and from the structures which make self-respect and self-kindness impossible, while also holding at bay the respect and kindness of others.

If we do not treat ourselves with love and compassion, it is a waste of time and energy to try to get other people to treat us that way. We only have the power to change our own non-physical structures, not those of anyone else. The feelings and actions of others are not within our sphere of influence. And unless and until we can treat *ourselves* respectfully and kindly, we will rarely receive such treatment from outside, no matter what we do.

When we experience rejection or cruelty from outside of ourselves, rather than the love, compassion and acceptance we need and deserve, it may feel as if God or life is punishing us. Yet what is occurring is actually a neutral energetic phenomenon, akin to the way in which water cannot enter a jar that is sealed. If, as adults, we repeatedly experience abuse or unkindness from others, it can only be because parts of us are internally "sealed" to more loving, compassionate energy, or internally configured in such a way that we expect and attract denigration. Of course, we can feel angry and hurt that life repeatedly reminds us of this inner state. But it is much more helpful to receive the message and take action on it than it is to blame the messenger.

Unsurprisingly, this internal configuration often comes about following childhood abuse. Was this abuse, too, our responsibility? On the human level, the answer is "Of course not." No infant or child ever wants to be abused, deserves abuse, or would knowingly set herself up to be abused. On the spirit level, the answer is less clear. There may be something our spirits are trying to learn through the difficult circumstance of being abused. Perhaps the lesson has to do with becoming able to fully value ourselves, no matter what kind of treatment comes at us from outside; perhaps the abuse we experience in a given lifetime takes place in a much larger context, as part of a vast trajectory of challenge, growth and healing too big for us to fully understand.

In any case, whether or not there is any spiritual cause of the childhood abuse, one thing is certain: we *do,* as adults, have the power to change our inner and outer circumstances. No matter what may have been done to us in the past, we *can* heal and transform, becoming able to value ourselves so deeply and completely that abuse can no longer enter our sphere.

Victim consciousness keeps us drained and distracted, always fighting or feeling hurt by forces "out there," and unable to focus our energy in the direction of true healing. Yet once we acknowledge that the source of the victimization originates within us, there are many different ways we can work to change that pattern, using the processes described throughout this book. The first step is always the same: *taking full self-responsibility*. That is the step that places power back in your own hands.

No matter what kind of mistreatment you may have endured, creating an internal climate of self-acceptance will change both your outer relationships, and your *experience* of those relationships. As you become able to love, honor and value yourself, many people will actually treat you differently; other peoples' behavior may remain the same, but you will be able to recognize that it has nothing to do with you or your worth, making it much less painful. Relationships that do not feed you will wither, while new, truly nourishing relationships will enter your sphere. As all of these changes take place, you will leave the drain and despair of victim consciousness behind you.

In Chapter 2, I described the process by which I permanently released the belief that said that I should not exist. Now, here's the back-story about what led me to do that piece of healing.

At the time, I was involved with a man named Miguel, who was in a committed long-term partnership with another woman. Because their relationship had not been sexual for many years, Miguel had obtained his partner's permission to have a sexual relationship with me—and, drawn to Miguel's warmth, honesty and sexual hunger, I had agreed to that condition. We saw each other one evening a week. Each time, I would cook for him, and after dinner, we would spend hours making love. Then he would rise from my bed, shower, and go home to his partner.

Miguel wasn't cruel, abusive or inconsiderate. In fact, he was kind and passionate, but our relationship was extremely circumscribed. He could call me on his way to or from work, but not from home. He couldn't see me at all on the weekends, except in the rare instances when his partner was out of town. Looking back on it now, I'm struck by what a perfect situation I manifested in order to bring my attention to my belief that I shouldn't exist!

But at the time, even though I had agreed to the conditions of our relationship, I began to feel victimized, mistreated and angry. It was easy to find ammunition for such feelings. Why, I fumed, couldn't Miguel stand up to his partner and give me more of his time and attention? Why were her needs so much more important to him than mine?

The crisis came on a weekend when Miguel's partner was out of town, so Miguel had invited me to spend the night at his house for the first time. He and his partner had agreed that their bedroom was off-limits, but that he and I could sleep together on the fold-out bed in the living room. But, being an ethical guy, Miguel became uncomfortable when I started kissing him in his kitchen—since he and his partner hadn't discussed the possibility of our having physical contact in other rooms in their house.

When Miguel rebuffed my kisses, I felt shattered inside. Fortunately, I had done enough internal work at that point to realize that it really wasn't his fault. Still, I couldn't seem to stop crying. My grief felt bottomless.

Yet even as I cried, I got curious. I'd almost forgotten about my experience on the cross-country drive with Jim many years before. Now it came back to me, and I remembered the feeling that had come up in me then: "I shouldn't exist." That was exactly what I was feeling now. I began to realize that that feeling, not Miguel, was the real source of my pain.

Fortunately, I had a healing session scheduled for the very next day. As I described in Chapter 4, I cleared the belief that I shouldn't exist within less than 24 hours. Within the next few months, as I dissolved the internal structures that had led me to consent to such a circumscribed relationship, Miguel and I parted. And although my subsequent relationships presented their own challenges, as relationships are designed to do, I never again repeated the pattern of being with someone who was only partially available to me.

This story offers a good example of why it's so important to *focus on our relationship to ourselves,* rather than on what anyone else is doing or failing to do. It was very tempting for me to analyze Miguel and his partner instead. Why were they no longer sexual, and why did Miguel remain in that relationship? Whose choice was it, really, that he could see me only one night per week? I *did* spend a fair amount of time focusing on these and similar questions, and trying to argue or manipulate Miguel into different behaviors, and it got me nowhere. It wasn't until I turned my attention fully toward myself—toward *my* reasons for participating in such an inherently unbalanced arrangement, and my own past-time sources of deep grief—that I was able to open myself to truly mutual partnership.

10

Identifying and Releasing Beliefs and Imprints

We have two alternatives: either we question our beliefs, or we don't. Either we accept our fixed versions of reality, or we begin to challenge them. In Buddha's opinion, to train in staying open and curious—to train in dissolving our assumptions and beliefs—is the best use of our human lives.

—*Pema Chödrön*

As we have seen, the beliefs and assumptions we develop early on about ourselves and others—often formed within our first few months of life, and based on confusion and distortion—create *imprints* which determine both what we draw to us, and what we are able to perceive. In other words, our inner pictures actually create what we experience in our outer lives. As the Pathwork puts it, "Unconscious or half-conscious feelings are self-fulfilling prophecies. According to your belief it shall be given to you."

In essence, we see and experience, again and again, what we have seen and experienced before—because it is what we expect, and what we believe is possible. Energetically, it is what we attract, and what we allow. Even if something else manages to show up in our lives, we may misperceive it by seeing in it only what we are used to seeing, or we may actually push it away. The net result is that although our theoretical field of possibilities is vast, most of those possibilities cannot actually come to pass in our lives—unless and until we change the imprints we carry.

The concept of "projective identification," developed by psychologist Melanie Klein, describes this phenomenon in more conventional psychological terms. As the Wikipedia entry on projective identification explains, "Projective identification can become a self-fulfilling prophecy, whereby a person, believing something false about another, relates to that other person in such a way that the other person alters their behavior to make the belief true."

This helps to explain why we find ourselves having the same kinds of painful experiences over and over again, and why attempts to change our lives from the "outside," by changing our job, home, partner, and so on, rarely achieve the effects we anticipate or desire. *It's actually far more effective to change what's inside of us first.* Once we've done so, our outer lives will automatically follow suit.

Yet it's admittedly challenging to change our beliefs and imprints before our outer lives have changed. We must open ourselves to believing in a reality different from what we have ever experienced—in order to become able to experience a reality different from what we have ever believed in. It requires a leap of faith, an act of grace, a concerted willingness, and, of course, help from higher sources. Fortunately, that help is abundantly available.

How can we identify and shift our deeply-held imprints? First, it helps to acknowledge that our beliefs about ourselves, others and life are just that: beliefs, rather than universal or absolute truths. For instance, a woman who believes that "Men always reject women" may have seen and experienced exactly that, over and over again. Yet if she intentionally looks around for evidence to contradict her belief, she will also see various other kinds of other things occurring: women rejecting men, men staying with women, men and women living happily together, and so on. Even in her own life, it's possible that she may have experienced something different from her imprint—for instance, a man who didn't reject her. Yet, if her imprint is strong enough, she will still be able to interpret everything she experiences through the distorting lens of her belief. For instance, perhaps the man who didn't reject her was different in some way from other men; the women who appear to be rejecting men are only doing so because they have already been rejected; the men who appear to be staying with women are only pretending, and will soon reject their partners; the women and men who appear to be happy together are doomed for an inevitable fall when the man rejects the women, as men always do… etcetera.

Imprints are essentially constellations of related beliefs. Because each distorted belief reinforces another, the combined effect can be extraordinarily powerful. When we are fully in the grip of an imprint, we may feel absolutely convinced that it is the truth. Some of us even take pride in the strength of our distorted convictions about ourselves, others and life. Yet this is a destructive, misplaced pride. It is as if we had blinders on, and then took pride in our "knowledge" that the world was really much narrower than others believed.

Yet sometimes we may be forced to notice that even if an imprint appears to hold true for us, other people seem to be exempt from it. It is extraordinarily painful to feel deprived of life's riches, and even more so when others seem to have escaped that deprivation. Is this because we are less deserving, or because life is cruel? No—it is because we are unconsciously or half-consciously reinforcing, experiencing and creating the reality we expect, over and over again.

Buddhist psychotherapist Tara Bennett-Goleman calls the consistent distortions in our perceptions of reality "maladaptive emotional schemas," and identifies the five most common schemas as *Abandonment, Deprivation, Mistrust, Subjugation,* and *Unlovability.* To identify which schemas we carry, we need only examine the kinds of pain we repeatedly experience. For instance, the stories I've told about my relationships with Jim and Miguel make clear that according to this system my main schema is *Deprivation,* the belief that "there will never be enough for me."

Dismantling Imprints

The first step in liberating ourselves from schemas or imprints is to realize that we have them. In other words, we must acknowledge that our deeply-held impressions of reality are not actually reality, even though they have shaped what we have thus far been able to see and experience. Although this realization might seem joyful and liberating, it can also be frightening and disorienting. Even if we hold imprints that make us miserable, the presence of a specific set of beliefs helps us to feel safe in an otherwise unpredictable world. Depending on which part of our consciousness we most identify with, we may be excited, terrified, or both by the realization that much more is possible than we had allowed ourselves to imagine. Realizing that our own imprints have been the cause of so much of our suffering can also bring up grief and shame. If those feelings are strong, we may need to work with them before proceeding further.

Next, it's helpful to inventory the nature of the schemas, beliefs or imprints we're carrying. There are several ways to do this. One is to make a list of painful or unwanted experiences that we find ourselves having again and again, and then work backward to identify the beliefs underlying those experiences. In every case, we can be certain that an imprint or belief is at work.

You can also discover imprints you carry by simply paying close attention to your inner landscape as you go about your daily life. Notice what ideas, feelings or images come up in you, and especially observe any feelings or beliefs with which you don't consciously identify—since those tend to be the imprints that wreak havoc from underground. The Pathwork encourages a "Daily Review," in which people write down every emotional spike or surge they experienced throughout the day, and then investigate the inner or outer conditions that triggered it.

You can also ask your guides to help you locate and write down every belief you hold in a given area of life—for instance, "Gender," "Sexuality," "Intimate Relationships," "Creativity," or "Work." (Most of us hold plenty of imprints related to all of these important life arenas.) For instance, if you are a man and pick "Gender," you might first write down every belief that exists in any corner of your being about men: what men do and don't do, what is required of men, what is "manly" or "unmanly," what is possible and impossible for men, what is "right" and "wrong" for men, etc. Then, you'd do the same about women. Even if your understanding of gender is more complex than can fit in a box labeled "male" or "female," this exercise is important, since it's likely that you're still carrying many beliefs and imprints regarding maleness and femaleness.

Next, ask your guides for help in remembering and recognizing instances in which reality has proven itself to be different from your imprints. Write down times when you or other men have "broken the rules" imbedded in your consciousness about men, and when women have contradicted your beliefs about women. If it's difficult for you to think of instances which disprove your beliefs, ask your guides to help you recognize such instances over the next few days, weeks or months. Consciously direct your intention to allow in a wider experience of life than has previously been available to you. If fear or resistance comes up, ask your guides to help you with that, too. Your statement of intention might be something like this:

I affirm my desire, my willingness, my choice and my intention to become more able to perceive the vast range of truth about men and women [or: about gender as a whole].

I ask for the help of my wise guides, inner teachers and higher consciousness in dissolving my limiting beliefs about men and women, and helping me see the much wider reality of both, or all, genders.

I also ask my guides for help in healing or releasing those parts of me that feel fear about entering into this wider knowing. Please, guides, help those parts to become stronger and more whole, or help them to dissolve them in the light of the larger parts of my being, whichever will best serve my highest good.

It's important to understand that the process of clearing your imprints is not simply a mental process. There *is* a mental component involved in consciously reminding yourself that your imprints represent a narrow, stuck distortion of reality, rather than reality itself. But that mental recognition alone does little or nothing to actually *clear* an imprint, and the part of you that holds imprints can't clear those imprints. That's why it's essential to call on larger forces in order to effect an energetic shift.

Here is a very simple yet powerful prayer that can help:

Releasing Prayer

Release what needs to be released.
Transform what needs to be transformed.
Bring in what needs to be brought in.

If you call in your guides, focus on the imprint you want to release or transform, and then chant this prayer, either inwardly or out loud, you may be surprised. You might feel a "whoosh" of energy in your system when you first say it, as if you've opened the door to let your guides begin their work—which, in fact, you have. You can repeat it again and again, even as you engage in other activities, to keep the healing and clearing process active.

Sometimes our beliefs and imprints were formed under very traumatic conditions. For instance, my client Jewel, who held the belief that "Men always reject women," had developed this imprint when her father left her mother, devastating her mother emotionally, logistically, and financially. Jewel was only three when this happened, and in many ways she not only lost her father, but her mother, too. Because there was so much emotional charge compressed into Jewel's imprint, she needed her guides' help in accessing, transmuting and releasing a great deal of grief, fear, and rage. This happened over a number of sessions involving soul retrieval, energetic clearing, drum healing and more.

If your imprints are highly charged in this way, you may need extra help from your guides, or even from a human practitioner, in clearing them.

Here is a prayer that can help:

Prayer for Clearing Imprints

As the storms of emotion move through me, please help me remain connected to you, my guides, and to the light of higher consciousness and love.

Please help me know that releasing this imprint will restore me to myself, to truth, and to the goodness of life itself. Please help me feel and hold to this truth with every cell in my body, and every iota of my being.

Please hold and help me as my grief, fear and rage pass through my body and return to the earth, where they can be composted. Please help me remain connected to you and to your love as I undergo this profound reconfiguration, and allow any emotions which are not mine to return to wherever or whomever they actually belong.

Sometimes clearing imprints can be easier than you might have imagined—as.simple as carrying a chair you no longer need out of a room where you had kept it. At other times it can feel as if you are trying to remove the foundation of your own house, even while you're living in the house. In that case, your healing process will be "nested," with each new process making possible the next.

As I described in the last chapter, my relationship with Miguel both emerged from the imprints I carried, and appeared to "prove" them to me. For instance, because I carried the belief that "I shouldn't exist," I manifested a situation perfectly designed to make me feel that way. As I explored further, I realized that I also believed that "There will never be enough for me." Obviously, these two beliefs reinforced one another, and being in an intimate relationship with someone who had a primary partner and could only see me once a week reinforced them both.

Although releasing the belief that "I should not exist" created a profound energetic shift, I still had more to do to clear the imprint. For instance, I realized that I felt resentful about cooking for Miguel on every one of our dates—yet then I remembered that Miguel had often offered to "pick up some take-out" on his way to my house, and I had always refused. I soon saw that although part of me resented Miguel for "taking advantage of me," another part felt very uncomfortable if I imagined a truly equal relationship. That part of me believed that I needed to give others much more than they gave me. In fact, as I explored further I discovered the belief that I needed to give my partners at least three times as much as I received from them!

Realizing that I carried these beliefs and imprints—and many more along the same lines—was a revelation to me. It allowed me to stop blaming Miguel and others for treating me unfairly, and to accept responsibility for having created the circumstances that I found so frustrating and unsatisfying. Once I understood that I had created them, I also knew that I could change them—and, over time, using the tools described in this book, I did.

Yet I did pass through some intense emotional storms in the process. I recall a three-day weekend when I had hoped that Miguel would be able to come over earlier than usual, since he had Monday off. However, ever the nice guy, he was spending his holiday helping some friends paint their house. Initially he told me he'd see me at 6:00, as he did on work nights. But at 6:30 he called and told me the painting was taking longer than anticipated. At 8:00 he called again, sounding apologetic, and promised he'd be there by 9:00. It was 9:30 by the time he finally knocked on my door.

Starting at around 7:30, I was lying on my couch, crying and shaking. From the outside, I probably looked like an addict in need of a fix. The "fix" that part of me craved and another part refused was blame. A big part of me wanted to rage at Miguel, to yell, refuse to talk to him, take revenge in some way. But since another part of me knew that I was equally responsible for the situation, I chose instead to use Miguel's lateness as an opportunity to do some intensive work with my deprivation schema. Instead of yelling at Miguel in my head, I covered my head with a blanket, sobbed, prayed, and asked my guides for help. I focused on dissolving my imprints, releasing Miguel from responsibility for my emotional needs, and remembering that the locus of power lay within me.

In the end, I was grateful that Miguel didn't arrive until 9:30. By then, the storm had passed and the emotional charge had dispersed. It was fine to see him, but I didn't need to see him, nor did I need to try to punish him. I'd gotten my power back.

11

Understanding and Shifting Emotional Postures

When you flip the switch in that attic, it doesn't matter whether it's been dark for ten minutes, ten years or ten decades. The light still illuminates the room.

– Sharon Salzberg

We've already seen the ways that our beliefs about ourselves and our lives determine our experience, and how we can shift those beliefs. In the process, it's also important to examine our habitual emotional postures, since those postures both emerge from and shape our beliefs.

It's easiest to understand emotional postures if we compare them to their physical counterparts. For instance, if you were leaning over for an extended period of time, your back would probably become sore. If you realized that your physical posture was causing the soreness, you could simply stand up straight, and the pain would go away. However, if you failed to make the connection between your posture and your back pain, you might continue leaning over, while also beginning to take painkillers for your sore back. You would then have embarked on the unfortunate path of medicating your symptom without recognizing or changing its underlying cause. If the painkiller gave you an upset stomach, you might then take a second medication to try to manage that symptom, which might then cause other problems, for which you might take a third medication, and so on—all without ever correcting the *easily correctable* original cause of your pain.

Many of us do exactly this in our emotional lives. When we understand the way emotional postures work, we can learn to hold ourselves in ways more consonant with our well-being, helping us to experience more free-dom, ease and joy.

Let's start with very different emotional postures that may seem to bear a surface resemblance to one another—for instance, *self-responsibility* and *self-blame*. People often resist taking responsibility for their inner lives because they have confused this movement with the pain of blaming themselves for their circumstances. Yet when we look more closely, we can see that the posture of self-responsibility is a wholesome stepping-forward into the universe; the statement it makes is, *I am here. I have choice, power and agency.* In contrast, the posture of self-blame says, *I should not be here. I hereby attempt to obliterate myself.*

Self-responsibility makes us larger, more powerful. It connects us to the harmonious force of life itself. In contrast, self-blame shrinks us and leaves us powerless. Its current of self-negation is an act of violence against the self—and, because we are part of life, it is also an act of violence against life. Therefore, self-responsibility is a posture that helps us to recognize and alleviate emotional pain, while self-blame both exacerbates existing pain, and causes additional pain.

In the previous chapters, I described my process of taking responsibility for the beliefs and imprints that had led me to attract and create painful, unsatisfying relationships. This self-responsibility allowed me to identify, heal and release the beliefs and imprints that were at fault, and thus to change my life.

If I had adopted a posture of self-blame rather than self-responsibility, this forward movement could never have occurred. Instead, I might have criticized myself: "What's wrong with me for attracting such lousy partners?" "Why don't I ever learn?" After a while, the pain of this self-blame would probably have led me to blame my partners, too. "What's wrong with [insert name here] for treating me this way?" (In fact, as I described, I was already doing some of that.) Of course, this would not have helped improve my relationships, especially since the real cause of the problem lay within my own psyche. The cycle of blaming ourselves and others is a painful, draining loop which can never bring about real change.

Many people get stuck on an inner seesaw of blame. When you're on the "up" end, you're blaming other people and feeling like a victim; when you're on the "down" end, you're blaming yourself and feeling like a stupid, worthless, hopeless, unlovable idiot. Both sides of the seesaw cause suffering, and the only way out of that suffering is to get off the seesaw and release blame entirely.

If you feel ready to take this step, here is a prayer that can help.

Prayer to Release Blame

I resolve in this moment, and in all other moments, to relinquish the illusion that anything in my life, past, present or future, is, was or will be in any way different from my destiny, my highest good. I resolve to allow and cultivate instead a profound acceptance of and gratitude for all of the circumstances, events and people in my life, for all that these configurations have taught me, and can and will teach me, when I permit them to.

I resolve to thank the universe and my own larger self daily for all of the circumstances and relationships in my life, exactly as they are. I resolve to meditate daily on the clear understanding that nothing is wrong *and to accept the help of the universe in living, seeing, hearing, breathing, experiencing this truth more fully and completely each day, and with each breath.*

I also resolve to bathe myself in a constant, undiluted solution of love, compassion and self-acceptance. I recognize that resistance to any phenomenon in or outside the self is resistance to life, and I resolve to continually and completely dissolve the misperceptions which have resulted in my current resistance to life. There is no one and nothing that has failed me, least of all life. I ask for help in recognizing, remembering and believing that life has served me perfectly and continues to do so, and I humbly ask for life's help in removing my blindness and resistance to its service.

As the Pathwork says, "When I withhold from life, I withhold from myself, for life and I are one. I recognize that it is this soul movement, rather than any other inner or outer change, that will bring the peace I seek."

This prayer was given to me by my guides during a very difficult period in my own life. Because I am a strong-willed person, my guides used very strong language to combat my tendency to find fault with life. If your patterns are different, you can alter the prayer in any way that feels right to you.

Another pair of emotional postures that may at first appear similar is *self-pity* and *self-compassion*. When we look more closely, we can see that these two postures are profoundly different. Self-pity says, *I am weak, helpless, a victim. Poor me. Life and others have turned against me. I am stuck.* Self-compassion says, *I am suffering, and I need and deserve help.*

As I worked to clear the relational imprints that made me feel resentful, victimized and deprived, a posture of self-pity would have led to thoughts like these: "I'll never have the kind of relationship I want." "My family damaged me irrevocably." "Either there is something seriously wrong with me, or life is just unfair." But the posture of self-compassion helped me understand how my problematic beliefs and imprints had been formed, and, even more importantly, created an inner climate in which I could shift them. Therefore, self-pity would have kept me stuck, while self-compassion enabled movement.

Guilt and *remorse* are two more postures that might superficially appear similar, yet are radically different on an energetic level. Guilt says *I did something bad; therefore, I am bad.* The posture is one of shrinking, cringing. Implicit in this posture is a belief that *I deserve to be punished. I do not deserve my full complement of life energy and compassion.* Again, this belief emerges out of a fundamental confusion, since anything withheld from the self is also, by definition, withheld from others. In contrast, the posture of remorse says, *I have done something which is out of alignment with what I know to be the highest truth or the highest good. I regret that action because it was not reflective of my true nature.* In remorse the posture is fully erect, without defensiveness or self-abnegation. The statement made by this posture is, *I wish and intend to align myself and my actions with the universal flow.* This posture allows both compassion for the self, and compassion from "outside" the self. Therefore, remorse can facilitate change and healing, while guilt will further entrench pain and make healing impossible.

If you have ever found yourself trapped in guilt, you know how paralyzing it can feel. Yet if you made a mistake, you may believe your guilt is "justified" or "necessary." The truth is that the posture of guilt is anti-life; it is never justified, necessary, or helpful. If you have made a mistake—as all of us do, and have—consciously choosing to shift from guilt to remorse can help you heal the internal conditions that led to that mistake, and also become ready to make external amends if it is possible and appropriate to do so.

Some people vigorously fight against acknowledging their mistakes or feeling remorse. Most often, this is because they are terrified of collapsing under the weight of guilt and self-rejection. An underlying structure of shame and self-hatred makes them fear complete annihilation if they admit wrongdoing of any kind. They therefore vehemently refuse to acknowledge any mistakes they may have made, and insist that any and all mistakes were made by others. Although this posture may look or even feel powerful on the surface, it is actually highly unstable. If you cannot allow yourself to accept and feel remorse for your own mistakes and must instead blame others for what you experience, you will inevitably find yourself trapped in victim consciousness. If you cultivate the ability to tolerate life-affirming, self-loving states of remorse, you will deepen your relationship to yourself, others and life.

Although people often confuse *discernment* and *judgment,* they are very different. Discernment is a neutral recognition of what is true on the human level at a given moment, while judgment is a value-laden assessment which labels phenomena as "good" or "bad," "better" or "worse," "right" or "wrong." While there are many areas of life in which discernment is necessary and valuable, judgment is an anti-life stance which is never helpful. Yet when we notice ourselves holding judgments, it is harmonious for us to acknowledge them openly and compassionately—since judging ourselves for having judgments would only compound the erroneous posture.

At first glance, it might appear more harmonious to feel proud than to feel ashamed, but in truth, both are energetically closed states. Although shame says *I am bad* and pride says *I am good,* both emerge from a framework in which a person conceives of him- or herself as separate, an individual self that, because it is cut off from life, needs to be reduced or enlarged in some way. The kind of enlargement that comes about through pride is energetically bloated and unstable, subject to collapsing in on itself in any moment and revealing itself as its "opposite," shame. Although shame creates pain and pride may at first appear to alleviate such pain, it will not lead to real healing.

In contrast, the posture of gratitude is a stable, balanced posture. In it, there is no attempt to "feel good" while holding oneself separate or apart from the universe; rather, there is a joyful acknowledgement of the connection between oneself and the universe. It's no surprise that numerous spiritual traditions promote the value of gratitude; researchers have even documented links between higher levels of gratitude and improved physical health. Some spiritual teachers suggest making "gratitude lists" on a daily or weekly basis, or saying gratitude prayers every night. However you nourish and cultivate gratitude, it will, in turn, nourish you.

Of course, it is not "bad" to blame ourselves, or to feel guilt or pride—nor is it "better" to feel self-responsible or grateful. It is simply that the former postures alienate and constrict the self from the universal flow, while the latter postures open and align us to that flow, thereby enhancing our joy and power. When we experience this difference, it makes sense to cultivate those postures which enlarge and empower us, simply because they *feel* so much better—and of course, they also facilitate our growth and evolution.

Some people believe that anger is a "negative emotion," and should be avoided. But that is a terrible oversimplification. If we look at the inner posture underlying anger, we can see that anger emerges from a place of resistance, an inner belief that something is wrong. Generally the statement being made is either, *I have been wronged*, or *Someone or something outside of me is wrong*. If we diagram these statements energetically, we will see a flow of energy leaving the person who believes they have been wronged, and going directly to the person they believe has wronged them. Anger has the effect of stripping away our life energy and gifting it to whoever we feel angry at. Although it is not "wrong," it is also not appropriate medicine for the pain it attempts to assuage, because it deepens rather than corrects energetic imbalance. Long-lasting patterns of anger often emerge from victim consciousness, or from a misguided attempt to protect ourselves from other feelings we might feel if the anger diminished.

Of course, judging anger as "bad" doesn't help. Instead, cultivating a posture of self-love will restore our energy to a more life-affirming posture. When we are in a state of self-love and in full possession of our own energy, we are unlikely to feel wronged, and we also become strong enough to feel whatever other emotions our anger might have been masking.

At times, anger is valuable and appropriate. As Isa Gucciardi says succinctly, "The purpose of anger is to put down a boundary." Particularly when we do not know how to establish boundaries in other ways, anger can be a valuable tool, just as flashlights can be useful when the lights go out. But once the lights come back on—once we have used the tools of love and compassion to heal our sense of self and create healthy boundaries—the flashlights and the anger can go back into the drawer labeled "for emergency use only."

Many people believe that "self-esteem" is good, and should be culti-vated, since most people prefer to "feel good about themselves" rather than experience the opposite state, "feeling bad about themselves" (although a surprising number actually have the reverse preference.) But to understand the true nature of this posture, we must explore what it is to feel "good about ourselves." Does this "good" feeling rely upon a sense of separation from others for its maintenance? Does it arise from feeling "better than" others? Does it contain any flavor of smugness or superiority? If so, this so-called "good" feeling is a trick knife-blade that will actually cause harm to the one who wields it, because any feeling that arises from or relies upon a notion of oneself as separate from others will ultimately cause pain. In contrast, self-acceptance, or any feeling that arises from an understanding of oneself as intrinsically and inextricably connected to all others, and to life, will promote joy and harmony.

Again, it is never helpful to judge, blame or criticize ourselves or others for holding emotional postures that reflect and further a sense of separation. Such judgment, blame or criticism only deepens the very split that we have already recognized as injurious. Rather, we can acknowledge where we have gone off course—where we are essentially leaning over in a way that causes us pain—while holding ourselves in complete compassion.

Sometimes people who feel committed to emotional and spiritual growth judge themselves even more harshly out of the mistaken belief that this will further their growth. A client of mine recently complained when she found herself feeling strong feelings of envy. "I don't like that in myself," she said, making a face. "It's so *unevolved*." Yet this kind of self-rejection makes it harder for us to feel whole—and when we do not feel fully whole in ourselves, it's natural to feel envy of others. In this way, self-judgment becomes a vicious cycle.

Human beings tend to judge emotions as "good" or "bad," "positive" or "negative," yet this act of judgment is as misplaced as judging a tree. Trees simply *are*; so, too, are emotions. Although certain emotions do contribute to suffering, while others are life-affirming, the act of judging an emotion as "bad"—or judging ourselves as "bad" for having "bad emotions"—only creates separation and suffering. The good news is that no matter what habitual postures we discover within ourselves, *any* genuine instance of compassion will restore harmony to our inner being, and in that way help restore us to our proper relationship to the universe.

12

The Transformational Power of Compassion

Compassion isn't some kind of self-improvement project or ideal that we're trying to live up to. Having compassion starts and ends with having compassion for all those unwanted parts of ourselves, all those imperfections that we don't even want to look at.

—Pema Chödrön

Compassion is one of the most powerful healing energies in existence, although its true nature is often misunderstood. We may confuse it with being "nice," or with empathy or sympathy. But to paraphrase Mark Twain, niceness, empathy and sympathy are to compassion what a lightning bug is to lightning. Compassion is not an emotional state; it is a transformational force. Like joy, it comes to us from beyond our human selves, although we can open ourselves to it, invoke it, invite it and cultivate it.

Used medicinally, compassion is highly adaptogenic—in other words, it's "good for what ails us," no matter what forms our ailments take. In fact, any time you find yourself stuck or blocked in any way, internally or externally, compassion can both salve your wounds and lever your tires out of the mud they've been spinning in.

The simple but powerful Buddhist practice of *metta*, lovingkindness meditation, is an excellent way to begin to experience the power of compassion.

Developing Compassion for Yourself and Others

1. First, say this prayer at least three times on your own behalf:

   May I heal
   May my heart open
   May I find joy
   May I live in peace.

   As you say it, attempt to take the messages of the blessings into your heart and body. It may help to lay a hand on your own heart or belly as you say the words.

2. Next, let yourself think of someone you feel loving feelings toward. Picturing his or her face, bless them, as well:

   May you heal
   May your heart open
   May you find joy
   May you live in peace.

   Again, say the prayer at least three times.

3. Next, pick someone about whom you feel neutral—a casual acquaintance, perhaps. Picturing his or her face, bless them the same way, slowly and repeatedly:

   May you heal
   May your heart open
   May you find joy
   May you live in peace.

4. Next, think of someone with whom you've struggled or had conflict. Picturing his or her face, say the prayer again, working to really feel it as you say it. Go over it at least three times; you may find it helps to say it ten, twenty, thirty times or more.

   May you heal
   May your heart open
   May you find joy
   May you live in peace.

5. Last, say the prayer on behalf of the entire world—remembering, of course, that that includes you, too. Let your mental gaze travel around

the country or world as you repeat the words, once again, at least three times.

May we heal
May our hearts open
May we find joy
May we live in peace.

If you truly give yourself to this process, repeating the phrases in sequence, you will feel the power of compassion soften your heart. Whether it happens in minutes, days, weeks or months depends on how calcified your tender emotional tissue has become. But it will happen.

There are many versions of *metta* prayers online and in Buddhist books. I composed the particular prayer above; you, too, can compose your own to create phrasing that feels just right for you. Words are carriers of energy, but the energy lives beyond the words; it comes through them or is summoned by them, and by your intention.

Traditionally, *metta* prayers were used to help people shift beyond a narrow conception of self-interest and into a state of benevolence toward others and the world. While of course that movement is still necessary, these days, as previously discussed, it's just as hard for many of us to direct compassion inward as outward. *Metta* practice is like a gentle, deep cleanse for our hearts. Some people find it helpful to say *metta* prayers every day for months or even years, allowing compassion to work its way into all the hidden crevices and gnarled knots of their being.

Of course, if you find yourself resistant to compassion, you can also work with your guides more directly to dismantle the inner structures involved. Here is the description of a shamanic journey that came after I asked my guides to help me open my heart.

I found my panther guide in a forest, where there seemed to be pieces of my heart scattered everywhere. He gathered them together and made them into a kind of heart-shaped pendant which he put around his neck and wore for a while to infuse it with power; then he got on top of me and infused the heart back into my chest.

Next he took me to the big light cave where the three beings who had visited me when I was four were waiting for me. They put me in the carved cradle I had as an infant and were completely loving and attentive to me, holding, patting, rocking and caring for me. I could feel part of me craving their attention and part of me completely, absolutely refusing and resisting it. As they continued to surround me with pure love and compassion, it became excruciatingly uncomfortable for me—I felt myself physically squirming, and was strongly tempted to end the journey. Instead I covered my whole face with my scarf because I felt so vulnerable. [I was doing this journey in a group setting.]

I understood that I needed to become able to allow this compassion in, in order to be able to feel more compassion for others. I asked the beings why there was so much struggle, and then realized that it felt like my heart would shatter if I let the compassion in. There was a hard wall around my heart, and part of me felt terrified of being made weak, of being disabled, by receiving love or compassion. It shocked me to feel how strong this was and how much of me was going into this refusal, keeping love and light out. However, the beings didn't seem shocked or dismayed; they just kept slowly, steadily emanating love and compassion, surrounding me with it, touching me with it. As they did so, I relaxed my self-judgment about not being able to let in their love, and eventually, relaxed my resistance to them as well. It wasn't dramatic; it was more like the way night slowly lightens into dawn. The change was gradual [within the space of the 10-minute journey] but profound. I understood that I could come back to this place for more "treatments" at any time.

As you can see, this journey showed that a part of me strongly feared and resisted the medicine of compassion—and yet compassion was the only medicine that could heal my fear and resistance. In fact, there is no condition, inner or outer, that cannot be helped by compassion.

Compassion is also crucial in helping us to heal our horror at our own misdeeds, as well as the misdeeds of others. The word "misdeed" sounds minor, like accidentally scratching a car's bumper in a parking lot and failing to leave a note, or not bothering to tell the cashier she's given us an extra dollar in change—but of course, in addition to these kinds of minor departures from integrity, most of us have at least occasionally been cruel, malicious, vengeful or caused serious harm. We may have lied to others in an effort to protect ourselves (even when we think we're lying to protect someone else, it's generally ourselves, or our image, or our perceived well-being that we're really protecting.) We may have exploited, manipulated or taken advantage of others. In fact, it would be surprising if we had never done any of these things, since they seem to be quintessentially human acts that have happened over and over again in the history of our kind.

A word we might use in place of "misdeed" is "sin." However, that word carries a terribly heavy burden for many of us because it has been so badly mistranslated, misused and misunderstood in religious contexts for centuries. Eckhart Tolle explains, "Literally translated from the ancient Greek in which the New Testament was written, to sin means to 'miss the mark' as an archer misses the target—so to sin means to miss the point of human existence, or to live unskillfully in ways that cause suffering."

In this sense, of course, all of us are "sinners," and compassion is the force that can eradicate both our sinning and our shame at having sinned. It is also the force that can help us heal our grief and rage at the sins of others. Thich Naht Hanh makes this point very powerfully in his poem, "Please Call Me By My True Names."

Please Call Me By My True Names

Do not say that I'll depart tomorrow
because even today I still arrive.

Look deeply: I arrive in every second
to be a bud on a spring branch,

to be a tiny bird, with wings still fragile,
learning to sing in my new nest,
to be a caterpillar in the heart of a flower,
to be a jewel hiding itself in a stone.

I still arrive, in order to laugh and to cry,
in order to fear and to hope.
The rhythm of my heart is the birth and
death of all that are alive.

I am the mayfly metamorphosing on the surface of the river,
and I am the bird which, when spring comes, arrives in time
to eat the mayfly.

I am the frog swimming happily in the clear pond,
and I am also the grass-snake who, approaching in silence,
feeds itself on the frog.

I am the child in Uganda, all skin and bones,
my legs as thin as bamboo sticks,
and I am the arms merchant, selling deadly weapons to Uganda.

I am the twelve-year-old girl, refugee on a small boat,
who throws herself into the ocean after being raped by a sea pirate,
and I am the pirate, my heart not yet capable of seeing and loving.

I am a member of the politburo, with plenty of power in my hands,
and I am the man who has to pay his "debt of blood" to my people,
dying slowly in a forced labor camp.

My joy is like spring, so warm it makes flowers bloom
in all walks of life.
My pain is like a river of tears, so full it fills the four oceans.
Please call me by my true names,
so I can hear all my cries and laughs at once,
so I can see that my joy and pain are one.

Please call me by my true names,
so I can wake up,
and so the door of my heart can be left open,
the door of compassion.

Of course, most readers of this book have never raped a twelve-year-old girl; we don't literally have "blood on our hands," and we are probably not dying in forced labor camps as we read these words. Yet within us lives the knowledge of all of these kinds of horror. And within us, too, is the door to our transformation—the door of compassion.

There are only a few times in my adult life when I remember consciously, deliberately withholding compassion from another human being. Here is the story of one such incident, which has been a powerful teacher for me.

After several weeks of traveling in India, I had learned to harden myself against the constant presence of beggars—the sea of emaciated, crippled, deformed sufferers, endlessly holding up their needy hands. On the last night of my trip, I went out to dinner with the express plan of saving my leftovers to eat on the flight home. Then, as I left the restaurant with my little white "doggie bag," I was approached by a young woman carrying a baby in her arms. She knew exactly what my little bag contained, and she asked me for it by pointing to it, then pointing to the baby's stomach and then to her own. But I wanted the food for myself. I didn't want to give it to her. And so I said No.

A moment later, after the young woman had disappeared into the crowd, I realized what I had done. I had plenty of money to buy other food to eat on my flight home, yet I had refused sustenance to someone whose need was obviously much greater than my own. Remorseful, I searched for the young woman, but was unable to find her.

Obviously, my action came out of a sense of separation. Yet somewhere in my being lived the sense—the knowledge—of connection, too. In fact, my sense of separation was so rigid largely because it imperfectly covered up a much deeper sense of heartbreak. The fact that there are people so poor and hungry that they literally beg for my money or food is shattering to me, when I let myself feel it. This means I need to direct compassion toward my own broken heart, as well as toward the panhandlers filling the streets.

Since I live in an urban area, someone asks me for money almost every time I go downtown. Of course, *what* I do in response matters much less than *how and why I do it.* It's possible to give money or food while withholding compassion—or to feel and emanate compassion, even while saying No to a given request. Learning to respond with compassion to the disowned, rejected parts of ourselves can help us retain compassion for the pain outside ourselves; responding compassionately to outer pain can also help us become more able to turn our compassion inward. Ultimately, the pain inside us and the pain outside us can both teach us about ourselves, and can both offer us the same opportunities for healing.

As poet Adrienne Rich writes:

> *The body's pain and the pain on the streets*
> *are not the same but you can learn*
> *from the edges that blur. O you who love clear edges*
> *more than anything,*
> *watch the edges that blur.*

13

Restoring Energetic Integrity

Without energetic boundaries, we can't share who and what we are with the world, and we can't receive the bounty the world has to offer us, either.

— Cyndi Dale

In order to move through our inner and outer landscapes with our full complement of life force and power, we need to cultivate the kind of integrity that Reiki practitioner Pamir Kiciman defines as "the quality of being whole or united, and of being unharmed or sound." In fact, if we are not whole and united within ourselves, we are very unlikely to be unharmed or sound.

"Soundness" in this context can mean many things; dictionary definitions include "free from injury or disease," "free from flaw, defect, or decay," "free from error, fallacy, or misapprehension," and "showing good judgment or sense." If we are disconnected or alienated from ourselves, *or* if we are connected to ourselves but do not appropriately distinguish between "self" and "not-self," we cannot enjoy these freedoms. If we do not have clear energetic boundaries, we become overly permeable to others; this leaves us either perpetually drained by others' suffering, or enforcing artificially rigid boundaries to prevent ourselves from being drained (as I did with the hungry woman in India.)

Because we are energetic beings, literally made of energy despite the illusion of solid mass, our energy fields can easily become tangled or blurred by the energies of other people. Energetic imprints from people we've known— parents, other relatives, ex-lovers—can become imbedded within us. Even energies from people whom we don't personally know can make their way into our energetic fiber, particularly if we have been wounded in ways that leave us energetically vulnerable. Just as a physical cut or scrape leaves us vulnerable to infection, non-physical wounding leaves us open to energetic intrusion. One shamanic term for this phenomenon is "energetic interference," since the presence of foreign energy does indeed interfere with our well-being. The restoration of our energetic integrity requires us to ensure that we are holding *all* of our own energy, and *none* of anyone else's.

Just as certain clothes are magnets for lint and pet hair, some peoples' energy fields tend to collect energetic detritus. If you are a sensitive, empathic, porous person, you've probably picked up a lot of energetic debris from those around you. At its most mundane, energetic clearing could be likened to using a tape-roller that peels off the pet hair, leaving your garment—or your energy field—looking like itself again.

Yet in other circumstances the process of energetic clearing is far more involved, complicated or emotionally challenging. If you've been violated or abused, the emotional and energetic currents of those who abused you may have become lodged within you, too. Particularly if the abuse began when you were very young, it can take a lot of work to separate out your own energy from that of others. After having carried the voices of your abusers inside you for so long, you may even have come to think of them as your own. It always takes longer to clear out things we think are *us,* because first we have to realize that they're not.

After relationships break up, we may hold on to the energies of our ex-spouses or ex-lovers; often there are parts of us that don't want to let them go, either because we miss them, or because we want to punish them—or both at once. Parents may hold on to their children's energies in an effort to try to protect them—or because their childrens' life energy is so much fresher and more vibrant than their own. Healers who do not carefully balance themselves may take on some of their clients' energies. Yet regardless of who or what may have become tangled-up inside us, we *can,* with work and consciousness, untangle it, clear it out, and restore our own energetic integrity.

It can be difficult in this clearing process to distinguish between the many diverse aspects of self—which, as previously discussed, may hold radically different perspectives and levels of consciousness, and be urgently in need of healing—and energies that are truly *not us,* and need to be released. Often it's helpful to work with an experienced human practitioner in this process. But you can also trust your guides to help you cleanse and heal whatever is truly yours, while also releasing what isn't.

When I first began studying shamanism, the idea of a person being inhabited or "possessed" by other energies seemed pretty far out-there to me. I felt both skeptical and fearful. Fortunately, my teacher was very matter-of-fact about the whole thing. She helped me understand this kind of "interference" as a common side-effect of trauma, analogous to an opportunistic infection which takes advantage of a lowered immune system.

In the years since then, I have led many clients through processes to release interfering energies. However, because I know that many people still harbor the kind of fear and disbelief I once had about this topic, I don't usually name what we've done. Occasionally, a client will spontaneously joke about it, saying something like, "Wow, that felt like an exorcism!" Usually I just smile and say something like, "That's one way to look at it."

Sometimes, however, the interfering energy makes itself known in a more obvious way. When this happens, my clients may be forced to adjust their view of reality. Here's a story about one such healing.

I had been working with Khadija for only a few weeks when she mentioned hesitantly that she "experienced suicidal ideation." Her phrasing caught my attention; I noticed that she hadn't said she "felt suicidal," but used more distanced language. I asked her to explain what she meant.

"Well," she admitted, "I frequently hear a voice in my head that says 'Just shoot yourself.' It doesn't seem to have any connection with what's going on in my life. It doesn't matter whether I'm depressed or happy, the voice is still there."

"How often do you hear it?"

"Oh, every day. Sometimes a few hundred times a day."

The fact that the voice said "Just shoot yourself" rather than "I want to shoot myself" or "I want to die" was an important clue; it indicated to me that we were probably dealing with a foreign presence, rather than a wounded part of Khadija.

In Khadija's next session, I asked her to tune into the place in her body where she heard this "voice," and describe the physical sensations associated with it.

She described what felt like a hard, greenish spot on the left side of her head. I suggested we speak directly with and to that spot, to find out why it kept telling Khadija to shoot herself.

"It's very angry at me," Khadija said. "It hates me. It doesn't want me to be happy."

"Why not?" I asked.

"Then it doesn't feel so alone," Khadija realized. "It's unhappy, so it wants me to be unhappy too."

We spoke with the voice for a few more minutes, and suddenly Khadija gasped. "It's Mr. Adams! He was the father of a kid I knew in grade school. He killed himself when I was ten."

Through Khadija, I helped Mr. Adams understand that his own long suffering and frustration would end if he left Khadija's body and moved into the light. Rather than trying to make Khadija unhappy to keep him company, he could become happy instead. He was understandably surprised by this idea, and initially quite suspicious. However, soon his dead mother—looking far more loving than she had ever appeared in life—came toward him from the light. It was touching to sense this destructive, unhappy spirit finally softening and allowing himself to receive love.

I drummed to help the energy move, and Khadija released Mr. Adams into the light. Then I advised Khadija to ask her guides to fill her completely with her own life energy, beginning with her own essential spark of life force and radiating it outward until her own light filled every nook, cranny and crevice in her being—including the spaces now left empty by Mr. Adams' departure. This kind of visualization is not only an important ending to the process of releasing interfering energies; it's also a powerful healing process in its own right, and helps render someone immune to further energetic interference.

After that session, Khadija never again heard the voice that had told her "Just shoot yourself" for so many years. Although she still had plenty of other healing to do, she could do it much more easily once her energy field was more her own.

The process of releasing a spirit that has taken up residence in a living person is often called "spirit releasement therapy." Psychiatrist Shakuntala Modi, M.D., comments, "I do not know whether these entities described by my patients are real or not… the only thing that is important to me is the result. And over the years, I have seen astounding results with spirit release-ment therapy."

From a shamanic perspective, this level of intrusion is not uncommon. However, it's even more common to find what Isa Gucciardi calls destructive "energy packets" within us. The imprint that told me that I shouldn't exist (see Chapters 1 and 4) was probably such a packet. I also encountered this kind of packet in my client Eileen.

Eileen had been born to an unmarried Chinese-American mother who was deeply ashamed of her, both because she was illegitimate and because she was half white. At home she wasn't Chinese enough, but at school she was picked on by the other children for not being white enough; they nicknamed her "Slanty," and, as she grew older, amended the name to "Slanty Slut."

Now in her mid-thirties, Eileen came to me to try to change her long-held pattern of involvement with lovers and friends who took advantage of her and treated her cruelly. Even though she was painfully aware of this pattern, she told me ruefully, "I just can't seem to put myself first."

I asked Eileen to tune into the physical sensations that arose when she said aloud, "It is right for me to put myself first." Immediately she responded, "It doesn't want me to."

"Who is this 'it'?"

"It's like a little black snake. It lives between my shoulder blades—oh, there's some in my forehead, too."

"And why doesn't it want you to put yourself first?"

"It says I don't deserve to. It says I'm—wow, this is weird." Eileen opened her eyes and looked at me with surprise. "It says I'm worse than rotten meat. It says I make people sick."

"Do you agree with it?"

"No, of course not!" Eileen's eyes filled with tears. "But it sounds just like the things people have said to me all my life."

"Is there any reason why you would want to keep this black snake inside of you, insulting you like this and preventing you from putting yourself first?"

"No. I want it gone," Eileen said firmly.

"Then hold onto your own understanding that it is right for you to put yourself first, and let's release it." I drummed, while Eileen asked her guides for

help in pushing the black snake out of her body and energy field. Although she had initially described it as "little," my perception as I drummed was that it was actually massive. It had extended bits of itself throughout her body, almost like a metastasized cancer. But as I continued drumming and Eileen continued working with her guides, I felt the black snake evaporate, dissolved by the presence of love and compassion.

"Wow," Eileen said after about ten minutes. "I think it's gone. It doesn't feel bad any more when I think about putting myself first. It feels like, 'Of course.'

If you sense that you may have energetic interference, it's probably best to look for a human practitioner who can assist you in clearing it. Initially it can be difficult to maintain enough strength, clarity and focus to do this level of work on your own. However, over time this type of healing can become as easy as cleaning your house. In fact, that's essentially what you're doing: cleaning your *inner* house, restoring your own power and energetic integrity.

14

The Challenge of Integration

We can't become centered in what I call the Self—the deep ground of our being—by trying to flatten, suppress, deny, or destroy the feelings we don't like in ourselves or others. To experience the Self, there's no shortcut around our inner barbarians… We must learn to listen to and ultimately embrace these unwelcome parts. If we can do that, rather than trying to exile them, they transform.

— Richard Schwartz

As we grow and heal, an essential part of our work involves *integrating* our new understandings and states of being. Otherwise, our healing will be shallow and unstable, and any expansion of consciousness we experience will be counteracted by the parts of ourselves that remain in shadow. To understand more about why that's so, we must look at what "we" actually are and contain.

As we've discussed, we each contain many split-off younger selves, coexisting uneasily despite radically different perspectives, priorities, and stages of development. In addition, we are energetically connected to the experiences and wounds of our relatives, ancestors, and cultural and subcultural groups. The truth is, the psyche you think of as "yours" as actually an aggregate of parts; there is no single "you." Although we are socialized to believe in the existence of a solid, consistent self, that self doesn't exist; the idea of the self is a fiction, a linguistic convenience, a social fantasy—and a source of enormous confusion for many of us.

Imagine that your psyche is like a gigantic house full of people. Some of them are crowded into a single room, but, like patients waiting in a doctor's office, they are each caught up in their own experience and may not interact much with one another. Other parts of you fill other parts of the house—some barricaded behind locked doors, some hiding in closets. In some rooms, two or more people may be fighting. At the same time, someone else might be out on the deck, serenely watching the sunset. Another person in the house may be sitting in front of an altar meditating. And each of these beings is you.

You've probably delegated one or more of these parts to be the "you" that goes to work, another one or few to be the "you" that interacts with your spouse, and others to fill all the usual roles in your life. But they may not know each other very well; they may also mistrust or abuse each other. "Why'd you drink so much again last night?" "Oh, give me a break." "When are you ever going to start going to the gym every day like you said you would?" "Fuck you." "I want my mommy." "Stop crying or I'll give you something to cry about, you big baby." And so on.

Now, imagine that a messenger comes to the door with a very important message for everyone in the house. Who will receive the message? And how can they possibly convey it to everyone else?

This is essentially the situation in which most of us find ourselves, unless and until we have made a concerted effort to create pathways of connection between our many parts. Lack of emotional integration is a common problem on the path of spiritual growth. We've all met people who seem wise, serene and loving—until their wounds are triggered, at which time their wisdom and serenity goes out the window, replaced by panic or rage. Many great spiritual teachers and leaders have been vessels of light with huge dark shadows—often expressed through alcoholism, seducing students or followers, or abusing people close to them. This lack of integration causes great confusion and suffering, both for the people who experience it and for others in their lives.

Unless we consciously work to move a given awareness throughout our being—or unless some radical dissolution of the being occurs, as happened to Eckhart Tolle and Byron Katie—the knowledge and wisdom gained by one part of us does not automatically become available to the other parts. This is why we can look and feel mature, competent and confident in some aspects of our lives, but turn into frightened five-year-olds or insecure teenagers in other situations. It's also why so many people contradict their public philosophies in their private lives. It isn't simply that they are hypocrites (although they may be that, too); it's that the beliefs and understandings held in one part of their being have simply not reached the other parts.

Of course, it *is* hypocritical to make public pronouncements that are in stark conflict with one's own private behaviors. Yet the phenomenon often underlying that hypocrisy is this: the man who seduces his teenaged foster daughter on Saturday night and the devoutly Christian minister who preaches an inspiring sermon on Sunday morning aren't really the same person at all, though they live in a single body and use one name.

Does it sound like I'm describing the psychological condition popularly known as "Multiple Personality Disorder"? In fact, every one of us has "multiple personalities," which some psychologists call "subpersonalities," and which Jung referred to as "the little people of the soul." The main difference is that people diagnosed with Multiple Personality Disorder—now re-named Dissociative Identity Disorder—often switch so completely from one aspect of self to another that they "lose time," surfacing hours, days or weeks later with no memory of who or where they've been. That doesn't happen to the rest of us—at least, not without a lot of drugs or alcohol. We generally remember exactly who and where we've been; we just have no way to make sense of our range of thoughts, feelings and behaviors.

We've all heard the dramatic versions of these stories: the happily married congressman who risks his career by emailing photos of his genitals to a college student he's never met; the anti-gay leader who regularly patronizes male prostitutes; the devoted young mother who deliberately drives her SUV into the bay to drown her children. Most of our life stories may not be quite so extreme, but Walt Whitman's famous words are true of all of us: "So I contradict myself? Very well then, I contradict myself. I am large; I contain multitudes."

If you're a novelist, these contradictions are endlessly fascinating. If you're a therapist, they'll keep you in business. But if you're a person who sincerely wants to grow and evolve, this multiplicity of selves presents a very real challenge. Here are some steps that can help you create channels of communication between the various "people" in the house of your psyche.

Emotional Integration Process

1. As usual, change starts with awareness. Before you can integrate various aspects of yourself, you have to know they're there! Meditation or self-inquiry can help you become more conscious of the usual cast of characters in your psyche. It can also help to start with a deceptively simple question: for instance, "How do I feel about X?" Whether X is your job, your partner, your home, sex, or some other circumstance in your life, it's a safe bet that different parts of you will feel different things. As you listen internally, you will become more able to "hear" these responses.

2. The second precondition for change is always acceptance and compassion. Even when you encounter aspects of self that surprise or distress another part of you, you can ask for help from the wisest parts of yourself, or from guides, in acknowledging what's there. Sometimes it's easiest to start by neutrally witnessing the various "little people" in your inner landscape, then gradually moving toward a friendlier emotional stance.

    Remember, this inner neutrality and even friendliness are not the same as "condoning" a part of yourself. It's possible to be aware that a part of you is wreaking havoc in some aspect of your life, yet still feel accepting and compassionate toward that part, especially when you also cultivate awareness of how and why your early life contributed to its way of being. If you have trouble feeling this kind of acceptance, turn to your guides for help. You'll find that they positively *emanate* the kind of acceptance you need.

3. It's also important to distinguish between wounded parts of yourself, and energetic interference from energies or spirits that aren't you at all. Exploring *why* a part behaves as it does can clarify whether or not this part is truly an aspect of you. If something inside you claims to want to make you suffer, it's most likely not you at all, and needs to be released. If you sense that you're dealing with something that truly *is* you, but has radically different priorities from your main persona, your guides can help you determine what kinds of reconnection are needed.

4. As you dialogue with parts of yourself, you'll discover how connected or conflicted your inner climate currently is. Sometimes the different aspects of self are relatively understanding and compassionate toward one

another; at other times, they are at each other's metaphorical throats. In this case, a soul retrieval or other healing process will be needed.

Of course, integration is a lifelong process. Even if we manage to move our entire "household" forward in healing and consciousness, we will always contain aspects of self at many different stages of development. Yet cultivating conscious communication with our many "selves" makes our inner lives more complex and dimensional—and makes us more able to accept and even appreciate other peoples' complexity, too. Although we will never completely eliminate our contradictions, acknowledging them can keep us humble and allow for more genuine intimacy, both with ourselves and with others.

I had to laugh at myself this morning. I've been staying in a little cabin for the week so that I could work non-stop on this book, and I've been doing exactly that, so I hadn't washed dishes for days. The cabin's kitchenette is more of an "ette" than a kitchen; there wasn't even room for the dish drainer on the tiny, cluttered counter, so I put it on the floor. A part of me started griping bitterly, "I don't like this place. I want a real kitchen." There was a regular sponge, but no scrubby-surface sponges of the kind I use at home. Griping voice again: "How am I supposed to get this dried food off the plates without a scrubby sponge? I can't believe there's no scrubby sponge. She advertised this place as 'fully equipped.' She said there were even spices. Well, there are exactly three spices in the cabinet—chopped onions, cinnamon, and garlic salt. And this stupid little electric hotplate is unbelievably slow. It takes ten minutes just to boil water. This place is overpriced. I should have gone somewhere else." As this part unleashed its litany of complaints, another, more light-hearted part of me began to tease gently, "Gripe, gripe, gripe. Gripe, gripe, gripe." Another part said thoughtfully, "Well, it's probably best that I didn't have a real kitchen; I might have spent too much time cooking. But I really wish there were a hot tub." The griping part of me, now emboldened, continued to complain. "And the sheets! Can you believe 100% polyester sheets?! Am I going to have to start bringing my own damned sheets every time I go away? Doesn't anybody know about cotton any more?" But by this time, even she had begun to find it funny. And by this time, the dishes were done.

I've spent at least sixty hours this week working on a book about healing and consciousness, and yet I'm still just as prone to inner snit-fits as most other humans seem to be. (In fact, working so much on the book may even have made me more *prone. See Chapter 45, "Forces and Counter-Forces," for more understanding of why.) Perhaps someday I will have transformed so completely that I will drift through life in a beatific haze of contentment, gratitude and bliss, unruffled by the things that irritate mere mortals. But I'm not counting on it. In the meantime, I can witness my inner petty tyrants with amusement, neither squelching them nor adopting their negative views, neither criticizing them nor letting them take over—and I can also remember that I am much, much more.*

And, from that awareness of "more," I can choose where to direct my consciousness. For instance, I've now moved my chair next to the wall heater so that I can enjoy its comforting warmth. (Someone made every part of this heater, metal grilles and pipes and levers and knobs, and all kinds of other parts I can't see; someone created propane, and someone brought it here; someone built this cabin, bought this heater, and installed it, all of which made it possible for me to feel this warmth right now...)

Outside the window, I see hundreds of pine trees climbing the hillside, and, closer to the cabin, one gracious, venerable Valley Oak, quercus lobata, *the largest of North American oaks, able to live six hundred years. It isn't just a tree, it's a work of art. My eyes get lost in its sculptural angles, twists, curves and knots. Its magnificently gnarled limbs are furred with bright green moss, and tufted with the paler green of Spanish moss. Some of its branches are broken or cut off, but most of them still reach toward the sky, each holding up its own bouquet of leaves like a celebration.*

Yes, there is much to celebrate. It's a beautiful world out there, and in here— polyester sheets and all.

15

The True Locus of Transformation

Our own life has to be our message.

– Thich Naht Hanh

Once we understand that the wounds, imprints and energies we carry within us create our experience of "reality" on both individual and collective levels, it becomes clear why it is more effective to focus on inner change, rather than outer. If we change or dissolve our beliefs, imprints and emotional postures, what shows up on the outside will inevitably and automatically change, too—but the reverse isn't necessarily true. For instance, we could exert enormous effort trying to change some outer circumstance, but even if we succeed, if we haven't changed what we hold within ourselves, we will inevitably continue to encounter or recreate similar circumstances elsewhere in our lives.

We must, of course, continue to do outer work as well; the material conditions of life require this from us. And when our outer work flows from a balanced internal current, it will create greater harmony in the world. It is also valuable for us to do outer work simply because of the ways in which it unfailingly illuminates the places within us which are in need of attention. The phenomena that show up in our outer lives give us a great deal of information about the imprints we are still carrying.

Of course, from the human perspective, there is a great deal that needs to be done in the outer world. Feeding the hungry, reforming the political system and saving the rainforests are all valid and important arenas to work in—as long as we can remain clear that within these arenas our *real* work continues to be the work of transforming our consciousness. At times physical reality is so consuming and distracting that we can lose sight of this bigger picture. This can lead to internal contradictions—for instance, when people working in peace movements become just as focused on "vanquishing the enemy" as those on the other side, whom they deplore.

No matter where we focus our energy in physical reality, the energy that fuels our actions is more impactful than the actions themselves. For instance, it is harmonious for us to be conscientious in our use of the earth's resources, as long as the attitudes underlying our actions are also conscientious. If instead we recycle our newspapers out of a grim insistence on being morally superior to others, we are committing an act of psychic violence rather than higher consciousness. Being "kind" to someone in a manner that depletes us is also an act of psychic violence—in this case, against ourselves. Of course, all acts of psychic violence affect both "others" and "self" because the current of violence cannot fail to run between, and thereby to pollute, both "sender" and "recipient." If we violently fight for peace, if we pollutedly fight against pollution, we create an energetic standoff in which nothing can really change.

Those of us who wish to "serve" or to "improve the world" are usually fueled by a genuine awareness of the life force and its beauty, and sincerely wish to feed and activate this beauty both within and outside of ourselves. Yet when one is not harmoniously internally oriented, any beautiful thing can become a weapon with which to bludgeon others or the self. Organized "Christianity" has accomplished this with Christ consciousness; who would ever have imagined that the source of such injunctions as "Love thy neighbor as thyself" and "Judge not lest ye be judged" could have been distorted so badly as to become an enormous machine spewing harsh notions of "sin," "repentance" and "damnation"? The human species has been adept at turning ploughshares into swords, and even the desire to heal, grow and cultivate higher consciousness can be misused as a weapon against others or self—for example, when people judge themselves or others for "not being evolved enough."

Clearly, therefore, the terrain of inner development is tricky and must be explored on the deepest levels—those levels on which any kind of violence, resistance, refusal or hostility, whether directed against oneself, "others," or life, is understood to be deeply in error. The barbs we direct at others cannot fail to pierce our own skin. The barbs we direct against ourselves cannot fail to harm others. The harm we do to ourselves and others cannot fail to harm the earth, the trees, the rivers, the animals and flowers.

If we see this truth only on a surface level we may use it to stab ourselves with the blades of despair, regret, or self-blame. Or we might use it to blame others, "the system," the Republicans, the Democrats, the corporations, our bosses, our parents, and so on. This is why it is so important to go deeper. We must understand that any of these inner movements actually enacts the violence we deplore, and that even the deploring itself can become a kind of violence against the violence. So we must instead take the violence—both "our own," and that of others—in our arms like a wailing and difficult baby. We must take ourselves in our arms this way, and our whole disturbed and disturbing, difficult and confused species. This is the only way to honor the life force which is in us, which is in everything and everyone. It is this life force that feeds and inspires us, and which we rightly know in our souls to be beautiful and worthy of nourishing.

The posture of being set against anything—whether inside or outside the self—will never serve us, or serve life. Life itself is not opposed to anything. Rather, there is a kind of immense and intricate harmony which emerges from life, and which *is* life. It is hardly the point to feel badly about ourselves or humankind because of how hard we have fought this harmony. The point is rather to recognize the harmony, to allow it into ourselves, to realize that we exist within it, that we are of it and not separate from it.

Each of us is the locus of transformation. Regardless of what any other human being does or does not do, what matters most in each moment is what we do in our own hearts. Directing psychic violence toward others, no matter who they are and no matter what they have done, cannot fail to inflict that same violence on ourselves and on the planet. Fighting against anyone or anything, whether inside or outside the self, is in essence fighting against life. It cannot be otherwise. We *are* life. So is every politician on every part of the political spectrum. So are our fathers, our mothers, our children, our bosses, the CEOs of giant corporations, and the homeless people who line the streets of our cities. So too is the Dalai Lama, and the oak tree outside my window, and the dandelion growing up through the cracked cement. Inner or outer violence against any aspect of life amounts to violence against ourselves, and violence against ourselves is violence against the collective. There are no exceptions.

Gandhi's famous words, "You must *be* the change you wish to see in the world," express this principle nicely. Yet it is far more easily said than done. If we find that in order to really "stop the violence" on this level we must turn ourselves inside out—we must die to who we have known ourselves to be, and allow someone else to be born—then, and only then, have we truly understood this principle. The prayer of St. Francis powerfully encapsulates these principles.

> *Lord, make me an instrument of your peace.*
> *Where there is hatred, let me sow love.*
> *Where there is injury, pardon.*
> *Where there is doubt, faith.*
> *Where there is despair, hope.*
> *Where there is darkness, light.*
> *Where there is sadness, joy.*
> *O Divine Master,*
> *grant that I may not so much seek to be consoled, as to console;*
> *to be understood, as to understand;*
> *to be loved, as to love.*
> *For it is in giving that we receive.*
> *It is in pardoning that we are pardoned,*
> *and it is in dying that we are born to Eternal Life.*

If you're not comfortable with the traditional language of this prayer, you can, of course, write your own. There are many ways to affirm your own power to transform yourself—and, in so doing, transform all that is. The most important thing to understand is that in each moment, no matter what may be occurring within us or outside of us, we always have the choice to embody compassion, peace and love.

16
Who are "You"?

When we quit thinking primarily about ourselves and our own self-preservation, we undergo a truly heroic transformation of consciousness.

– Joseph Campbell

As we've discussed, the self is not a single, discrete entity; what each of us thinks of as our "self" is actually an amalgamation of many different strands, a braid of wildly different aspects. Whoever you are, it is likely that some of these aspects are ancient, wise, and highly evolved, while others are at a more primitive stage of development. Some of them may be from other planets or realms, while others are almost certainly of the earth. Some are in need of healing, while others—no matter what may have happened in your human life—are intact and unscarred. Who, then, are "you"?

Of course, there are many possible answers, since you are actually a vast collection of diverse parts and aspects. However, identifying yourself as this entire unwieldy bundle of aspects makes it very difficult to move in any single direction. While some parts of you push toward evolution, others may hide or stockpile internal weapons. While some parts expand into deep states of generosity and love, others nurse grudges and plot revenge. While some parts of you gravitate toward the possibility of experiencing radiant well-being independent of outer circumstances, other parts actually gravitate away from that expanded consciousness, and toward addictive behaviors or numbing anti-life cycles.

This is why concepts like "self sabotage" have emerged in the contemporary psychological vocabulary, although they are not quite accurate. It is not really that any part of ourselves is attempting to sabotage "us" or itself, but simply that different parts of the self hold different beliefs about what will make us safe or happy. This is why many contemporary therapies and self-help methods, including Inner Relationship Focusing and Inner Family Systems, focus on dialogue between parts of the self. If we do not find ways to work deliberately and skillfully with our many parts, we are likely to become stuck—just as we would be stuck if we sat in our cars with one hand turning the steering wheel to the left while another turned it to the right, and one foot pressed down on the brake while another pressed on the gas pedal.

So the answer, "*I am all of what I contain*," is true, yet not conducive to movement. Another answer might be, "I *am who I believe I am*." This answer is also true, as we can see by observing those around us. We all know people who are intelligent and competent, yet who do not *believe* themselves to be these things, and so are unable to make much use of the capacities they actually possess.

This is why many healing and therapeutic techniques focus on identifying and clearing inaccurate and limiting beliefs. It's also why the use of affirmations is so popular; people hope that by affirming, "I am intelligent and successful," the parts of themselves that believe otherwise will dissolve or disappear. Some schools of thought, including Science of Mind, recommend acting and speaking as if the desired reality has already come to pass, positing that in this way we can re-align our inner landscapes in accordance with the outcomes we wish for. And some people do in fact experience internal and external shifts through such approaches—since what we believe does shape both what we perceive and what we experience.

This book offers many practices and tools to help you change your beliefs and imprints about yourself and life, and that work is valid and necessary. Yet because there are so many aspects of self, this process can also seem nearly endless. So there is another answer to the question, "Who am I?" which has even more transformative power, when it is used in a conscious manner and at an appropriate stage in your healing journey. That answer is, "*I am whichever parts of myself I choose to identify with*."

Of course, this answer is not the whole truth. In fact, you are *all* of your parts. An even wider truth is that you are—or you contain, somewhere within you—every part and aspect that exists within humanity. As the ancient Roman playwright Terence said, and many others have echoed,

"Nothing human is alien to me." But since you cannot act and live effectively from all of those parts at once—just as you cannot drive effectively while pressing down on the gas and brake pedals at once—choosing which aspects you will claim, feed and support as "yourself" allows for movement.

The Cherokee legend, "Two Wolves," often circulated in spiritual circles, describes this in simple yet dramatic terms:

"A fight is going on inside me," a grandfather told his young grandson. "It is a terrible fight between two wolves. One is evil. He is anger, envy, sorrow, regret, greed, arrogance, self-pity, guilt, resentment, inferiority, lies, false pride, superiority, and ego. The other is good. He is joy, peace, love, hope, serenity, humility, kindness, benevolence, empathy, generosity, truth, compassion, and faith. The same fight is going on inside you—and inside every other person, too."

"Which wolf will win?" the boy asked anxiously.

"The one you feed," answered his grandfather.

In other words, although we each contain many contradictory energies and aspects, we do have choices about "which wolf we feed"—which aspects of self we cultivate and strengthen. Using a different metaphor, Thich Naht Hanh compares all of the aspects of consciousness to seeds, and reminds us that we can choose which seeds to water.

It will not serve your growth or evolution to ignore, deny, repress or disown those parts of you that feel angry, envious, sad, regretful, greedy—or anything else that another part of you might judge, or would rather not feel. Repressing or disowning aspects of ourselves only relegate them to the shadow, and as Carl Jung discovered, our shadows often end up running much of our lives from underground. Categorizing aspects of self as "me" and "not-me" can also foster a sense of separation which runs counter to the shift in consciousness we need to make, as individuals and as a species. Yet it is easier to refuse food and water to your anger, envy, sorrow, regret and greed if you understand them as states passing through you, temporary manifestations of being, rather than as your true self.

Buddhism refers to emotions like anger and sorrow as "negative emotions," but this term is often misunderstood by Western practitioners. Although these emotions are often negative in their *impact* on us, they are not "bad," nor are we bad for feeling them. They impact us negatively because they emerge from parts of ourselves that dwell in states of pain and separation, rather than connection and joy. Those parts of ourselves need and deserve our compassionate attention in order to heal. Yet, if we think of those parts of us as "us," believe the sad, angry stories they tell, and give that sadness or anger free reign in our bodies and energy fields, we are much less able to help them heal.

It's tricky to hold an inner posture in which we can recognize the wounded parts of ourselves from which such "negative emotions" emerge, dismantle their erroneous beliefs, and offer them compassion and healing— all while also understanding that these parts of self are not truly, or not fully, "us." Eckhart Tolle likens this to identifying with the unmoving depths of the ocean, even as tumultuous waves continue to swell and break on the ocean's surface. Craig Hamilton suggests that although human beings always contain a diverse range of levels of consciousness, we can still choose "who to be," which self to live from, on a day-by-day, moment-by-moment basis. Using Einstein's wording, we might think of this as identifying ourselves with the level of consciousness that can solve our problems, rather than the levels of consciousness on which we created them—while still holding those other aspects of ourselves within loving arms.

17

The Role of Human Support

At times our own light goes out, then is rekindled by a spark from another human being. Each of us has cause to think with deep gratitude of those who have rekindled the inner spirit.

— Albert Schweitzer

No human being can ever offer us the same constant availability or absolute neutrality, compassion and wisdom as our inner guides. If we expect to get this level of support from other people, we will be sorely disappointed. But since we are living physical lives on the physical plane, it's also true that our fellow humans can sometimes understand and assist us in ways that our inner teachers cannot.

Human support may come to us from many sources, including healers, therapists, teachers, clergy, spiritual communities, or growth-oriented friendships with peers or relatives. Of course, in the bigger picture every person and relationship in our lives is supporting our growth in one way or another, even without consciously intending to. Although it can be difficult to recognize incidents of abuse and conflict as "support," pain often pushes us toward growth in a way that few other experiences can. Yet we all benefit from relationships in which the spiritual friendship and support provided are much more direct, deliberate and intentional—and from providing such support to others, even as we each walk our own paths.

If we are committed to self-responsibility and to our own most harmonious development, we can accelerate and strengthen our internal process by forming relationships whose consecration, or deepest intention, is to help us grow. In Buddhist traditions such friendships are called *kalyana mitta,* usually translated as "noble friendship" or "admirable friendship." The Wikipedia entry on *kalyana mitta* explains, "Since early Buddhist history, these relationships have involved spiritual teacher-student dyads as well as communal peer groups. In general, such a supportive relationship is based on shared Buddhist ethical values and the pursuit of enlightenment."

In 12-step programs, the relationships in which group members share their "experience, strength and hope" with one another are called *fellowship.* According to one anonymous writer, the purpose of such fellowship is to aid individuals in making contact with their inner divine spirit, the "liberator-comforter-redeemer-teacher within." Twelve-step program literature asserts that people cannot consistently access this inner teacher without the support of other people who are similarly inclined. This understanding parallels a reported conversation between the Buddha and his disciple Ananda, in which Ananda declared that admirable friendship was half of the holy life—to which the Buddha replied, "Don't say that, Ananda. Admirable friendship, admirable companionship, admirable camaraderie is actually the whole of a holy life."

Elsewhere, the Buddha also declared, "'With regard to external factors, I don't envision any other single factor like admirable friendship as doing so much for a monk in training, who has not attained the heart's goal but remains intent on the unsurpassed safety from bondage. A monk who is a friend with admirable people abandons what is unskillful and develops what is skillful." Although most readers of this book are not literally monks, I believe that all of us with strong commitments to inner development are, in a sense, lay monks, nuns or priests in training—that is, people to whom the spiritual life is at least as important, or even more important, than our ordinary-reality material existence.

When we connect with another person or people with whom we share spiritual understandings, an instant *sangha* (the Sanskrit word for "community," commonly used in Buddhist circles) is created. As Christ said, "When two or three have gathered in My name, I am there in their midst." This chapter focuses on two kinds of *sangha*: the support we can receive from human teachers, healers or therapists, and the support we can both give and receive in peer-level spiritual friendships.

In order to receive support at this very deep level, we must trust its source. Yet humans by our nature are not and cannot be completely trustworthy; all human beings have biases and distortions, wounds and limitations. There-fore, it is most appropriate and harmonious for us to place *relative* trust, rather than *absolute* trust, in human sources of support. We do well to re-member that e must check whatever a would-be "admirable friend" says to us against our own inner knowing. A Buddhist expression advises us to "bite the teacher with our teeth to see if he or she is really made of gold." At the same time, since we, too, have biases, wounds and limitations, we must also continually check our inner sense of things, using discernment to ascertain where and when we are clear and balanced, and where we ourselves might need a course correction.

Each of us also has imprints and habits related to trust. Some of us may appear to trust easily, perhaps *too* easily; others may tend toward suspi-cion, and struggle with trust. The harmonious relationship to trust involves becoming able to open ourselves where, and to whom, we discern that it is wise and helpful to do so—and also to close ourselves again when our growth will be best served by our doing so.

Here are some guidelines and tips you may find helpful if you are seek-ing a human teacher, healer or source of guidance.

Criteria to Use in Selecting a Human Teacher or Healer

1. In order to help you connect and work with your own sources of guidance, a teacher or practitioner must have access to her own. The best way to find out if this is the case is simply to ask! If someone isn't able or willing to speak freely about his own non-ordinary sources of support, he's not likely to be able to help you connect with yours.

2. Practitioners who work directly with higher consciousness call themselves by many names—for example, you might work or study with a spiritual director, an intuitive counselor, a hypnotherapist, a psychic, a shaman or shamanic practitioner, an energy healer, a transpersonal or holistic psy-chotherapist, a teacher of Buddhism or other spiritual practices, or even a mystically-oriented priest, rabbi, monk or nun.

    Physical-world credentials don't tell you much about who is best-suited to give you this kind of help. It doesn't much matter what letters someone has or doesn't have after their name, or whether they've written bestsellers, led expensive workshops, studied with big-name healers, or trekked the world apprenticing themselves to faraway shamans. What's most important is that your healer has a strong connection to higher consciousness.

3. It's also important that your healer, teacher or advisor has a deep commitment to her own path of healing and evolution. Shamanism is often called "the path of the wounded healer;" knowing that your healer has been through challenges of his own can rightfully build your confidence. All human beings on growth paths are and should be in process; anyone who tells you that she has "arrived" is probably deceiving herself. Yet someone who is still very much caught in his own muck may not be able to be of much help, either. Look for someone who is able to reflect easily and honestly on challenges she's already overcome, while acknowledging that her personal work is ongoing.

4. Avoid healers or teachers who imply that their guides or methods are the best or only valid approach, those who charge exorbitant fees, those who seem intent on being an authority, and those who clearly long to be adored. Narcissism is a common malady among human beings, but it is very problematic in healers and spiritual teachers. Seek someone who is sincerely committed to helping you access your own power, rather than impressing you with his. The best practitioners tend to be neither self-deprecating nor self-aggrandizing. They inhabit their abilities with comfort and grace, while acknowledging that their gifts come from higher sources.

   Of course, anyone you would trust as a human helper should be kind, grounded, compassionate, humble, smart, trustworthy, a good listener—and accessible to you in terms of physical location (or phone or Skype access), schedule, and fees. It's a good idea to interview at least a few possibilities by phone or in person before making an appointment. If someone is pushy or seems to be trying to "sell" you on their services, move on. A good practitioner should seem warm, knowledgeable, responsive, and happy to work with you—and should maintain their warmth and equanimity even if you decide not to work with them.

5. All other criteria aside, you should trust your gut, honor your intuition—and ask your guides, if you're already in contact with them—as you choose a human helper. If someone "doesn't feel right" to you, look for someone who does.

6. All of these guidelines continue to apply even after you've begun studying or working with someone. If, after one or several classes or sessions,
something feels "off" to you, again, trust your gut. If your therapist or
teacher tries to tell you that your hesitance is due to resistance, check
what she says against your own inner knowing. It's true that sometimes
people get scared when we sense real transformation at hand. It's also
true that some teachers and therapists are simply not good fits for us, or
not in full alignment themselves. Only you—with the help of your inner
guidance or guides, of course—can determine what is actually occurring
in a given situation.

The "Bibliography and Resources" section of this book lists a number
of practitioners and resources I have personally found helpful. Most cities
have newspapers or magazines in which healers and therapists commonly
advertise, including "new age" or spiritually-oriented publications. Meetup.
com is an international website which can help you connect with people
with similar interests; many healing practitioners lead Meetup groups, or
group leaders could be sources of referrals. Of course, an internet search will
turn up many possibilities too. (Out of curiosity, I just googled "shamanic
practitioner Des Moines" and got 187,000 hits, although I seriously doubt
there are 187,000 shamanic practitioners in that city.) You'll find various
practitioner listing services online, too. Working by phone or Skype is just
as effective as working in person, and can exponentially increase the number
of practitioners available to you.

Some people find the teacher-student, therapist-client model nourishing and easeful; others prefer to give and receive support on a peer level. And
of course, many of us do both. Although this chapter is written primarily
from the point of view of the student or client, it's equally important for
those of us who are teachers and healers to consider these issues, and work
honestly, humbly and mindfully with them.

It can be extraordinarily valuable to work closely with a teacher or healer. At their best, such apprenticeships can exponentially increase our healing
and growth, radically transforming our lives. Yet most of the people I know
who have worked closely with spiritual teachers or healers have also, at some
point, found themselves severely disappointed. I have heard so many stories of teacher-student betrayal, inappropriate demands, attacks and shun-
ning that it's clear that this is a widespread phenomenon, not an isolated

occurrence. Yet while it can be devastating to have a beloved teacher or mentor appear to turn on you, such events take place as part of our larger trajectory of unfolding. Throughout history, most students have eventually had to split with their teachers and mentors in order to follow their own authentic paths. It's also true that many students—myself included—have inappropriately attempted to give over our self-responsibility and life-force to teachers whom we revered and loved. Although the desire to surrender to larger or higher forces is appropriate, it is a mistake to confuse or conflate our human teachers with those higher forces—or, if we ourselves are teachers, to believe that the higher forces we channel are actually *us*.

Of course, this dynamic works both ways; students and clients sometimes turn on their teachers or healers, as well. As in any deep human relationship, teacher-student or healer-client relationships can become extremely fraught, with the potential for a great deal of projection, confusion and pain in both directions. In such circumstances we may find ourselves in the grip of what Buddhism calls "ancient twisted karma," re-enacting the accumulated residue of many other lifetimes. Even if we confine our gaze to the present lifetime, we can still understand whatever occurs as part of a much larger learning process—and we can still find ways to use these difficult experiences, like all others, in the service of our growth and healing.

Although peer relationships are not completely free of these dangers, their mutuality does tend to create a more level playing field, and they are therefore often more sustainable. The support we receive from and give to our peers may not be quite as catalytic, as dramatically life-changing, as that we may receive from teachers and healers, but it is no less valuable, especially over the long term.

There are numerous structures available to help people create growth-oriented peer relationships. Focusing, a self-inquiry and self-presence practice, encourages students to form partnerships in which people take turns giving each other Focusing sessions. Many students of shamanism also form partnerships or groups to do shamanic journeys together. Twelve-step programs encourage new members to be "sponsored" by more experienced members, and then to sponsor others in turn. Some longtime Pathwork students work together in Pathwork Process Groups. Spiritual teacher Leslie Temple Thurston encourages her students to meet in "processing groups," to support one another in engaging in Thurston's spiritual clearing exercises. The Spirit Rock meditation center in Woodacre, California helps local Buddhist practitioners form *kalyana mitta* groups, and other Buddhist organizations help far-flung Buddhists to connect with similarly-inclined pen pals. Of course, outside of all of these structures you can also create your own process groups, study groups, support groups, or "noble friendships" with others who share your deepest understandings and commitments.

This model of friendship is very different from friendships in which people get together to "have a good time," or to support each other in less conscious ways. In these generally unexamined friendships, conversations are often superficial, maintain "us/them" polarities, or support victim consciousness. In contrast, spiritual friends pledge to compassionately support each other in feeding and watering the parts of themselves which gravitate toward healing, evolution and higher consciousness. In this way, the friendship itself becomes a contribution to the higher good—the kind of friendship Mahatma Gandhi meant when he said, "With every true friendship, we build more firmly the foundations on which the peace of the whole world rests."

Of course, since even those of us who are very committed to growth also contain aspects of self that hold different priorities—priorities like comfort, stability, maintaining the status quo, "people pleasing," and so on—this kind of friendship can feel scary at times. It takes courage to point out a friend's blind spots, spur her to assume greater self-responsibility, or guide her to connect more deeply to her own sources of wisdom—or to allow a friend to support you in those ways. Yet all human beings do have blind spots, and all of us experience times of resistance, fear, confusion, denial or despair. Allowing ourselves to give and receive compassionate, challenging, growth-oriented help is one of the most sacred forms of human connection.

When a friend reminds us to own up to our own part in a problematic dynamic or to identify our deepest intentions in a given situation, it helps to remember that she is actually helping us to *reconnect to our power.* In contrast, when you allow a friend to "vent" and simply listen sympathetically to his stories of being neglected or mistreated, you are enabling him to remain disconnected from his power. It is amazing how many "friendships" actually rest on this dynamic, which 12-step programs call "pity parties." When you really think about it, why would you ever want to strengthen someone else's imprints of helplessness and victimization, rather than helping him to reconnect with himself and make positive change? And why would you ever want a "friend" to support you in a posture of unconsciousness and suffering? Instead, spiritual friends can lovingly witness each other in their times of greatest challenge, and support each other's deepest unfolding.

18
Nourishment for the Journey

People usually consider walking on water or in thin air a miracle. But I think the real miracle is not to walk either on water or in thin air, but to walk on earth.

– Thich Naht Hanh

The farther we travel on a path of growth and healing, the more intense and profound are the challenges that arise. The path doesn't get easier; in fact, as we grow larger and stronger on a soul level, we actually *need* challenges in order to exercise our newly developed muscles. It's important, therefore, to understand that the continued appearance of challenges is neither a "punishment," nor a sign that something is wrong. In fact, it is quite the opposite. As a child gets better at reading, he will naturally choose to read more difficult and complex books; as an athlete continues with her training, she will naturally choose to take on more difficult feats. Continuing to read basic primers or confine ourselves to simple exercises once our skills are more advanced would be both unsatisfying, and an inefficient use of the skills and power we have gained.

And yet at times we may feel weary of so much challenge. Our human selves also need rest and replenishment, opportunities to simply soak in the goodness of life itself. Fortunately, such opportunities are everywhere. When we open ourselves to the beauty of our place in the cosmos, it becomes possible to experience every aspect of our lives—even, or perhaps especially, those we had dismissed as trivial, mundane, not worthy of our mindful engagement—as a form of blessing.

For example, simply sitting by a window and sipping a cup of tea or water can be a deeply nourishing act. Thich Naht Hanh advises, "Drink your tea slowly and reverently, as if it is the axis on which the world earth revolves—slowly, evenly, without rushing toward the future." As we do so, we can connect with the world outside the window, allowing our eyes to rest on the exact patterns and configurations of the landscape, whatever it contains. Leslie Temple-Thurston recommends the meditative practice of "gazing," simply looking with softened gaze at a tree, flower, cloud or other aspect of nature for ten minutes or more. Even if we live in a completely urban environment, some aspect of that natural world is likely to be visible to us; as we gaze at it, its energy field and our own can interpenetrate in profoundly restful and nourishing ways.

As we sip our tea we can also connect with our own bodies, with the wise intelligence of our breath as it brings in oxygen and releases carbon dioxide, with the miraculous, ever-present effort of all of our vital organs, and with the physical senses that enable us to see, hear, smell, taste, and feel the sensation of the cup in our hands, and the warm liquid in our mouths.

We can also turn our appreciative attention toward the water in the cup, remembering that it is gifted to us by the vast forces of the natural world. Perhaps its origin is a mountain stream that has been piped hundreds of miles into our urban dwelling; perhaps it comes to us from a well that draws water up to us from deep in the earth. Wherever it comes from, it has probably been made available to us as a result of the labor and inventions of many other human beings.

Most readers of this book can probably access water simply by turning a faucet. Yet when we allow ourselves to remember that our ancestors, at some time in their history, had to haul every drop of water they would drink in buckets or jugs, often across long distances—and that many people living today must do that, too—we can feel profound gratitude at the much greater physical ease of the lives we are privileged to live. We can also remind ourselves that this privilege is lent to us, not promised to us forever. The ease we take for granted now may not always be available to us. Rather than causing us alarm, this knowledge can instead prompt us to more fully celebrate the gifts we enjoy today.

Each small thing we do can be a doorway into the miraculous. For instance, preparing a meal gives us a chance to celebrate the many gifts of the earth, the many forms of life energy, human and non-human, that went into growing and nourishing the vegetables, fruits, nuts, grains, or seeds we ingest in order to sustain our own life force. If we eat meat or fish, we owe gratitude to the animal whose flesh we are taking in, an animal who once lived, walked or swam, breathed, and experienced its own life on earth. When we take vitamins or medications, we can remember that we are inviting concentrated substances into our bodies with the intention of enhancing our physical health and vitality, so that life may flow through us more fully, and we may more fully participate in life. When we shower or bathe, we can consciously greet and welcome the water touching our skin, remembering that it is the life-giving substance of which we are largely made. We can invite it to cleanse us both physically and spiritually, to enliven us and to remind us of our connection to all of the other life-forms with which water intimately engages.

Often lighting a candle can help bring us into contact with the sacred dimension of life. Of course, even this small act connects us to a vast evolutionary process; our life as a species changed forever when we became able to generate the power of fire at will. Fire warms us, soothes us, cooks our food, heats our water, and makes possible the creation of almost every single object we now use in our daily lives. Because we deeply know and biologically respond to its power, it is an important source of nourishment to our souls.

At times we may feel daunted by the individual healing and clearing work we have before us, and by the vastness of the challenges currently facing our species. In such moments it is important to remember that we are not alone in our efforts, either as individuals or as a human collective. This remembering will help us most if it is not only cognitive, but visceral—if we remind ourselves through myriad, daily, embodied actions just how connected we are, and to how much. As Pema Chödrön reminds us, "Rejoicing in ordinary things is not sentimental or trite. It actually takes guts. Each time we drop our complaints and allow everyday good fortune to inspire us, we enter the warrior's world."

In the San Francisco Bay Area, fall comes late, and spring comes early, so it is not uncommon to see a fiery golden maple tree in the process of losing its leaves, right next to a dogwood tree covered in tender new pink blossoms. Many of us may find ourselves in a similar time in our own lives, a time in which endings and beginnings live side by side within us. We can draw understanding and comfort from the poignant beauty of these two currents as they come together, both in nature and in ourselves. And we can cultivate within ourselves a sense of appreciation for both, for the areas within us that feel like spring, the many buds beginning to open in our spirits and hearts, and also for the places inside us where leaves are falling. We can allow ourselves to behold both inner seasons, and their role in the larger cycles of life, with a sense of welcome and wonder.

As we continue to move toward new beginnings, even amid the falling leaves of endings, it can be helpful to go beyond our concepts of either simply "sitting with" or "pushing against" what currently exists within us and in our lives. Instead, we can open ourselves to the concept of *pushing with.*

We know, of course, that we don't have to push the spring into coming; it comes on its own. Everything in the universe is lined up to enable it to come. And in fact, everything in the universe is similarly aligned toward our own growth, healing, and evolution—which means that when we tire of working so hard, we can move ourselves into one of life's flowing currents and allow ourselves to let it carry us. Metaphorically speaking, we can sit in a canoe and allow the river of life to move us along; or, if we choose, we can paddle, too. Each is its own kind of *pushing with,* since in each case we are being supported by forces far larger than our small personal selves.

As we paddle or feel ourselves carried, we can also turn our attention to the underground streams of our hearts. Each of us contains the spiritual and emotional equivalent of vast, powerful rushing rivers that had been frozen and are now beginning to thaw. As that thaw continues, much greater amounts of power and energy becomes more accessible to us. Some parts of us may become frightened when we sense that power; we may be tempted to try to dam it up, rather than letting it flow. If this happens, we can remind ourselves that in fact, we *are* the river; the river is us. We are simply developing a deeper relationship between the small constructed persona that we usually think of as ourselves, and the much larger, more powerful self that is also us.

It can feel difficult to bear the sense of expansion, the breaking up of the ice. It can be frightening to have more of ourselves accessible, both to us, and to the world. Yet nothing in our lives is random or mistaken; everything fits together in such a way that no misstep is possible. Remembering this, we can welcome whatever happens, inside or outside of us, with a sense of wonder and curiosity. This, too, offers us ground on which to rest.

II

The Big Picture

19

Our Purpose on Earth

There is a vitality, a life force, an energy, a quickening that is translated through you into action, and because there is only one of you in all time, this expression is unique. And if you block it, it will never exist through any other medium and will be lost.

– Martha Graham

We've been discussing how we can personally heal and transform, and why our personal shifts help shift human consciousness itself. But why are we even here, individually or collectively? What is the purpose of our lives on earth?

The simplest, truest answer is that each of us is here to fulfill our inner design. The *inner design* can be understood as a kind of soul-level blueprint; when we fulfill it, we grow into our truest selves. What that means—what that looks like, on the level of physical form—is up to each of us to discover and determine. In other words, your most important task on earth is to discover what it means to be *you,* and then to embody your own being and essence as fully and as authentically as you can.

Most of us deeply sense the importance of becoming fully ourselves, although we may get diverted from this process by fear, self-doubt, and the attempt to fit into familial, cultural or social norms. Bronnie Ware, a nurse who spent years caring for people in their last few months of life, recounts that the most common sentiment she heard from her dying patients was, "I wish I'd had the courage to live a life true to myself, not the life others expected of me."

When we look at other life forms, it is obvious that their purpose is to become fully themselves. For instance, we know that the purpose of a dandelion seed is to become a dandelion; we would never imagine that it should try to become a rose bush or an oak tree instead. If that seed found itself pushing its way up through a crack in the sidewalk, rather than growing in a lush, moist patch of dirt, the plant that grew from it might remain small and scraggly—but even so it would still be a dandelion, and it would still be fulfilling its purpose. No matter how small it remained, it would not judge itself as lacking, nor would it be judged by life. The dandelion seed fulfills its inner design by becoming a dandelion plant; the dandelion plant fulfills its inner design, what we might think of as its essential blueprint, simply by *being*.

Perhaps you have noticed the exuberant well-being that emanates from dandelions—and, in one way or another, from all living things. That emanation of well-being is the natural byproduct of a life lived in harmony with one's inner design. The human name for that emanation is *joy.* When we are living in ways that fulfill our inner design, we frequently feel joy. When we are living in ways not consonant with our inner design, joy is absent. For this reason, joy can serve us as a navigational aid, always able to let us know whether or not we are living in accordance with our inner design.

Life forms that lack fully individuated consciousness have a much easier time fulfilling their inner design; in fact, it isn't possible for them to stray from it. Only human beings are capable of making choices so incongruent with our inner blueprints. When we make such choices, we can recognize them by our lack of joy. Yet if we have lost the ability to deeply sense ourselves and respond to our inner signals, this recognition sometimes comes slowly, and we may misunderstand its significance.

Our inner design never requires—or proscribes—specific choices on the level of form. There is no single "right" destiny for any of us; we are not specifically designed to become lawyers, artists or monks, to be married or to remain single, to have children or remain childless, to become famous or to live a quiet, externally ordinary life. Our destiny is simply to become fully ourselves within whichever forms we choose, create, or find available to us, just as the dandelion seed's destiny is to become a dandelion wherever it lands. Or, as the ancient philosopher Lao Tzu said, "The snow goose need not bathe to make itself white. Neither need you do anything but be yourself."

For instance, if our inner design involves deeply nurturing other beings, we might fulfill it by having children—or by becoming a teacher, a social worker, or a veterinarian. We might fulfill it by being a bus driver who cares deeply for each passenger on her route, or a waiter who cultivates warmth with the people whose food he brings, or a volunteer at an animal shelter or soup kitchen. One childless woman I know has close relationships with her nieces and nephews, volunteers as a Big Sister, and teaches writing to children and adults. All of these forms make use of the same parts of her being that could also have been utilized by becoming a mother.

Is it "better" to use our nurturing energy among a few people or many, in our own families or outside of them? Life has no preference in this regard. On the level of form there are always myriad ways to fulfill your inner design. Yet if that design requires you to nurture others and you cut yourself off from other people because of wounds or fears, you will suffer an absence of joy.

In one sense, the fulfillment of your inner design is a solitary pursuit. You are the only one who can recognize and align yourself with what astrologer Steven Forrest calls "that deep soul-feeling inside yourself to which you must be true if your life is to stay on course." Yet in another sense, the fulfillment of your inner design is intricately connected with the life tasks of many other beings, human and non-human. As you fulfill your own inner design, you invariably make it easier for others to fulfill their inner designs, too. At times this will be apparent to you; at other times you may fear that fulfilling your inner design could harm someone else. Yet since at a deeper level we are all connected, your fulfillment cannot fail to contribute to the fulfillment of the greater whole. For this reason, the work of aligning yourself with your inner design is never "selfish." In fact, it is the most effective and evolutionary way you can connect to life, yourself and others.

It's easier to understand how this works by observing the life cycles of other living things. A flowering plant, for instance, fulfills its inner design by growing and flowering. It must do this on its own; no one else can complete this task for it. And yet it is constantly supported in fulfilling its inner design. Life is highly efficient and synergistic; each life form exists within an intricate, mutually interdependent web of receiving and giving. The earth, sun and rain make it possible for the plant to grow and flower; when it is time for it to spread its seed, it is supported by wind, sometimes by animals, and by bees and other insects. As it grows, it also provides support to other life forms—sheltering them, feeding them, or delighting them with the beauty of its fragrance or color. Then, usually after it has reproduced, it "dies"—or rather, transforms its aliveness in such a way that life can continue to make use of it by feeding and replenishing the soil from which it came. And then, of course, the cycle begins again.

Each human being is part of a similar process. Like the flower, we are constantly receiving support from other humans, other life forms, and the earth itself, and we are also supporting others in myriad ways. Even if we do not physically reproduce, our lives perpetuate the continuation of our species, and the continuation of life itself. Although our lives are far longer and more complex than a flower's, they are part of the same supportive web that encompasses all living beings on earth.

I now understand that the non-physical beings who visited me when I was four—who told or showed me what I was here to do with my life, and then made me forget the details—gave me exactly the experience I needed. The knowledge that my life was not random, that I did have a purpose and mission, was instrumental in leading me to the teachers and processes that have given me my life's work. At the same time, if I had been able to remember the details of what my guides showed me, my freedom of choice would have been too compromised; I would have felt as if I was living out a pre-determined script, rather than exploring, making discoveries and decisions for myself.

A few years ago, while at a conference of holistic psychologists, I began telling another participant the story of my visitation. Midway through, he interrupted me: "And then they made you forget the details, right?" I was shocked. "How did you know?" "Oh," he said, "They always do that." It turned out that he had studied this kind of visitation, which, he told me, happens most commonly between the ages of three and five. Far from being unique, my early meeting with non-physical teachers followed a pattern clearly designed by a higher intelligence.

20
The Role of Choice

If a path exists in the forest, don't follow it, for though it took someone else to the Grail, it will not take you there, because it is not your path.

           – Joseph Campbell

Because our individuated consciousness leads us to conceive of ourselves as separate *selves*, we have the chance—and in fact, the obligation—to exert freedom of choice in our cycles of growth and development. It is as if we are flowers capable of choosing to transplant ourselves to the desert or the mountains or a heavily wooded forest, to conditions of drought or flooding or moderate rainfall, to gardens filled with other flowers or to barren, isolated patches of earth—and then also choosing the nature, size, color and fragrance of our blooms.

Although this level of freedom is a terrific creative opportunity, for many of us it is also a source of great confusion and stress. We may fear making the "wrong" choices; we may mistrust the deep wells of knowing within us, and struggle against our own inclinations. We may feel ourselves torn between different levels or aspects of ourselves, or between various conflicting familial and social structures. These are challenges which no other species on earth experiences.

In limited ways, most of us enjoy getting to make our own choices—for instance, when we are handed a menu in a restaurant. Yet in our lives, the choices available to us are so many and so constant that it's easy to become overwhelmed. Some of us therefore attempt to exempt ourselves from the responsibility of making choices. We may adopt a passive stance toward our lives and surroundings, trying to simply "take what comes," rather than acting in accordance with our own preferences. We may strive to have no preferences at all—or to pretend that we do not have preferences. Some people even have the misconception that this is a "spiritual" way to be, a sign of our willingness to accept life as it is. Of course, it *is* deeply helpful to accept life as it is, since the alternative—refusing to accept life as it is—pits us against life in a battle we can never win. But the idea that we should therefore resist having preferences, or acting on those preferences, reflects a misunderstanding of our role on earth. Accepting life as it is does not preclude our acting to change any aspect of what lies within our sphere of influence, a sphere defined by the contours of the individual self.

The Serenity Prayer recited in thousands of 12-step meetings worldwide acknowledges the distinction this way:

> *God grant me the ability to accept the things I cannot change,*
> *the courage to change the things I can,*
> *and the wisdom to know the difference.*

It's self-evident that each of us possesses the ability to change certain things, and lacks the ability to change others. Yet when we are not in possession of "the wisdom to know the difference," we waste tremendous amounts of time and energy trying to change things that are not within our sphere of influence—for instance, the lives and emotions of other people—while neglecting myriad opportunities to change the things we can, i.e., the things within ourselves.

The availability of choice is encoded within us; we cannot escape it. Even choosing to attempt to escape it—or choosing to resist, deny or ignore it—is itself a choice. Although there is nothing "wrong" with choosing to refuse to choose, it's like being an artist who has millions of beautiful colors of paint available to her, yet who blindfolds herself as she paints. Whatever emerges will still be her creation; in fact, her creativity is inevitably at work even in her attempt to surrender to the principles of randomness, her choice to let life make her choices for her. And yet few of us in our lives truly wish for this degree of surrender. Most of us have quite distinct preferences. It is, in fact, very human to have preferences. And so it is harmonious to life, since we ourselves are a part of life, to honor those preferences with our choices, when and where we can.

From the highest perspective, no choice we can make is right or wrong. Yet some choices *are* better-suited or less well-suited to our own inner design, and therefore bring us into fuller harmony with life and with ourselves. Since we can fulfill our inner design through a vast number of different external forms, what matters most is not *what* we choose, but why and how we choose it, the quality of energy that flows through our choice. The same external choices can have radically different internal meanings; we cannot know the energies involved when we view peoples' lives from outside. One person might get married as part of the fulfillment of his inner design, while for another it might be a way of evading or ignoring that design. One person might have children out of a soul-level yearning to become a mother, while another might do so simply because her parents or culture expect her to. Some people choose paths of religious celibacy as part of the fulfillment of their inner design, while others do so in a misguided attempt to escape or repress their sexual nature.

It also happens that choices which align with our inner design at one point in our lives may later cease to align with our souls' blueprint. As our spirits grow and change—which they must, since growth and change are the hallmark of all living organisms—we may shift in ways that require us to change the outer forms of our lives, as well. It takes courage to heed these messages from within, particularly when they tell us to leave behind identities, circumstances or relationships in which we have become socially or emotionally enmeshed.

Many people automatically interpret a radical change of plan or direction as a sign of "failure," yet in fact it can be a way of deeply honoring ourselves and our soul-level needs. On the other hand, a change in course could also represent a misguided attempt to escape pain and refuse self-responsibility. Only you can know what is true for you in a given instance—and you can only know by exploring deeply within.

As we deeply explore ourselves and our choices, we are likely to find that in most parts of our lives there are a variety of energies at work, some more harmonious, others emerging from inner places of confusion or distortion. This is inevitable, since we each contain so many parts of self at so many different levels of healing and development. The point, therefore, is not to strive toward some kind of mythical purity of motive, but rather, to cultivate awareness of all of the different kinds of inclinations and impulses at work within us. That kind of awareness and self-honesty allows us to continue working toward the fulfillment of our inner design, no matter what choices we make on the level of form.

Some choices we make may fulfill us for a lifetime; others serve as rafts that carry us to other shores, where we will need to get out of our boats and keep walking. Even choices that satisfy deeply-held needs may bring about a shift in those needs—not because we have acted in error, but because fulfilling one part of our blueprint readies our souls for whatever comes next. Our challenge is to remain sensitive and alert to the changing tides within us as well as outside of us, and to cultivate flexibility in our responses to inner and outer conditions.

Tao practitioner Kelli Thomaides describes this process beautifully in her personal essay, "More Will Be Revealed" (available online). First, she recounts how depression and anxiety led her to alcoholism; her drinking led her to hit bottom, join Alcoholics Anonymous, be sponsored by another member, and sponsor someone else in turn. When, after 18 months in the program, she felt she had a spiritual plateau, she discovered Tao, a set of spiritual understandings and practices which provided her with a deeper level of support. Through Tao, she gained the courage to pursue her lifelong dream of becoming an actress. Thomaides writes, "In order to do so, I had to quit my current teaching job and break the lease on my apartment—both of which were scary ideas to me. One of my Tao teachers was instrumental in providing me with the support I needed to take the right action in order to realize my dream. When I felt paralyzed with fear, he reminded me that I was doing this for myself, and if I did not do it, I would have to live with my own regret. So I sold my furniture, quit my job, broke my lease, and drove to New York City."

If Thomaides' story was a Hollywood movie, she would have become a successful actress and then lived happily ever after. Instead, pursuing her dream of acting led Thomaides to a host of other challenges and changes. First, she found that she felt alienated by the "temptation and indulgence" of the drinking, drug-using entertainment industry, and also felt envious of other peoples' material success. In order to resist the temptation to drink, she deepened her spiritual practice; after that, she says: "I was able to see how empty my material desires were. I finally realized that I was there [in New York] to reevaluate my investment in the material world and make a commitment to a spiritual life... Cultivating Tao brought me the point where I could see that my dream to become an actress was inauthentic, because it was merely a manifestation of lower desires. I wanted to become an actress in order to receive attention and connect with people in power. In order to get out of this 'ego trap', I needed to gain wisdom... Once I could intuit that my dreams and wishes were artificial, I began to walk down an authentic path towards my True Heart. The True Heart is the part of ourselves that is in harmony with the universe, so it can only be revealed when we are acting authentically and with good intention."

What Thomaides calls the "True Heart" is a beautiful synonym for the inner design. And as her story makes clear, each step of life is instrumental in leading us where we need to go.

Yet on the human level, a level on which we are often encouraged to make lifelong commitments or at least five-year plans, this kind of inner openness, receptivity and willingness to change course can be very challenging. At moments it might appear far easier to force ourselves to stay within a structure we have chosen than to remain responsive to the shifting climates of our soul. Or we may seek external authorities to guide us, rather than taking responsibility for adhering to inner signals. There is no shortage of religious leaders, politicians, friends or relatives who are happy to tell us what is "right" or "wrong" for us according to their own viewpoints—which, of course, may contradict one another. Yet when we attempt to live in accordance with other peoples' preferences, standards or paradigms, we are robbing ourselves of the biggest gift our individuated consciousness can offer us: the opportunity to make choices for ourselves, in accordance with our own deepest knowing and inner design.

In one of Carlos Castenada's books, the shaman Don Juan tells his young apprentice, "All paths are the same; they lead nowhere. So the question to ask is, 'Does this path have a heart?'" Of course, the "heart" or "lack of heart" is not intrinsic to the path itself; it is the interaction between the path and your own spirit that determines whether a given path has a heart for *you.*

21

How and Why Our Choices Matter

It is a painful thing to say to oneself: by choosing one road I am turning my back on a thousand others. Everything is interesting; everything might be useful; everything attracts and charms a noble mind; but death is before us; mind and matter make their demands; willy-nilly we must submit and rest content as to things that time and wisdom deny us, with a glance of sympathy which is another act of our homage to the truth.

—Antonin Sertillanges

Our choices are very important, although they are rarely important in the ways we believe them to be. For instance, an absence of joy in our lives is a reliable indicator that something is amiss; there is some way in which we have departed from, or are not fulfilling, our inner design. Yet changing the outer form of our lives—ending a relationship, leaving a job or career, moving to a new locale—will not necessarily bring us closer to that inner design, and may not be necessary at all. It's entirely possible to make radical changes on the physical level, yet remain essentially in the same place emotionally and energetically, continuing to enact the same types of dynamics we had hoped to change. And so it makes sense that the reverse is also always possible: to remain in the same place physically, yet engage with the externally unchanged forms of our lives in a completely different way.

From the spirit's perspective, it is not necessarily better to change the outer form, nor is it better to refrain from changing it. There is never only one possible harmonious choice. In fact, the more fully we understand the true nature of our inner design, the more we realize the possibility of fulfilling it through almost *any* choice. Again, this is why what we do is always

153

less important than how or why we do it. It's also important to understand that no matter what choices we make, we will face profound challenges—not because we have erred, but because such challenges are necessary to our souls' development.

Obviously, we can serve life and ourselves most easily when we choose forms and structures that resonate with us and bring joy. If you marry, it is harmonious for you to choose a spouse with whom you feel a deep affinity, rather than someone you dislike. If you work, it's harmonious for you to choose a career path you enjoy rather than one that bores or alienates you. Yet whatever you choose, no matter how well it suits you, you will encounter cauldrons at many points along your path. The lessons you need to learn and the soul-level challenges that are yours to grapple with will find a way to come to you, no matter where you go or what you do.

For instance, if you yearn to have children, it is harmonious for you to do so—not because your life with your children will be easy, but because a life with children is the context in which you wish to engage with your share of life's challenges. If you would rather remain childless, that, too, is a harmonious choice—and of course, your childless life will also present you with challenges. In either case, with children or without, by conscious choice or by accident, you can still fulfill your inner design. It is simply a question of creating more or less easeful circumstances for your own spirit.

Our lives are designed so elegantly that regardless of our outer circumstances—whether we live in the city or the country, marry or remain single, work as a carpenter or a psychotherapist—we always have opportunities to fulfill our inner design. Of course some of us would prefer to be married carpenters in the city, and some would prefer to be single psychotherapists in the countryside—or married psychotherapists and single carpenters, or live in the jungle or beside the sea—and on the level of form, all of these options and many more have been provided to us. They are the field in which we get to play. They are the palette of colors with which we get to paint. As we have seen, nothing we do is "wrong" or "right" from life's point of view, although some choices align better with our own preferences than others.

For instance, Kelli Thomaides chose to leave Alcoholics Anonymous once she became a Tao practitioner, and then to leave New York and acting behind in order to honor her evolving sense of her inner design. Yet someone else in her shoes might have chosen to remain in A.A., or in the entertainment world, and worked to find her "True Heart" there.

Thomaides discovered that her desire to act came from superficial or, as she put it, "inauthentic" sources in her being. Yet actress Shirley MacLaine, who has used her movie-star fame to bring visibility to her spiritual beliefs and practices, sees acting as an authentic part of her life's work; in fact, to her the work of acting and the spiritual search seem very much the same. MacLaine says, "I knew I wanted to be a communicator from the very beginning. So I communicated through fifty films, many TV and stage shows and ten books. For me the search for Truth is paramount...The truth of a character I'm playing, the truth of the subject matter I write about or the truth of why we are alive and how it relates to our destiny."

Some people believe that physical or emotional limitations, financial circumstances or family obligations make it impossible for them to follow their soul's path. Yet since our souls are connected to all other souls and therefore to all circumstances, this cannot ever really be true. What is deeply right for one person's soul must also, on some level, be right for the souls of others in their life. Therefore, if you feel trapped by circumstance, it's worthwhile to probe more deeply. For instance, are you being held back by fear? By the need to please or impress others? By the need to maintain a certain income level or lifestyle? By questions about identity—"Who would I be if I made this choice?" Any of these mental or emotional states can be shifted, if you are willing to choose on behalf of yourself and life.

If you believe you are denying your soul's calling out of a sense of responsibility to another person or people, it's worth exploring whether your love for that person or those people could still be served—in fact, could perhaps be even more fully served—if you chose on behalf of your own joy. On the other hand, perhaps you have a misunderstanding of what your inner design requires. Even if part of you wants to go travel the world, perhaps it is an even deeper expression of who you are—an even more precise way of fulfilling your inner design—to move back to your home town and care for an aged parent. Pleasure and joy are not the same thing; a choice which sounds like more fun to one part of us may not be what our soul most deeply yearns toward, or what will most help us fulfill our inner design.

Only you can discern what is true for you. What's most important is *why* you choose what you choose—whether the energies fueling your choice are composed of self-love, self-honoring and an affirmation of life. If so, no matter how difficult the path may be, joy will grow within you, and you will feel increasingly delighted to be yourself. As the groundbreaking surrealist artist Salvador Dali put it, "Each morning when I awake, I experience again a supreme pleasure: that of being Salvador Dali."

Obviously, there are circumstances in which certain choices are truly not available to us on the level of form. For instance, unless you started serious training in your youth or early adulthood, you are unlikely to become an Olympic-level athlete. Yet the soul never requires specific forms in order to fulfill its inner design. If devoting yourself to a particular sport or activity brings you joy, ribbons, medals, cheering crowds and cash prizes are not required.

Even those of us who face very limited options in our external lives still have a vast array of inner choices available to us in each moment. Even physical immobilization or confinement does not remove our ability to choose our level of consciousness, and to deeply harmonize that consciousness with the design of our soul. The Dalai Lama tells the story of a Tibetan monk who spent most of his adult life in a prison run by the Chinese government, being abused and tortured. After his release, he told the Dalai Lama that each day of his imprisonment, he had been quite afraid. "I didn't fear for my life," he explained. "I feared every day that I would lose my compassion for the Chinese."

Evidently, sustaining a sense of compassion for others was a deep soul-calling for this monk. Although it's difficult to imagine feeling joy in a life of imprisonment, abuse and torture, the monk's choice to keep compassion alive within him brought him more joy, under the circumstances, than any other choice he could have made. Even in horrific conditions, moment by moment, day by day, he chose on behalf of himself and life, and in that way fulfilled his inner design.

As the monk's story makes clear, nothing and no one can take away our ability to make choices—choices that either connect us more fully to ourselves and to life, or further our sense of separation. Life offers up an endless stream of ways, forms and contexts in which we are continually challenged to learn what we need to learn, heal what we need to heal, and bring forth what is within us—and we can do that learning, healing and bringing-forth regardless of our circumstances, whatever outer forms we create or find ourselves confined within.

This is why we never have to fear missing out on opportunities, or making the "wrong" choice. Whichever paths we choose, and whatever our intentions, life will continually offer us opportunities and possibilities that fit our trajectory. Such opportunities are everywhere; the field of possibilities which contains us, and which we contain, is much larger than we can conceive. It's as if we are artists with billions of colors at our disposal—yet, since no palette could possibly hold all those colors, only the colors or options relevant to the picture we are currently painting will present themselves to us. When we choose to begin a different picture—when we re-set our intentions—then a different palette automatically becomes available.

I reached a crossroads in my fifth year of full-time college teaching, one year before I would have received tenure. Teaching creative writing full-time was no longer satisfying me, but I had no idea what came next. My restlessness made me more open than I would otherwise have been. Although I had never had any interest in hypnotherapy—and in fact, knew almost nothing about it—I followed my intuition, which led me to my teacher. As it turned out, that first hypnotherapy course was the gateway to my study of shamanism, energy medicine and Transpersonal Psychology. Soon I decided to leave academia and become a self-employed healer.

"Don't quit your job. The economy is bad. It's too risky. You can always do healing work on the side," many people counseled me. When I submitted my resignation, the chair of my department was shocked. "A lot of writers would give their right arm for your job!" he told me. Of course, being human, I did feel some fear about leaving behind a guaranteed income, job security and benefits to strike out on my own. Yet I also knew what felt deeply right to me.

I believe my private practice thrived because I made my choice for reasons aligned with my soul. If I had left academia because I was angry at my colleagues, or because I was too insecure to let myself stay in such a desirable position, the energies fueling my choice would have been inharmonious, and this would have been reflected in the results; that anger or insecurity would have followed me into whatever I did next. Yet if I had forced myself to stay in my teaching job because it offered more prestige or because I was too frightened to give up the guaranteed income, this, too, would have been inharmonious and would have led to an absence of joy.

I have worked with many people who faced similar crossroads in their own lives. Some have been able, whether quickly or slowly, to follow the call of their souls, often leaving the security of long-term jobs or relationships in the process. Others have ignored or suppressed the inner call for years or even decades, forcing themselves to remain in circumstances that do not feed them. Sadly, this inability to follow our soul's path invariably leads to depression, physical illness or other symptoms. These negative consequences are the inevitable result of a misalignment between our human choices and our soul. When we use tools in ways for which they were not designed, they usually break. The same thing happens when we use our lives in ways not consonant with our inner design.

Every form in existence is equally valid, and any form can potentially offer a vehicle for fulfillment of our inner design. Yet some forms truly are a better fit for each of us than others. This is why it is so important to become your own authority, to develop the ability and willingness to discern what is harmonious for *you,* and make choices accordingly. Anything you choose can become a way to participate more deeply in the larger web of life—or to internally separate yourself from it.

My guides once gave me a vision which helped me to understand this principle:

I am looking down at the earth as if from another planet, through the eyes of someone who knows nothing about human life on earth. In this state, without any preconceived notions or interpretations, I see people engaged in many different tasks. Some are bringing plates of food to other people; some are driving big trucks filled with things; some are attending to people who are lying in bed; some are standing up and talking in big rooms filled with other people; some are sitting, staring at small boxes and making tapping sounds with their fingers, and so on.

Since, in this vision, I have no idea of the meaning or purpose of these actions, all I can see is the quality of energy flowing through each person. I notice that some of them are filled with an energy that looks bright, light, clear and sparkly, like the bubbles in club soda, while others have thicker rivers of light running through them. In some people, the light is bright white; in others it has more of a golden or pinkish hue. Whatever the nature of the energy in each person's body, I see how it flows through them into whatever they are doing, and also flows into the other people with whom they come in contact.

In some people, however, I can see no light at all. In others, there is light that seems to be stopped-up or dammed; although it flickers inside them, it isn't able to move through them and infuse the work they are doing. In this case, no matter how valuable or worthwhile their work may be on a worldly level, it is energetically empty. I see other people whose bodies are filled with dark, sticky-looking energy—the kind of energy produced by bitterness, resentment or despair. Even if these people are doing "good work," the impact they have on others—and the impact they experience within themselves—cannot possibly be positive, because they are working against, rather than with, the current of life itself.

Theologian and civil rights leader Howard Thurman sums this up beautifully: "Don't ask yourself what the world needs. Ask yourself what makes you come alive, and then go do that—because what the world needs is people who have come alive."

22

Joy as Navigational Aid

Joy is the infallible sign of the presence of God.

—Madeleine L'Engle

Few of us were taught to recognize and honor our joy, much less use it as a compass on the byways of our lives. In fact, many of us were taught exactly the opposite. I've talked with people who had trouble even allowing themselves simple pleasure, much less choosing on behalf of joy. "If I start doing something I really enjoy, I always feel like I should be doing something else," one person told me. Another admitted, "Joy makes me anxious, because I can't control it. I don't want to feel it because then it'll just go away again."

As children, all of us naturally recognized and followed joy as easily and spontaneously as cats seek out warm places to sleep. But some of us had parents or circumstances that punished or shamed us for "wasting time" if we were reading, drawing, sitting quietly in nature, dancing, imagining, storytelling, writing, playing, or any of the many other things which may have brought us joy. And as adults, we live in a culture that encourages us to suppress many of our inner signals. For instance, few of us go to sleep when we first feel tired; most of us feel we have "too much to do," and push ourselves further—only to find that when we do finally go to bed, sleep doesn't come. Few of us eat only when we are truly hungry, and only foods that genuinely nourish us. So it's no surprise that we are also unused to navigating by joy. Just as many people who have developed unhealthy relationships to food and eating must learn, over time, to pay close attention to the inner sensations of hunger and fullness and to their bodies' actual *physical* cravings— the cravings that come from a deeper, more wholesome level than the desires for "junk food"—we may also need to learn how to differentiate between very different kinds and levels of impulses and longings within our being.

Joy is qualitatively different from other emotional experiences we may think of as "positive," like happiness, pleasure and contentment. Although joy sometimes co-exists with those other states, very often it does not. Happiness, pleasure and contentment can emerge from experiences that satisfy us on more shallow levels of being. Although there is nothing "wrong" with superficial satisfaction—in fact, it can be both nourishing and instructive, particularly if we do not become overly attached to the conditions which appear to produce it—it does not bring us into contact with the deep wisdom of the soul.

In contrast, joy is a kind of musical tone which reverberates through all levels of the being. It is an experience which is very much of the personal self, yet transcends that personal self at the same time. And, because it comes to us straight from the soul, joy is our most accurate navigational aid. We might compare it to a GPS, which can tell us exactly when to turn left or right, turn around, or hold our course.

Of course, we do not have to obey the GPS in our cars. We are free to turn right when the GPS tells us to turn left, or to keep going straight when it tells us to turn around. The GPS has no emotional investment in our following its instructions. It does not need to prove itself, nor does it ever become offended or hurt. It never attempts to control or manipulate us; it doesn't get impatient, frustrated or angry with us, even when we travel very far off course. And no matter which turns we make or do not make, the GPS is always ready, willing and able to instruct us in how to reach our destination from our new location.

Our souls use the presence or absence of joy as a way to communicate with us as we steer and make choices within the vehicles of our lives. Although we may sometimes judge ourselves, or grow angry, frustrated, impatient, depressed or despairing, our souls never judge us. In fact, like a GPS, the soul is incapable of judgment. Yet many of us are so used to judging ourselves, or acting in response to the feared or perceived judgment of others, that it can be difficult for us to shift out of paradigms of "wrong" and "right" and keep our focus on the fulfillment of our inner design.

Fortunately, when we look for it, support is everywhere. Even the common objects around us can help us understand these principles, if we allow them to. For instance, as I write this, I am sitting on a chair, with a steaming cup of tea on the table next to me. The cup's inner design makes it well-suited to hold hot liquid; its handle enables me to bring the liquid to my mouth without burning my hand. The table is well-designed as a surface on which a cup can rest, and the chair's design gives me a place to sit comfortably.

Now, I *could* sit on my table and rest my cup of tea on my chair—there would be nothing "wrong" with doing so. Yet it clearly works better the other way around. I *could* pour my tea onto the surface of the table, and then crouch underneath the table to try to catch a few drops of tea in my mouth; again, while this would not be "wrong," it would be inefficient, would leave me thirsty, and might damage the surface of the table. I *could* attempt to sit on my cup, pour my tea onto my chair, and tilt it toward me to try to drink from it—not "wrong," but again, certainly uncomfortable and unsatisfying. In fact, my cup might break in the process of being used in a manner so ill-suited to its inner design.

For each of us, as for the table, chair and cup, there are roles, tasks, choices for which we are more optimally suited, and toward which our spirit naturally gravitates—and other roles for which we are not so well-suited, and toward which we do not gravitate. Few of us would literally attempt to sit on our cups, pour tea onto the surfaces of our tables, and drink from the tables' edge. And yet, how many of us do indeed attempt to use ourselves—to direct our own life energy—into forms and pathways just as ill-suited to us?

Often we may be aware that our souls are urging us in a particular direction, yet still find ourselves making choices that are not in accordance with our souls. Living in ways that are out of sync with our inner design may offer us social rewards, and we may experience some limited satisfaction in amassing those rewards. But making choices that are out of alignment with our own souls, or for reasons that are not aligned with our own souls, will never bring *joy*. Joy is a state of being which can neither be manufactured, nor disguised. When we feel joy, it is an unfailing indicator that we are working in harmony with our inner design.

We've all experienced times or aspects of our lives in which we feel energized, interested, engaged, motivated, excited, and grateful. This is evidence that we are living in alignment with our inner design. Many of us have also experienced times or aspects of life in which we've felt restless, bored, unhappy, self-doubting, trapped, despairing, and angry.

These emotional states serve as an indicator that we are doing the equivalent of attempting to sit on our cups and drink from our tables. When joy is not present, something is out of alignment in our relationship to ourselves, others, or life.

Mythology scholar and author Joseph Campbell famously said, "Follow your bliss and the universe will open doors where there were only walls." In contrast, Andrew Harvey, the originator of Sacred Activism, suggests that we follow our heartbreak. The truth is, work that attempts to change whatever breaks our hearts is very often the work that brings us bliss, or at least deep soul-level satisfaction. As Campbell also advised, "Find a place inside where there's joy, and the joy will burn out the pain."

Each of us is unique, both in what evokes our deepest heartbreak and pain, and in the creative responses we formulate to burn that pain out with joy. In a recent *New York Times*, I found glimpses of three human lives lived in accordance with very different inner designs.

John Henry Browne *is a lawyer who has spent his life defending people no other lawyer wanted to defend. Currently, he is working on behalf of the American soldier who has admitted killing seventeen Afghan civilians, including nine children, in the middle of the night. About the case, Browne said, "People have to understand that we have created these soldiers. Your tax dollars, my tax dollars are funding this. We all have responsibility... In the Frankenstein movies, Frankenstein was not the monster; the monster was Dr. Frankenstein, who created him."*

Christina Beckles *is a former Golden Gloves boxing champion who now spends her time working without pay for the dog rescue organization she founded, which brings abandoned Puerto Rican dogs to the United States and finds homes for them. It all started when she went to Puerto Rico on vacation and found a starving pregnant dog in a restaurant parking lot. "No one wanted to help. It broke my heart," she explains. Given that Puerto Rico is estimated to have 150,000 unwanted dogs, the 81 dogs she has saved so far could seem like a very small drop in an overwhelming bucket. But, says Beckles, "A saved dog is a saved dog." One tiny chihuahua weighed only one pound and had lost much of her fur, but Beckles nursed her back to health with scrambled eggs, salmon and chicken—and, two weeks later, put her on a plane to a new home in Las Vegas, now weighing two pounds and covered in a healthy new coat of fur.*

Matt Green, *a former civil engineer, now spends his days walking. He began in 2010 with a five-month walk from Rockaway Beach, New York, to Rockaway Beach, Oregon. After that he worked odd jobs for a year and a half, saving up money for his next walk. He has now decided to walk every street in every borough in New York City, a distance he calculates at roughly 8000 miles, counting parks, paths and cemeteries. He lives on $15 per day, sleeps on friends' couches, walks all day, and updates his blog and Web site by night. About his passion, he says, "Some people have asked if I'm on a quest to figure out what to do with my life, but it's almost the exact opposite. When I'm outside, I get so immersed in wherever I am that it's sort of impossible to think about my long-term future." In his first two months of walking New York City, he has passed slaughterhouses in the Bronx and a hit-and-run accident in Queens; he has swum off the coast in Brighton Beach, Brooklyn, and prayed beside Khmer Buddhist monks at a temple near Prospect Park. "This walk is a way of understanding a place on its own terms, instead of taking someone else's word for it," he says.*

I find it inspiring to see how fully each of these people is following his or her own inner blueprint, responding to what brings joy, causes heartbreak, or both. The life that fulfills your inner design may look more ordinary than this on the surface—or it may be just as quirky, just as magnificently specific to you, as the lives of the people described above.

Yet "quirkiness" does not necessarily indicate fulfillment of one's inner design. The *New York Times* also recently profiled Beth Shak, a woman who by her own count owns over 1200 pairs of high-heeled shoes. She estimates that she has spent approximately $500,000 on those shoes, many of which she has never even worn. When Shak discusses her shoe collection, her wording makes clear that she has bought these shoes out of compulsion, not joy. "I went through a period in my life where I was really unhappy," she says, "and the only thing that made me happy was buying a pair of shoes." Now divorced, Shak adds, "I'm in a better place now. I buy less."

Most of us have at least occasionally attempted to "make ourselves feel better" with addictive or compulsive behaviors. Whether it's food, alcohol, drugs, sex, shopping, pornography, Facebook, video games, reading, work, or something else, we are, as a species, capable of using almost any substance or behavior as a means of escaping from ourselves and from life. But distraction, escape and self-medication never actually bring joy. If we find ourselves engaged in these behaviors, it's simply a sign that we have in some way veered off course from the design of our souls. Fortunately, a course correction is always within reach.

23

The Nature of the Soul

If the grandfather of the grandfather of Jesus had known what was hidden within him, he would have stood humble and awe-struck before his soul.

– Khalil Gibran

Imagine a vast plant that could somehow seed itself in many parts of the world, and even in other parts of the universe, at once. Imagine that this single plant could take different forms each time it seeded itself—some as small as a clover, others as delicate as a rosebush, others as vast as a gigantic redwood tree, and so on. Now imagine that each of these many forms—which might appear to the human eye like many kinds of plants, yet are actually one—could stretch "forward" and "backward" in time as we understand it, so that a single plant might be forming roses in Germany in the year 1940, making pine cones in Illinois in the year 1860, and sprouting thistleheads in India in the year 1150, all at the very same moment.

Now, imagine that each of the forms of this single plant were somehow in communication with each other across time and space, so that anything it learned or experienced became part of the knowledge of the whole organism. The aspect living as a redwood tree would gain a visceral understanding of silken, fragrant, brightly-colored petals; the rose would access the power and strength of a hundred-foot-tall tree; both the rose and the redwood would gain the knowledge of a thistle plant, with all of its softness, prickliness, and ability to travel long distances to seed itself. Of course, such a plant could never die, because even when one or many of its aspects reached the end of its life, the plant would always have many more aspects, each in different forms and places, and each containing all of the knowledge of those that had come "before" it, those that existed "at the same time" as it, and those that would exist in what we think of as "the future."

Although it is difficult for us to conceive of such a magical, multidimensional plant, this crude analogy can help us begin to grasp the nature of the soul. It helps to explain how the soul's life can span what appear to us as many human lifetimes, and also why each of us is able to access pools of knowledge far greater than our individual human minds. Given its nature, the soul cannot possibly accomplish all of the learning, growth, exploration and healing it needs in a single human form or lifetime. Therefore, it takes many forms over a period of many lifetimes, allowing itself myriad opportunities to learn, grow, create, make colossal "mistakes" and redeem or rectify them, experience tremendous damage and heal it, and much more.

Seen from this angle, it might appear not to matter much what happens in a single human lifetime, since the soul has such a great number of opportunities to live, grow, develop and experience life. Yet each human lifetime does deeply affect the soul. After all, although a single toenail may seem insignificant in the scale of your entire body, if that toenail becomes ingrown, its pain will get your attention! And once it does, you will probably do everything in your power to restore the well-being of your toenail, because what is good for your toenail is also good for you. Similarly, our well-being feeds the well-being of our souls, and our souls never tire of helping us fulfill our inner design.

Human beings tend to think it is "better" to complete things quickly. However, the soul is in no hurry for us to grow. Nor does it have any resistance to our growth. In other words, it neither pushes us nor drags its feet. It is our choice how fully we will take on the work of our soul—how fully we will embody our inner design—in each lifetime. The only incentive life gives us is the feeling of joy that comes when we are living in harmony with our own nature, and with our inner design.

Whether it happens rapidly or slowly, under conditions of tremendous hardship or with apparent ease, most of us do manage to grow in ways consonant with our inner design in each human lifetime. This growth may be partial, stunted, or relatively confined to certain aspects of our lives; again, there is nothing "wrong" with that, although it is likely to result in uneven allotments of joy in different parts of our lives. We may, for instance, choose to spend a lot of time and energy on our career, fulfilling one aspect of our inner design, even while other aspects of our lives and our being remain somewhat underdeveloped. Or our paid work may feel relatively unimportant to us, and we may give our best energy to, and experience the major part of our joy in, the process of raising children. Or we may come most fully alive while making art or music, or while gardening, or while experiencing the infinite permutations of love and sexuality in one or many intimate relationships. Each of these paths can be a way of fulfilling a part of our inner design.

Regrettably, however, some of us spend the greater part of our life energy in ways that do not contribute much to the fulfillment of our inner design. For instance, if you have an externally successful corporate career but your soul actually thrives on gardening, your work may be contributing very little to the fulfillment of your inner design. Perhaps tending to the potted plants in your office is the only part of your workday that truly feeds your soul.

Even if we are engaged in activities which in and of themselves *are* consonant with our inner design, it is possible to do them in ways that do not bring joy, especially if we lose sight of the real purpose of our endeavors. For instance, if your soul thrives on gardening and you leave your corporate job to become a landscaper, but bring a corporate work ethic to your new life, that pressured, deadline-driven approach may still keep you from joy; you may spend more of your time hunched over your computer than working with the plants that you love. If this is the case, a realignment is needed— not a change in *what* you are doing, but a shift in the consciousness you bring to your endeavors.

I've seen artists and writers who become so concerned with the commercial aspects of their work that they lose contact with their real reason for creating. Even people whose focus is not external success can veer from their inner design; for example, some healers become so overwhelmed by the amount of suffering in the world that they exhaust themselves by trying to serve as many clients or patients as possible. All of these attitudes emerge from misunderstandings about our souls' purpose. Since all outer forms are simply vehicles for our souls' development, any strain or tension in our human lives is an indication that we need to recalibrate the connection between our human selves and our souls.

Several years ago, I worked with a client who reminded me a great deal of my sister. Like my sister, Luce was sweet, radiant, lovely and creative—and had a vicious eating disorder. One night she called me to tell me that she had just spent the past twelve hours buying food, eating it and throwing it up, over and over again. Although Luce had a strong connection with her guides, she was stuck, despite what seemed to me to be her best efforts and my own.

The pain I feel about other peoples' pain has been one of my biggest challenges as a human being, and as a healer. The morning after Luce's phone call, still feeling deeply shaken and sad, I took that pain with me to a small chamber music concert in my neighborhood. As I leaned back and listened to the music, I silently prayed for assistance. To my surprise, I soon perceived the presence of Jesus Christ. He isn't one of my usual guides, but perhaps he was the being most suited to help me with this particular issue—or maybe he just liked the music. Tears covered my face as I viscerally felt Him patting light into my heart like a potter working with clay. Then, in my mind's eye, I watched an astonishing transformation: my anguish morphed into a radiant emanation of compassion. It was like a mathematical equation: anguish plus light equals compassion.

In the years since then, I have returned to this vision many times. I see clearly that I can be most useful to my clients by witnessing them with deep compassion, no matter what they may choose or do. When I am able to be with clients in this way, I feel joy—a clear indication that I am fulfilling my inner design. Yet if I start to believe that my work is actually to "help" people, I can become frustrated and drained by working with people who do not seem—from my limited vantage point—to be receiving that help. This induces the state many caregivers know as "burnout" or "compassion fatigue." ("Compassion fatigue" isn't caused by having too much compassion; there is, in fact, no such thing as "too much compassion." Rather, it's caused by not receiving enough compassion ourselves *from non-physical sources.)*

If I didn't understand the source of this burnout, I might think that it meant I needed to stop working as a therapist. Yet if I did not address my underlying confusion, I would most likely continue to find myself in similarly misaligned roles with friends, family members, coworkers or other people, who also might seem to need and yet to refuse my help. On the other hand, if I remain focused on the quality of energy that flows through me when I work with clients, rather than on the outcomes that are visible to me, joy returns.

24

The Multidimensional Tapestry of Reality

…The chaos of textures that went into each strand of that eternally complex tapestry…each one resonated under the step of the dancing mad god, vibrating and sending little echoes of bravery, or hunger, or architecture, or argument, or cabbage or murder or concrete across the ether… Every intention, interaction, motivation, every color, every body, every action and reaction, every piece of physical reality and the thoughts that it engendered, every connection made, every nuanced moment of history and potentiality, every toothache and flagstone, every emotion and birth and banknote, every possible thing ever is woven into that limitless, sprawling web. It is without beginning or end. It is complex to a degree that humbles the mind. It is a work of such beauty that my soul wept.

- China Miéville

Our human lives exist as part of the phenomenally complex, multifaceted lives of our souls—and our souls exist within a vast multidimensional tapestry, extending inward and outward, forward and backward, upward and downward, in every possible direction. This tapestry incorporates all of what we think of as the "past," the "present," and the "future." It contains within it not only what we have physically actualized, but every other potential we hold. It is a web of love, compassion and synergy far greater than we can begin to imagine.

Because this tapestry is so vast, our human minds can grasp or see only a tiny segment of its pattern at one time. It is as if our eyes are fixed a mere inch away from its surface, rendering us unable to see its larger design. For this reason, we can be easily distracted by details which are actually minute in relation to the whole.

If you have ever looked at an actual tapestry or painting from very close up, and then moved across the room to look at it again, you have probably noticed that the design "made more sense" when seen from further away; its images or patterns resolved and became more recognizable to you when you looked at it from a distance. Since we rarely have the opportunity to stand back and gain this perspective on our own lives, much less on the vast design of which our lives are only a tiny part, there is much that we cannot see, and much else that we inevitably misinterpret. Remembering this can help us hold our experiences, beliefs, desires and disappointments more lightly, and allow us to more easily see the humor, even the grace, in what occurs. When the energies of lightness, humor and grace enter our being, they create a different momentum in our lives; they help us to uncramp ourselves, relax our inner muscles, and behold ourselves and our lives with more equanimity.

There is nothing wrong with our limited vantage point, and nothing wrong with us for having it. It's the nature of the human experience, and it allows us to learn and develop in some very specific ways. Our relative lack of awareness, at this period in our evolution as a species, is actually an integral aspect of the tapestry—not a mistake, not something to struggle against, bemoan, or resist. And yet when we are able to briefly glimpse the larger reality of which we are part, such glimpses imbue our lives with a much deeper sense of meaning, purpose and joy.

An individual flower cannot comprehend the larger forces which propel it to sprout, nourish it into blooming, and allow other beings to "give" to it and "receive" from it at every point in its life cycle. But, because the flower does not conceive of itself as separate from the web of life, it also cannot feel fear or self-doubt. The individuated consciousness of human beings leaves us very vulnerable to such feelings, despite the great web of life which is supporting us, and is available to support us, at all times. For this reason, it is helpful for us to consciously observe, remember and remind ourselves of our interconnectedness, and of the true size of the tapestry of which we are part. If we feel alone or disconnected from life, it is actually a trick of our consciousness, a blind spot, and not reality. We are, in fact, never alone, and never unsupported, just as no flower or tree is ever alone or unsupported. Life is always with us, always moving through us and available to us, regardless of how things may appear.

Throughout human history, there have been certain exceptional people, Jesus Christ and the Buddha among them, who have seen, lived and taught from a larger view of the tapestry. In fact, every culture in human history has had its seers, mystics, monks, priests, artists, poets and other visionaries who have done the same. Most cultures have also made use of rituals and practices, including meditation, prayer, yoga, and ingesting sacred plant substances, to help people access a larger view of ourselves and our place in the universe. The visions and understandings reached by people in many different places, using many different practices and substances, have been remarkably similar.

Even people who have never engaged in explicitly spiritual practices occasionally experience moments of profound clarity, in which we are able to sense our intrinsic connection to life, and to life's many forms. For most of us, these glimpses remain brief; we cannot sustain this expanded perspective day to day, moment to moment. Nonetheless, our memory or awareness of the larger truth can remain with us, continuing to inform us on deeper levels, even as we go about the business of living as individual human selves, with all of the unique gifts, opportunities and challenges of the human state.

René Daumal writes, "One climbs and one sees, one descends and one sees no longer, but one has seen. There is an art of conducting oneself… by the memory of what one saw higher up. When one no longer sees, one can at least still know."

When my sister became pregnant after more than two decades of struggle with eating disorders, drug addiction and mental illness, my first response was horror. I knew that there was no way she could adequately parent a child. And because my work brings me into daily contact with the devastation caused by mentally ill and addicted parents, it was hard for me not to feel that her pregnancy was a terrible mistake. I wondered whether I should pray for her to miscarry.

Then I reminded myself that from a higher perspective, there are no mistakes; things simply are as they are. When viewed with enough distance, the patterns of light and darkness, health and illness, connection and disconnection in our lives look like branches on a tree, gnarling, knotting and reaching out in ways that are always beautiful—even when limbs die, are stunted, or get cut off.

From a human standpoint, it didn't seem "fair" to me that a child would have to gestate in the womb of someone so unprepared to receive him, and then endure whatever trauma his life with my sister might bring. However, my guides had taught me that life is neither fair nor unfair; it simply extends its creativity into every nook and cranny of existence, exploring all the possibilities available.

When I tried to sense into the spirit of the child who would be my nephew, I got an impression of a joyful, adventurous being who loved roller coasters, literally and figuratively. A roller coaster seemed an excellent metaphor for what life with my sister was likely to bring—careening wildly around curves, shooting down steep hills, chugging up seemingly impossible slopes. I myself am not a fan of roller coasters, but I certainly wouldn't presume to say that other people shouldn't enjoy them. Nor could I possibly know what this spirit might be able to gain or learn from the trauma he will experience. I could only remind myself that the picture is far bigger than I could see.

Eight years have passed since then, and after much trauma early in his life, my sister's child is now a lively, bright grade-schooler who is being raised by my mother and her partner. I am curious to see who he will become.

25

The Role of Hardship and Pain

There's a crack, a crack in everything. That's how the light gets in.

- Leonard Cohen

If it is true that life is always supporting us, and always available to support us, then why do so many human beings have to struggle with such difficult conditions? From the human perspective, so many lives are so terribly stunted or distorted by circumstances like poverty and oppression, abuse, neglect, and physical or mental illness. When we look at the tapestry from this vantage point, it seems tragic that these conditions limit the potential each human being might otherwise reach.

Of course, if we broaden our gaze, we see immediately that it is not only human beings who face this challenge. For instance, some flowers must struggle to grow through drought, or through floods, or through extremely hot or cold temperatures, or must push their way up through cement.

It is hard for us to see, from the human level, that life equally values, and is equally present within, *all* conditions—conditions of "hardship" as much as "ease," "insufficiency" as much as "plenty." Life pours itself out equally toward and into all circumstances and life forms; life trusts in itself and supports itself in ways more generous than we can imagine, and in so doing creates a marvelously diverse universe filled with surprise, variety, ingenuity, creativity and adventure. If we look closely at what we call the "natural" world, and if we allow ourselves to deeply *feel* that world, we will know the truth of this in our cells.

And yet as human beings we are fated to perceive ourselves as "individual selves," knowing little or nothing of the conditions in which we came to be. Like all other living things, we are determined to grow, fueled by the force of life within our cells—and in our growth process, each of us will encounter conditions of "hardship" and "ease," "insufficiency" and "plenty." We are certain to struggle in some ways and thrive in others, and through all of this we are life, and are completely held and supported by life. Life's support is no less present, no less generous or real, in our times of "hardship." It is only because of the limitations of our human vision that we view pain and difficulty as "bad," as a sign that something must be wrong with us, or with others, or with life itself.

The great mystic Julian of Norwich put it this way: "If there be anywhere on earth a lover of God who is always kept safe, I know nothing of it, for it was not shown to me. But this was shown: that in falling and rising again, we are always kept safe in that same precious love."

Hardship is not—cannot ever be—a barrier to the fulfillment of our inner design. In fact, if we were able to stand further back from the tapestry, we would see that each hardship is a creative variable, lovingly introduced by life, on behalf of life. There is no circumstance which cannot serve our growth and development if we allow it to. For instance, the suffering that feels as if it will shatter us may actually serve to shatter the rigid shell of the individual selves we believe ourselves to be; this breaking-open can be a great gift to our souls. The guide who has helped me write this book began speaking to me after a very painful and confusing period in my own life; several well-known contemporary spiritual teachers report that they achieved lasting states of higher consciousness after being "shattered" by long-term depression. Just as a seed needs to break apart in order to germinate, to be able to grow up through the earth and fulfill its inner design, so we, too, often need to break apart, or be broken apart by life. When we can fully embrace this experience, rather than struggling against it or believing that we have been wronged, we are far better positioned to receive its transformational gifts.

Of course, most depressed people will not experience sudden, dramatic and sustained spiritual awakenings. Instead, we may feel as if our lives, or the lives of others we know, have been warped or truncated by inner or outer difficulties. We may be haunted by the sense of "wasted" or "lost" potential. While understandable on the human level, this perception emerges from a misunderstanding about life and about our own purpose within it. It is true that no one among us will ever reach the particular expression we might have reached if every condition and circumstance we had encountered had been optimal. Yet what is also true is that *it was never our purpose to reach that "optimal" expression*—nor to experience a life without apparent hardship or "damage."

What or who we might have become without hardship or damage is not the point. Rather, the point is what we do *with* and *through* the damage and hardship of our lives. When we let go of the idea that our lives should have been different in some way, we can see more clearly the way light both enters us through our wounds, and radiates out from them.

From our vantage point here on earth, the moon appears to go through cycles of growth and diminishment, waxing and waning. At times we see the moon as round, and we call it "full." At other times, we barely see the moon at all; it seems to have disappeared. Yet the truth is that the moon is *always* full and round. All that changes is the angle from which *we* are able to see the moon. In just that way, we, too, are always "full." Everything we could have been and done, including the fullest and most glorious expression of every single one of our potentials, exists somewhere in a dimension we cannot usually perceive from our earthly perspective. It simply would not be possible to embody all of that within a single human body and lifetime; if it were, then having a human body and lifetime would be unnecessary. So, rather than grieving for the parts of our own moon that appear to be "missing," we can choose instead to celebrate all the parts of ourselves that are present and glowing, here and now—all of the ways in which we are still filled with creativity, love, and the infinite self-healing capacity of life itself.

For many years I was haunted by grief about my sister's suffering and wasted potential, as well as guilt about my own much greater well-being. Even once I began communicating with inner teachers, I often argued with them about the pain in my sister's life. I remember one such fight, in which I practically screamed at my guide, "Why is there so much pain in the world?" Of course, my guide remained completely equanimous. "Because pain is such a good teacher," he answered calmly.

Even though I wanted to argue, I knew he was right. The lion's share of my own growth and learning has come about through the most painful experiences in my life. I don't know how my sister's pain has helped her grow, but I do know that my pain about *her pain has been one of the major forces behind my drive both to heal, and to help others heal.*

In another meditation, I asked to see my sister's higher self or spirit. To my surprise, I was shown a graceful, supremely confident being who joyfully accepted the challenge of incarnating into such a troubled human life. I realized that in some ways I had always perceived this aspect of my sister, but had misunderstood its true nature. I had grieved the fact that this spirit was not more visible in my sister's daily life. I had thought that represented an error in the universe. Now, as I was able to glimpse more of the tapestry of reality, I could see that this spirit had deliberately chosen a life in which much of her light would be unavailable to her, in order to learn from that experience.

Can I know for sure that this is "the truth"? Of course not—but neither can I, or any of us, know anything else for sure. I am reminded of the parable of the blind men and the elephant—and how the man who touched the tail was convinced that an elephant is like a rope, the man with his hand on the elephant's tusk believed that an elephant is like a spear, and the man whose hand had landed on the elephant's leg knew an elephant to be like a tree trunk. Each man was right, of course; and because none of the men had the whole picture, each was also wrong.

My sister's life is tragic. My sister's life represents the perfect learning opportunity for her spirit. My sister's life has caused me great pain. My sister's life has spurred me to learn, grow and heal, and to devote my life to helping others do the same. Each of these things are true, and many more things are true, too. I often think of it this way: I have only one finger on one strand of hair in the elephant's tail. That's it; that's all the reality I can see. So I'm grateful when a brief glimpse of the larger tapestry can bring me greater peace and understanding.

26

Releasing Life on its Own Recognizance

Life is a series of natural and spontaneous changes. Don't resist them—
that only creates sorrow. Let reality be reality. Let things flow naturally
forward in whatever way they like.

– Lao Tzu

As our consciousness expands, and as we deepen our contact with the realms of support available to us, we experience new levels of hope, purpose, and joy. Yet we are also likely to find ourselves slamming up against internal patterns that stunt our growth and keep us from joy. One such pattern is a basic posture of resistance to life itself.

Many of us feel that life has committed crimes against us. We may feel we did not receive what we needed or deserved, or that we received treatment we did not deserve, from our parents, siblings, schools, spouses, friends, children, workplaces, or other people or circumstances in our lives. And in many cases, from the human perspective, we are absolutely right. There is a great deal of unconsciousness, abuse, violence, cruelty and neglect among human beings, and most of us have been the recipients of these damaging behaviors at least some of the time. (Of course, though we may wish it were otherwise, we have likely been the perpetrators at least some of the time, as well.)

It is also true that damage and pain are not apportioned equally or "fairly" between all human beings. Some people, in some lifetimes, endure far more abuse and hardship than others. If we are among those people, we may feel angry, bitter, mistrustful and scarred—and we may believe we are entirely justified in feeling this way.

From a human perspective, no one ever deserves cruelty, abuse, neglect or hardship—so when these things occur, they seem "wrong" to us. Yet when we view such phenomena as part of the larger tapestry of reality, we see that "hardship" is simply part of the diversity of life's creative expression. "Deserving" and "not deserving" are not concepts relevant to the way life works. The dandelion that grows up through a crack in the cement, rather than in lush soil, is not being abused or neglected by life; it neither "deserves" this circumstance, nor deserves a different one. Life has not turned against it, nor against any one of us, no matter how difficult our circumstances may be. In fact, life demonstrates its love for itself and for us by extending itself into every corner and crevice, every circumstance imaginable.

In one sense, it is no different for a child to be molested by her father than for a dandelion seed to find itself struggling to grow through a thin crack in a sidewalk. Neither the child nor the dandelion seed are experiencing ideal conditions; the major difference is that the dandelion's hardship is caused by forces that we can clearly see are impersonal, while the child's abuse is perpetrated by a human being with individuated consciousness—someone who experiences himself as separate from her, and is capable of harboring an *intent* to harm.

In addition, the child's own individuated consciousness means that the abuse is likely to shape the beliefs she holds about herself, others and life. A dandelion growing up through cement never thinks, "This must be my fault, I must deserve this, I must be bad." If it finds its growth stunted by harsh conditions, it will struggle to survive. Perhaps it will wither shortly after sprouting; perhaps it will manage, against the odds, to create a straggly little flower, and then, just before it is able to go to seed, someone will step on it or mow it down. Or perhaps it will successfully send a few seeds out into the world, and if these seeds land in dirt, they, too, may sprout. Whatever happens, the dandelion will not blame itself, nor anyone else, nor life for its hardship.

Yet because the nature of our consciousness leads us to experience ourselves as separate from other people and from life, human suffering tends to spur us toward blame. Often, people who have been abused or neglected blame themselves. The belief that we must have "deserved" our harsh treatment, or that it would not have happened if we had been somehow different or "better," frequently takes root in childhood and persists throughout our lives. Or we may blame our parents, or whoever else treated us badly. If we recognize that what happened was neither our fault not even truly our parents' fault—if, for instance, we know that our parents were also abused, and were merely re-enacting a cycle—we may blame life itself, or God, however we understand God. And of course, many people ricochet internally between all of these potential targets for blame.

The problem with blame is that it is a vicious internal loop. No matter what or whom we blame, the act and energy of blaming will keep us feeling both wrong or wronged, and will separate us from ourselves, from others, and from life. Even though someone who is accustomed to blaming herself might think it would be "healthier" to blame others, or vice versa, the truth is that blame does not, will not and cannot heal us. No matter where we direct it, blame can never help us connect more fully to ourselves, to others or to life. And blame is also never "true," in a larger sense, since pain is neither fair nor unfair, and is never personal. So blame is an emotional and energetic dead-end, an inner posture that saps our energy, keeps us re-telling the same stories, and thereby blocks us from the healing we long for.

In order to facilitate true inner peace and healing, we must dismantle this internal blame machine and commit to the work of accepting ourselves, our lives and our circumstances, exactly as we and they are. It is impossible to feel blame and acceptance at once; they are opposing currents. If we cultivate acceptance, the blame in us will wither. It also works the other way around; if we dismantle blame, we create fertile ground for acceptance to begin to grow.

Although making these inner shifts may feel frightening, destabilizing and disorienting at first, we will soon find that they free up a great deal of life energy. Since blame is a vicious loop, cycles of other-blame, self-blame and life-blame keep us running in circles, rather than able to make real movement. It takes conscious intention and work to shift this pattern, but help is available from higher sources when we ask for it.

A dandelion seed is blown onto cement rather than dirt; a forest fire burns a tree; a child is sexually abused by her father. These situations are very different, and yet they are not. In each case, an organism experiences conditions less than optimal for its growth. The fact is, life rarely provides completely optimal circumstances to anyone or anything. Of course, this isn't "fair." Neither is it "unfair." Fairness is an important concept among human beings, precisely because our individuated consciousness can lead us to behave *unfairly* in a manner that is simply not possible for any other being. However, the concept of fairness has no relevance in the natural world. Cats are not being unfair to the birds they kill and eat, nor are birds unfair to the insects and worms that make up their own diet. The concepts of fairness and unfairness are irrelevant in these circumstances because none of what occurs is personal. Each actor involved is simply being itself.

A child's individuated consciousness may lead her to take it personally when a parent abuses her—yet on the level of life itself, hardship and abuse are never personal. People who are abused are simply the unfortunate recipients of other peoples' confusion and pain, just as trees burned by forest fires are the unfortunate recipients of a particular combination of fire, dry wood, and wind. Trees do not "deserve" to burn, nor do people "deserve" abuse. And yet anyone who experiences abuse, and any tree that burns, can be sure that many millions of other people and trees have experienced similarly painful circumstances. Although it is sometimes possible to identify and hold responsible the perpetrators of specific acts of abuse, in the largest sense, the fact that such things come to pass is no one's fault. It is simply the way life works on this plane of existence.

Yet not only in situations of childhood abuse, but throughout most of our lives, human beings' consciousness predisposes us to experience the generalized phenomenon of difficulty as a personal attack or affront. When we feel pain, we often erroneously conclude that life is cruel, does not value us, or is punishing us. In turn, we may decide to punish life. Emotionally, we "arrest" life for the crimes we believe it has committed against us.

The sad truth is that when we adopt such a posture, what we actually arrest is our own development. We cannot grow and develop in healthy ways by pitting ourselves against life. We *are* life, so by pitting ourselves against life, we pit ourselves against ourselves. And when we are pitted against ourselves and against life, it is much harder for the nourishing energies of life to reach us. We become like dandelions growing up through cracks in cement that respond to their hardship by erecting metal boxes around themselves—metal boxes that ensure that neither the rain nor the sun can reach them. In this way, we greatly increase our own suffering.

What is the alternative?

When someone has been arrested for a crime, our legal system sometimes releases them from police custody "on their own recognizance," without requiring them to pay bail. This is an act of good faith and trust on the part of the court. Releasing life from the internal house arrest of our own judgment and resentment—releasing life on its own recognizance—is also an act of good faith and trust. Beyond that, it is a profound soul movement, a movement that is necessary if we are to live in harmony with ourselves, our circumstances, and the larger tapestry of reality.

One way to work toward releasing life on its own recognizance is simply by *ceasing to pray or wish for anything in your life to be other than as it is.* If, in this process, you encounter parts of yourself that *do* wish for things to be other than as they are, then you can step back a bit further and cease wishing for *those* parts to be different. You can accept them as they are in this moment, in all their confusion and striving, without identifying them as *yourself.* You can be the watcher, the seer, the holder of all that is, both "inside" and "outside" ourselves. And as you do this, an internal reconciliation can occur.

If, for example, you have an illness, do not pray to get well. If you have physical or emotional pain, do not try to make it go away. Allow the illness or pain to be there, just as it is. Most of us tend to respond to pain with resistance. Ironically, this resistance actually increases our pain by increasing our separation from ourselves. So, try to focus your energy not toward re-sisting, but toward a deeper and deeper allowing. Allow yourself to remem-ber and to know that there are tremendous forces both inside and outside of you, which are always available to help you reach fuller alignment and harmony with the universe. Your conscious intention to align yourself with their compassionate stream will serve you better than any other intention or effort you could possibly hold.

If part of you does wish for the illness to go away, or for the pain to diminish, then you can also focus on deeply acknowledging and accepting *that* part of your being. Let it know that you understand its wish to experi-ence something different, to feel better. Let it know that you accept it, too, exactly as it is.

Physiologically, of course, we are designed to flinch from pain—and if we touch something that physically burns or cuts us, it is wise to quickly move away. So it's not surprising that so many of us have learned to do the same thing with our emotions. The problem is that this very leads to our moving away from the vulnerable, hurting parts of *ourselves,* and also moving away from life—which is what happens when we close ourselves to, or reject, any aspect of our experience.

Life, however, does not ever move away from *us*. Life offers itself up to be lived in us, and through us, no matter what we experience, and no matter how we respond. Whether we embrace it or curse it, life remains perpetually with us and available to us. It is endlessly generous and abundant in that way. And so when we are able to meet life in a spirit similar to that with which life meets *us*, we are more likely to feel joy. When we resist any aspect of ourselves, our experience, or life, we are likely to feel pain.

Life has no particular preference for joy over pain. Life recognizes all states of being as equally valid, and embraces all of them, and all of us. Yet since most of us would prefer to feel joy rather than pain, we can use the presence of pain as a sort of warning light on the dashboards of our psyches. Our pain will remain illuminated for as long as is needed to get our attention—that is, until we recognize and shift the ways in which we are separating ourselves from ourselves, from our own experiences, or from life.

It's not exactly that life is "trying to teach us a lesson," as some parents say when they punish their children. It is simply an energetic principle. We cannot fail to feel pain when we separate ourselves from life. We cannot remain connected to life when we attempt to escape or evade any part of it. It is only by embracing, rather than rejecting life, that we can move from pain to joy. In the process, of course, we must also embrace *ourselves*—since we are part of life, and can never be separate from it.

If we accept the challenges our lives bring to us, and embrace them—if we live our way into those challenges fully, bringing ourselves to the tasks at hand with all the depth of courage, wisdom, spirit and heart we can find within ourselves—then we will serve life. And if at the same time we can also remember—not only in our minds, but in the very depths of our beings—that this life as it appears to us is only a tiny part of the larger tapestry of reality, and that the whole of our existence and being is much bigger than we can presently see, then life will find us more receptive, and will have an easier time serving *us*.

My own struggle to "release life on its own recognizance" has been fueled both by my pain about the suffering in my family, and by a deep sense of alienation

from much of human culture. For instance, the thought that "my" country has a military—that adult men and women dress up in costumes and deliberately go to other countries to kill people, and that the taxes I pay actually fund this activity—seems not only wrong, but completely bizarre to me. I have often felt as if I come from another planet. And so, in my most difficult moments over the years, I often wished to leave earth behind and go back "home." "When are they sending the spaceship?" I used to joke with a friend who felt similarly.

Some years back, I went through a very difficult passage. Within the space of a year I separated from a beloved mentor, confronted an escalating series of crises in my family, sold the house that I loved and moved cross-country, then changed my mind and moved back. I felt as if I had lost my mooring on earth. As I began the challenging process of reconstructing my life, my guides let me know that I had some serious work to do on the inner plane, too. Because I was only partially and reluctantly committed to life on earth, much of my energy and power were elsewhere. It was as if I was sitting in my car with one foot on the gas and the other on the brake, both pressing down.

Of course, I could remain in this position if I chose to, but my guides made it clear that it would limit what I was able to experience and accomplish on earth. Or I could choose to say a more definitive "No" to life on earth—not necessarily through suicide, but through a more complete withdrawal of my energy from physical life. The third option, they told me, was to say a wholehearted "Yes" to life on earth, difficulties, alienation and all.

I knew I wanted to choose Door #3. But it wasn't easy. I encountered a lot of internal resistance as I attempted to release life on its own recognizance, and truly accept its conditions. Truthfully, a big part of me didn't want to—but the part of me that did was even bigger. So I set my intention, asked my guides and larger forces for help, and worked to realign my being to say Yes to life.

I went through several intensive weeks of prayers, soul retrievals, shamanic journeys and energetic clearing—and my life did change. Manifesting what I wanted became much easier; for instance, I was able to get a home loan at a time when my circumstances made it look nearly impossible. I will always believe that I got that loan because of the inner work I had done. Determining what I wanted became easier, too. In the years since that difficult passage, my life has become more and more fully my own—since I have also given myself so much more fully to life.

27

Saying *Yes* to Life

Whatever the present moment contains, accept it as if you had chosen it. Always work with it, not against it.

– Eckhart Tolle

Releasing life on its own recognizance is a crucial step on the path toward saying *Yes* to life. But saying *I will cease to fight and resist life* is still not quite the same as saying *Yes*.

For most of us, it is very hard to say a full, complete *Yes* to life in all of its aspects. In fact, few people ever do. Yet this refusal to say *Yes* to life has many consequences. It means that we do not and cannot fully say *Yes* to ourselves, since we are a part of life. It robs us of the deep peacefulness that comes from aligning ourselves to the larger movements of the universe. And it diminishes our power, our ability to manifest changes in our lives. After all, how powerful can we be when we're pitting our small human fists against the much larger body of the world?

Essentially, when we do not say *Yes* to life, to the great stream of energy which contains us and which we contain, we condemn ourselves to living a kind of half-life in which we must always remain frustrated and at odds. Since we are a part of life, there is no way for us to be at odds with life without also being at odds with ourselves.

We often have misconceptions about what it would mean to say *Yes* to life. From the human perspective—remember, that perspective in which we are so close to the tapestry of reality that we can see very little of its actual design—life is full of cruelty, injustice and suffering. So we might imagine that saying *Yes* to life would mean saying *Yes* to war, rape, child molestation, concentration camps, and torture, as well as to many smaller acts of harm. If our childhoods were abusive, we may think that saying *Yes* to life means saying *Yes* to whatever abuse we received.

It's understandable that we don't want to grant approval to these kinds of phenomena. They do not deserve our approval. And yet, these disturbing phenomena do exist on earth. In fact, the basic error in consciousness that causes them to exist also exists within us. And by attempting to separate ourselves internally from "sin" or abuse, *in the very act of separation itself,* we are also separating ourselves from ourselves from life, and from love. Because the essence of love is non-separation, *any* separation, any act of rejection or judgment, distances us from love. This means that the remedy for the terrible problem of separation—and for its terrible consequences—is, and can only be, love.

From the distance at which human beings generally view the tapestry of reality, the idea of love as a remedy for terrible acts of cruelty and injustice may seem impossible, or even morally wrong. And yet if we observe ourselves closely, we will notice that when we withhold our love from these disturbing phenomena, we become filled up with the emotional and energetic current of lovelessness. When we respond to horrors with hatred, resistance, judgment or refusal, these energies flow from us out into the world, adding to the heavy load of hatred and judgment already present in the world. Thus we add to the very state of non-love which we deplore, and also condemn ourselves to live within that bleakness.

This is one reason why people who devote their lives to "service," to "working for good," sometimes grow so cynical and despairing. Over time, so much resistance to what is "wrong" in the world becomes braided into their beings that it essentially poisons them. On one level, they are perceiving things accurately. From the human perspective, there *is* a great deal that is wrong in the world. Yet of course, despite the greatest effort anyone can make, these wrongs appear to continue unceasingly, and by resisting them, we only add more fuel to the fires of separation. The energy of condemnation is a boomerang; it condemns both "subject" and "object," those who condemn as much as that which is condemned. Hatred, judgment, resistance and condemnation are cognitive and energetic states that are essentially anti-life. No stance that is anti-life can truly work in favor of life. It is that simple.

And so if we truly wish to work on behalf of life, we must love what seems to us utterly unlovable. From the human level, this can be difficult to imagine—even though we are being shown this sort of love all the time. The love of the sun, for instance, shines equally on everything. The love of the rain falls equally on all things, without judgment or discrimination. This kind of encompassing, non-discriminating love is available constantly, to all of us, from the unseen realm. This is the sort of love that prefers nothing, and rejects nothing. It is the love that says *Yes* to all of us, no matter where and who we are, no matter what we have done or left undone in our lives. When we can allow ourselves to feel and receive this *Yes,* we become more able to extend the same *Yes* both outwardly and inwardly, toward all we see and experience. Saying this kind of *Yes* to life does not render us unable to change internal or external realities; on the contrary, it is the position from which we are *most* able to make change, because we are working with rather than against the forces of life.

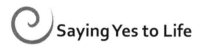 Saying Yes to Life

Using this prayer is like setting your inner GPS toward the destination "Saying Yes to Life." Your arrival won't be instantaneous, but it will happen. The prayer is simple enough to repeat to yourself throughout your day, even as you're driving, showering, walking, cooking, doing dishes, cleaning, or anything else that doesn't demand 100% of your attention. You can repeat the four statements in any order, allowing them to become a rhythmic chant with the power to profoundly internally reorient and rearrange you. The more often you use this prayer, the more quickly you will feel yourself shift.

Help me accept
Help me assent
Help me embrace
Help me say Yes

Help me embrace
Help me accept
Help me assent
Help me say Yes

Help me assent
Help me embrace
Help me accept
Help me say Yes

Help me say Yes
Help me accept
Help me embrace
Help me assent

28

What and Whom to Serve

As we cease to resist our lives, become more able to say *Yes* to our inner and outer circumstances, and feel more peace and joy, we often wish to help other people experience the same thing. The desire to serve other people, or to serve life itself, spontaneously emerges as a result of our growing sense of love for others and for the earth. Yet it is important to understand just which forms of "service" can truly serve our own unfolding and the unfolding of others.

Many religious and spiritual traditions promote "service to others" as an important path for soul growth, yet they do so out of a well-intentioned error in perception. Other people don't actually need our "help;" no one and nothing actually needs us to "serve" it. The tapestry of reality is so vast, and we are so small in relation to it, that we cannot ever know what another person needs from us; the most we can ever hope to know is our own next step in fulfilling our inner design. As we have already seen, the fulfillment of our inner design is our true purpose, and joy is our only reliable navigational aid. When we navigate by joy, we are serving life itself—and when we are serving ourselves and life, we are inevitably serving all other beings, too.

Perhaps at an earlier time in human history, before our individuated consciousness had become so easily twisted into patterns of self-rejection and self-hatred, it came easily and naturally to each of us to "serve ourselves." At that point, the idea of "serving others" may have been useful as a reminder that the "self" extends beyond our own physical frame. Yet now the idea of placing others' needs over our own has become institutionalized in many of our individual psyches—and in many religious traditions, institutions and cultures—in ways that cause great distortion and damage. For instance, the Indian nun Mother Theresa was venerated during her lifetime as a living saint who brought food and care to thousands of the most down-trodden, suffering people in India. Yet since her death, biographies have revealed that Mother Theresa was a deeply tormented woman who was often cruel to the nuns who worked with her. She was also chronically exhausted, spiritually depleted, and profoundly out of contact with the God she wished and claimed to serve. If it is true that beneath the surface of *what* she did, the *why* and *how* of Mother Theresa's "good works"—the energies that fueled them—were truly those of despair, pain, anger and self-abnegation, then she unwittingly strengthened the force of those energies in the world.

When we remember that at the deepest levels of being we are all connected, the idea that it is "better" to serve others than to serve ourselves is clearly revealed as illogical. Since others *are* us and we *are* others, serving "ourselves" in ways that honor the soul—through true presence, nurturing, nourishment, attention and compassion—cannot possibly be any less worthwhile than serving "others" in such ways, and serving "others" while repressing, denying, harming or debasing the self cannot possibly bring more light into the world.

Yet it is also true that the experience of "being used for a purpose greater than ourselves" is one of the most profound sources of joy available to human beings. When we are able to open ourselves in such a way that we can allow the larger spirit of life and light to flow through us, enlarging and expanding us, nourishing and loving us more widely and deeply than "we" (in the small sense) could ever love ourselves, we are indeed in heaven—and heaven is, as singer Belinda Carlisle sang, a place on earth. The problem is that when others attempt to force us into such postures, or we attempt to force ourselves, what results is a rape of our spirits rather than a state in which we can truly give, receive and "make" love. It is only possible to make love—in any sense of that term—by navigating according to what brings us joy.

So what, then, can we make of the desire to "serve"? A broader way to understand this desire is as an impulse to participate directly rather than indirectly, consciously rather than unconsciously, in the evolution of our planet and of our species. Of course, everyone is always participating in this evolutionary process; there is no one who is not, and no way to exempt oneself. But those of us who have inquired more deeply into the nature of the human experience do have an opportunity to participate more deliberately, to make choices based on a higher level of understanding about the nature of our participation.

As human beings with physical bodies, we are in a very powerful position. As Isa Gucciardi puts it, these bodies give us a license to operate on the earth plane. As physical beings, we can influence physical matter far more easily than non-physical beings or forces can. In addition, because of the freedom of choice afforded to us by our individuated consciousness, we can consciously choose to be vessels for non-physical energies like love and compassion, just as a cup is a vessel for tea. When we make this choice, we serve ourselves, because holding wisdom, compassion and love inside of us feels so good! We also serve those energies by giving them opportunities to fulfill their inner design. And of course we do serve others too, just as the tea cup serves itself, the tea it holds, and whoever drinks from it. This state of mutual benefit is what the Dalai Lama calls "enlightened altruism."

However, it is important for us to remember that our role as vessels is limited to *holding energies.* What others do or fail to do with those energies cannot be our concern. The cup does not become frustrated when someone holds it improperly, spills most of its tea while drinking it, or transfers the tea to her mouth with a fingertip rather than by sipping directly from the cup. The cup *knows* (in a manner of speaking) that it has a handle by which it can be held, and a rim to which people can put their mouths. It is well-designed as a vessel from which people can drink. If people do not drink from it, or do not drink in the most efficient manner, the cup will still have fulfilled its inner design simply by existing.

In just this way, we fulfill our inner design as vessels of consciousness simply by holding the energies of love and compassion, regardless of whether or not these energies appear to be received by others. There are many ways we can transmit these energies: through written and spoken words, through actions, or through gestures or touch. We even transmit them simply by holding their frequency, even when we appear to be doing nothing. There is documented proof of this phenomenon; for instance, when a large enough percentage of people in a given geographic area begin to meditate, the local crime rate goes down. The energetic state of peace and equanimity achieved by the meditators has a statistically measurable impact on everyone else in the local environment, *even though the meditators are not consciously trying to prevent crime or alter the mind-states of those who commit it.*

Of course, consciously holding the energies of love, peace and wisdom will increase our own state of joy. And even if it appears that others have not received our transmission, that perception need not interfere with our joy. Regardless of what happens—or what we *perceive* is happening, which of course is never the full reality of the larger tapestry—simply being a vessel is a source of joy. A tea cup is designed for the purpose of providing tea; its joy (so to speak) comes from its holding of tea—regardless of whether or not someone drinks from it, or how efficiently they imbibe it.

It is not that we do not, cannot or will not help others; very often, in fact, we will. But it is important for us to understand that helping others is not our *purpose*. This understanding will keep us from attempting to intervene inappropriately in other peoples' lives, or becoming frustrated when they appear to refuse the "help" we have offered. There are always those who will not accept help or whom we cannot help, at least on the levels we are able to perceive—and if we think that our purpose is to help, this will feel to us like failure. From a higher vantage point, of course, "failure" does not exist. On the level of the larger tapestry, the level on which our souls reside, there is no such thing as failure—and there is also no such thing as success. There are only degrees of unfolding, alignment, and harmony. Focusing on our own unfolding and alignment, our own joy, is the way in which we can best serve others, and serve life itself.

29
Loving the Gap

Human mistakes and inaccuracies are no less important than divinity.
The human condition creates divinity in the higher self.

— Lena Lees

As we grow in consciousness and wisdom, we may notice a disconcert-ing phenomenon. We know that higher realms exist to support us; we receive their support and bask in their wisdom, compassion and love, at least some of the time. We understand that we are connected to everyone and everything, and increasingly, we actually feel that connection. And yet we are also still our human selves, still prone to feeling grumpy, depressed, selfish, impatient, and still sometimes deceptive or even cruel toward our-selves or others. We live from our larger selves, from higher wisdom, *some* of the time. But some of the time, we don't.

As we recognize this gap between our awareness and our human lives, we may become frustrated with our limited human selves in a whole new way. We may even begin to fear that our human selves are insufficient, "not enough" for our lives, higher selves, or God. Then, because of the ping-pong effect between what we fear and what we experience, we may also fear, para-doxically, that life may be insufficient or "not enough" for *us*. We may begin to feel that it would be better not to be human at all.

When we hold a perspective and a knowing far larger than our human personality selves, it has the potential to set us free; however, given a slight distortion in our thinking, it can instead lead us to feel confined within, and frustrated by, our human lives. It can be very painful to feel inadequate to *live* what we know—to feel too small and wounded to live a life as large and as free as the wealth of possibilities we can sense. And we may also fear that we are disappointing our larger selves by failing to fulfill all the beautiful potentials we sense are available.

Yet there is a fundamental misconception at work here, a way in which we have confused the small personal self with the larger, transpersonal self. We have forgotten that we are *both,* and have both to draw on, and to be fed by, as we live out our "personal life"—or what appears to be our personal life—on this plane. It is almost as if we have turned our higher or transpersonal self into a parent who cannot be satisfied no matter what we do, when in fact the opposite is true. Our larger selves are always satisfied! They find no fault with us. Rather, the problem originates within the confusion of our small self, the human-level of personality self, which so often fears not measuring up. We might compare that aspect of self to a young child who believes she is already supposed to be an adult, and feels a sense of failure because she isn't.

The answer to this dilemma, as to all dilemmas, is love. Love is the only substance that can free us from this bind of our own making. We are like flies caught and struggling in a spider web, but love has the capacity to dissolve those sticky strands and leave us free.

This love is available to us at all times from the level of higher consciousness; when we have difficulty feeling it, it is not because our souls or inner teachers have rejected us—they are not capable of rejection. It can only be because distortions in the personal self have rendered us temporarily unable to experience the true nature of that connection, and to be supported by it.

If we find ourselves struggling with this gap, it can be helpful to contemplate the following questions:

How do I understand God, or my larger/higher self? What is its nature?

How does my higher self feel toward me? What does it want from me?

What does my higher self have to offer me? How do I feel about accepting what it offers? What would prevent me from accepting what it offers?

If I believe I need to be different in order to fulfill the design of my higher self, from where has that belief come?

How can I heal my wounds and correct my misconceptions related to my higher self?

Sensing the true answers to these questions will enable us to restore balance and harmony within our being. In fact, part of the work of our human selves in this lifetime is to unravel these fundamental misconceptions in our being and to heal them, and ourselves, with love. In this process we will fully connect our larger and our personal selves, and become able to live from and within that connection. So it is important for us to understand that our current struggles and confusions are not keeping us from our real work; instead, they are actually pointing to it. Once we straighten out the knotted-up channels in our being so that that knowing can flow freely into and through our human lives, the ways in which we can fulfill our inner design will naturally emerge.

Whenever we feel drained or inadequate, we can be sure that somewhere within us there is a misunderstanding of life, its relationship to us, and our place in it. In fact, if we allow it to, life can wrap itself as tenderly around us as we might tuck a blanket around a small child whom we deeply love. The precise tenderness which we need is readily available to us. The universe holds us with that kind of love; we need only change the internal structures and misunderstandings which are preventing us from *feeling* that love, and our lives will change, too.

About a year after my guide began talking to me, I started to feel like a failure. Although having a direct channel to higher wisdom had created many changes in me, I found that I often asked my guide the same kinds of questions over and over again. For instance, I would ask what I should do in a given circumstance, even though I knew he would say—as he had so many times—that it didn't matter so much what I did, but why and how I did it. Eventually I developed trick ways to ask my questions; rather than asking what I should do, I would ask, "What are the issues involved in my decision about X?" Sometimes the answers that came then provided more illumination—but sometimes they simply illuminated the stuck places in my own being. Even after a whole year of directly accessing higher consciousness, I still had plenty of those.

I made an appointment to speak with a woman who had been channeling a wise guide for sixteen years, and explained to her what was going on. Her eyes lit up. "Ah," she said. "That's the gap. You have to learn to love the gap."

Love the gap?! How could I love being stuck in my narrow, petulant, limited human consciousness, especially once I was also in contact with something so much wider, deeper and more wondrous?

Yet her words stayed with me. And over time, through further reflection as well as more conversations with my guide, I realized that we human beings don't access higher consciousness in order to become *higher consciousness through and through. We are here on earth to be human, and human we will remain. In fact, it's the chemical reactions that occur between the diffuse nature of higher consciousness and the individuated nature of human consciousness—the sparkles, crackles, pops, fizzes and openings—that enable us to serve as bridges between the human and the divine.*

After all, the purpose of a bridge is to connect two bodies of land. It doesn't make two bodies of land into one, nor does it need to! It exists to help others cross from one land into another, and in order to do so, it must keep part of itself on each of the two different shores.

To have a gap is to be human. We aren't here on earth in human bodies to stop being human; we are here to introduce higher consciousness as fully as we can into the human frame. It won't fit all the way. It can't. It's not supposed to. And we're not wrong or defective because we don't stop being human, even when higher wisdom is available to us.

This doesn't mean, of course, that we should cease to take responsibility for our destructive, hurtful inner postures or outer behaviors. And working to narrow the gap—to bring more and more of ourselves into the light of our highest knowing, and to act from that higher knowing more of the time—invariably brings joy. Yet, when we fall short, we haven't failed. These physical human bodies just weren't made to fly. We are composite beings—part divine, part earthly. And it's important for us to refrain from self-blame, self-criticism or self-rejection when we see our gaps in action—because of course, directing those judgmental energies at ourselves will only widen the gap!

Our wise inner teachers are never disappointed or frustrated by us; they never judge us. Their essence is always radiant and compassionate. So when we extend that same quality of compassion to ourselves, we actually narrow the gap between their level of consciousness and our own.

30
The Oxymoron of Human Happiness

A warrior chooses a path with heart, any path with heart, and follows it; and then he rejoices and laughs... He sees that nothing is more important than anything else.

— Carlos Castenada

There is an inherent contradiction within the notion of "human happiness." Human beings tend to believe that our happiness requires the establishment and maintenance of a particular set of conditions—conditions which may or may not be in accordance with the larger harmony. Even if these conditions are initially harmonious, the attempt to maintain them in a fixed and static way, or to ensure that their evolution proceeds in a fixed form or direction, cannot possibly be in harmony with the larger, ever-changing order. This means that to achieve what we think of as "happiness," we end up working against the flow of life itself. And yet happiness cannot possibly result when we work against the flow of life! The only possible source of happiness lies in the onrushing stream of the life force. That is the only medium which can carry happiness, the way a rushing river moves itself, and whatever it holds, to the sea.

Although many of us can intellectually recognize this truth, we often remain deeply divided within ourselves. We allow this understanding to exist in one region of our consciousness, yet wall off large segments of the inner being from the dramatic changes that would ensue if we were to fully integrate what we know. We may even feel an attachment to what we perceive as the "human condition," which is understood to be one of suffering. This leads us to believe that since we are human, we must continue to suffer. In

199

fact, it is the other way around. It is the decision on deep levels of our being to continue to suffer, that perpetuates "humanity" as we know it. We could stop this suffering at any time by following Krishnamurti's path to happiness. "My secret," he said, "is that I don't mind what happens."

Of course, from a higher level there is nothing wrong with suffering. Yet what we fail to recognize it that this suffering is not inevitable. We could end it at any moment, while still continuing to live our physical lives.

The human plane is currently at a crossroads on every level—from the tiniest biological phenomena we are capable of perceiving with our sophisticated scientific instruments, to the largest "global changes" we can measure. This crossroads includes all of the phenomena within the sphere of the individual and collective human body—from physical and mental disease, to holocausts and wars. We have created unsustainable conditions as a result of our "humanness," our individuated consciousness. Our consciousness is thus something like a parasite that must eventually kill its host—and yet we are also the host who insists on harboring the parasite; we refuse to let it go.

Which "we" are we, really, then? Are we the parasite, or the host, or the entity dreaming them both—dreaming the entire dilemma?

We are the sole cause of all of that which we experience as suffering. This is equally true on both the individual and the collective levels. This is also why attempts to "help" or "serve" humanity in its current configuration are deeply misguided; by making the oxymoronic existence slightly more bearable, such efforts actually serve to perpetuate the condition that must be overturned. There is no moral imperative here; it is more of a biological imperative or a physical law. The collective human organism is so sick that it must die to itself, in order that life may life. Or to put it another way, the human organism is not sick at all, and never has been, and never could be, but its illusion of sickness and its misunderstanding of its true nature—the true nature and being of life itself—has become so pervasive that it can no longer support life.

The problem of being human is an insoluble problem. But on the level of real truth, not only are there no insoluble problems, there are no problems at all. Life is only life, and is always life. Consciousness is continually shifting, evolving, mutating, experimenting, playing, exploring, experiencing itself. We are tiny particles of that consciousness and also holograms— each "we" contains the whole. Even that sounds metaphorical to us, when it is actually literal; each of us *is* the whole—which indicates, of course, that we are not the "we" that we think we are! Given that, there is really no problem, of course. And yet we are caught in such a profound and disturbing dream of a problem that we must be awoken, so to speak.

At this time there are many changes taking place both in our outer world, and in the individual consciousness of each human being, which are contributing to that process of awakening. As the inner design of our plane continues to unfold, many of us will come to understand these truths much more deeply. Each of us has trained and prepared for this, without knowing it on the level we think of as "ourselves." All biological processes are prepared for by a phenomenally intricate and coordinated orchestral sequence, much of which is invisible to us.

The time has come for the consciousness of the larger tapestry—the consciousness of ultimate reality—to integrate itself fully within human consciousness, or rather, within the consciousness of we who think of ourselves as human. It is time for that split to dissolve, for the fields to merge. Each of us involved in this endeavor—which is all of us, of course; but particularly those of us capable of having some degree of individual consciousness about it—will experience the changes in our own ways. Yet for all of us it will entail a dissolution of membranes which had previously held separate the different regions of our consciousness.

Again, our language must use figures of speech to point toward deeper truths. There is no individual consciousness, for instance. But since we believe that there is, there is really no way to communicate about any of this without leaning on the essentially non-existent structures which we have confused with "reality," and on which we rely. It is like the old story about the prisoners in separate cells, who communicated by rapping on the wall between them. The wall was what separated them, yet it was also what allowed them—in their separate state—to communicate.

Our work at this time, then, is to dissolve the wall between what we understand to be "us" and "not-us," so that we may at last experience direct communication—with *ourselves.* (Because, of course, what we have imagined to be "not-us" is also, in reality, *us.*) Or rather, the work of the universe, of which we are both a part and the whole, is to dissolve this wall which does not in fact exist, and never did. Then, and only then, will we become able to experience real happiness, though our human consciousness will be so radically different as to render us nearly unrecognizable to ourselves.

31

The Necessary Illusion
of the Personal Self

*Bondage is the life of personality, and for bondage the personal self will
fight with tireless resourcefulness and the most stubborn cunning.*

– Aldous Huxley

There is a secret which is right in front of us, a secret which holds the
key to our experience of joy. The secret is this: there is no personal self.
It does not exist; "you," as you conceive yourself to be, the separate, isolated,
disconnected "you," do not exist. The personal self is a fiction, a construct, a
clever façade, like a two-dimensional stage set for a high school play.

Some people on spiritual paths believe that they need to dissolve their
personal selves, or banish or vanquish them. But of course, we cannot dissolve, banish or vanquish what does not exist! What can happen instead is
that when this personal self in which we believe becomes strong, whole and
healed enough in our experience of it, then "we," who have seen life through
narrowed blinders for so long, become more and more willing to allow in
the knowledge and experience of the larger self—that aspect of self that is
everything and everyone, that has no illusion of fixedness or constancy.

There is great confusion about what it means to have a separate body, a
distinct physical form. Our physical form is not irrelevant; it's more like the
personal viewing screens now available on many airplanes which allow each
passenger to watch a different movie. The individual physical form, personality and life have great utility as teaching and learning devices. The problem
is that we have confused this form with "ourselves," with some separate self
that does not truly exist.

Trying to live within the personal self is limiting, isolating and confining. And yet at times we actually welcome that confinement, because we are frightened of our true freedom. We are terrified of perceiving existence without all the mirrors, false starts, dead ends, imagined paths, reflections and distortions with which we live; we balk at stepping out from this narrow and echoing chamber into the light of day. Yet the chamber does not actually exist; we are already free in the light of day, just unable to see it.

The fiction of the personal self does have a purpose. Essentially, it provides us with a means to explore our options on the physical plane. Just as we can learn from a table about some of the many ways of interacting with external matter, we can learn from the "personal self" about the many varieties of inner freedom and imprisonment, clarity and obscuration, harmony and distortion. It is necessary that we "believe in" the table; if we did not, we could not use it as a surface on which to rest our cups. In the same way, it is necessary that we believe in the personal self, because it is a vehicle through which we can experience the effects of our choices.

Physics tells us that the table on which we place our cup is, in an ultimate sense, not "real," yet it remains useful to us as a surface on which to rest our cups. Metaphysics has told us that the personal self is not "real," yet it is equally useful to us as a microcosm, a hologram, a miniature landscape which contains all the same features as the larger landscape.

The construct of the personal self is valuable because if we believe an emotion or issue is "ours," there is an opportunity for us to engage with it much more deeply. This provides us with a means to learn about, and ultimately to transform, the specific energetic configurations that correspond to what we think of as our "selves." Yet in fact, because there truly is no personal self, the work we do on "ourselves" is not work on "ourselves" at all. Any work we do on "our own" distortions is work on the distortions of the world. *There is no difference.* What each of us does and chooses in her or his "personal life" can have an impact as great as the actions of an Adolf Hitler, on the one hand, or a Dalai Lama on the other. The work we do with "our" fear, anger, or confusion about love, *is* work on the world. In fact, it is the most immediate and direct means available to us to work on, and thereby serve, the world.

Although the illusion of the personal self does serve an important purpose, at this point in the evolution of our species it would be helpful for us not to believe quite as much, or quite as fervently, in this fiction. Beyond a certain point, it gets in our way. When we think that the laws of physical matter are real and immutable, we cannot understand how people can sometimes walk on hot coals without getting burned, or heal someone thousands of miles away with only "their thoughts" (which of course are neither only "theirs," nor only "thoughts"). And yet these things do happen. When we confuse ourselves with the fictitious, constructed personal self to too great an extent, we miss out on the opportunity to play joyfully in the fields of the universe—to use this "self" as a vehicle which can bring us to those fields, and through which we can experience joy.

We use our tables, of course, but we do not take them so very *seriously*. In the same way, we can use our illusion of the personal self as the miraculous teaching and learning device that it is, without losing sight of the larger task in which we are truly engaged. The small self is a portal through which to enter the larger; the larger can also come through that porthole to inform the small self and infuse it with light.

Nothing of what we do matters in exactly the ways we think it does, or for the reasons we think it does—yet it is still very important that we bring ourselves to the tasks at hand. When we do not become too attached to the level of form—our "own" form, or the form our efforts will take, or produce—then our "individual" work can aid rather than impede the larger flow. And when we understand everything that happens as a metaphor, or as a tiny piece of a much larger process—when we remember that we "ourselves" are in some sense a metaphor for, or held within, a much larger process—then we can work with the currents rather than against them, knowing that we are held within a larger stream of compassion, harmony and well-being.

III

Challenges on the Path

32

The Family as Teacher and Crucible

If you think you're enlightened, go spend a week with your family.

– Jack Kornfield

Our families are the most important teachers most of us will ever have. As the first and primary shapers of our inner world in this lifetime, they determine much about the contours of our souls' work—or perhaps, as some people believe, our souls actually choose our families and early life circumstances in order to have the opportunity to wrestle with particular challenges. Either way, we are likely to find echoes of that original configuration, or those original relationships, in every difficulty we encounter throughout our lives.

From a higher perspective, it is neither a mistake nor unfortunate that most of us will spend our lives working to clear the imprints of our first few years on earth. Family relationships were actually *designed* to give us a lifetime's worth of material to work with, and no matter how and in what contexts we work with this material, our efforts are never wasted. Each lesson we learn, each hard-won piece of healing we achieve, is a contribution to the larger human collective; as we unknot what we experience as our own knots and tangles, we clear pathways in consciousness that others can access, too.

When we understand our "individual" healing and clearing processes in this way, we see that there is no reason to be impatient with our own progress, or to think that we should heal more quickly. After all, when we do manage to finish one piece of inner work, we simply move on to something else! If we somehow managed to heal all the wounds and distortions created by our family relationships, we would simply need to find other work to do.

There is no end of work to be done on the human plane—and that is as it should be, since work is what we came to this plane to do.

Yet even once we understand the larger purpose of our personal healing, we must still go through it, step by challenging step. It is only by experiencing the necessary storms of confusion, anger, grief and fear that we can actually heal. Even when parts of ourselves already see the bigger picture, it doesn't work to try to suppress or overcome the reactions that emerge on one level with the perspectives from another. Rather, the level of the emotional storms and the level of the bigger picture must have a chance to encounter one another, to interpenetrate and embrace. Otherwise we end up riding the rails on the "Transcendental Express"—taking mental shortcuts to "transcendent" perspectives which we cannot actually embody in our lives.

My father has been a great and difficult teacher for me. He was (and still is, as of this writing), a brilliant, selfish, generous, narcissistic, charismatic, manipulative, creative, mentally ill physician, researcher and drug addict. Of course, it took me a very long time to realize and accept that all of these things and many more were true about him at the same time.

As a child, I adored my father. As a teenager, I rebelled against him, but still admired him. He tried in many ways to crush my spirit; after my parents separated, he literally broke down my door to force me to spend time with him. Yet he also praised my intelligence and competence, and told me over and over that I could do anything I wanted to do in life. He helped me develop the boldness and self-confidence that has let me chart my own course, yet he also sexually molested me when I was very young. In all of these ways he helped shape me into the healer and writer I have become.

In my early adulthood, my relationship with my father began to alternate between periods of feuding and uneasy reunions. Although he let me down in many ways over the years, I still turned to him for certain kinds of help, and often, in crises, he came through. "I'm best in a crisis," he would often say, and it was true.

In my thirties and forties, as I learned more about spiritual and emotional healing, I also tried to help my father—though most often in inappropriate, codependent ways. When his third wife left him, I encouraged him to work with a good friend of mine who was a healer. When he didn't pay my friend, I covered the cost of his sessions myself. I also lent him money when he asked for it, knowing even as I did so that I would never be repaid.

I remember visiting my father when I was in my late thirties. Even then, he took off all his clothes, lay down on his stomach and asked me to rub his back, just as I had done so many times as a child—and although I felt uncomfortable, I did as he asked. (Several years later, my first soul retrieval addressed the soul loss those backrubs had created in me and helped me understand why I had been so unable to say No to my father.)

Just before my 44th birthday, when I read online that my father was about to lose his medical license for "thousands of unaccounted-for narcotics prescriptions," the truth broke through my decades of denial. The extent of my own grief shocked me. I cried for months. A very young part of me felt inconsolable. She simply could not bear to see how deeply disturbed and unreliable her (my) father really was. I spent many hours working to help that part of me connect with trustworthy guides who could serve as non-physical "father figures," and also connecting with her and nurturing her myself.

Each time I thought I had finally come to terms with who my father was and what had happened to him, I received a new piece of information that sent me back to the inner drawing board. For instance, one night I received a call from a woman who identified herself as my father's ex-girlfriend. She told me that my father had blacked out while driving her car, made her tell the police that she'd been the one driving, and then refused to take her to the hospital. Later, my father supplied my sister, also an addict, with drugs, then told lies under oath in a failed attempt to help her regain custody of her son. Shortly after that, he became the caretaker for his elderly mother, and began spending all of her money to feed his habit.

As each new revelation about my father surfaced, it felt as if the structure of my psyche was crumbling. I hadn't realized how much my sense of myself had been constructed around an image of who my father was. Since he was smart, strong and capable, so was I. I began to wonder if he had ever been the person I had believed him to be. If he had, what had happened? If he hadn't, what did that mean for me?

Eventually I came to see that my father is a classic example of a profoundly unintegrated person. When I was a teenager, he would often quote the great Jewish mystic Martin Buber: "I'm waiting for the deed that intends me." He devoured the Carlos Castenada books, studied the Kabbalah, and read other mystical texts. I believe that a big part of him yearned toward healing and evolution. Yet he also had a very big shadow which he was never able to acknowledge or accept help with. "I was wrong once," he was fond of saying. "I think it was back in, oh, 1963." In all of his communications, everything that went wrong in his life was always someone else's fault.

As I struggled to come to terms with the combination of vulnerability and arrogance that had destroyed my father, and led him to cause a great deal of destruction to others as well, I also had to look hard at myself. In many ways, I am very like my father. His life story is a cautionary tale for me. When I cultivate humility, when I acknowledge wrongdoing, when I admit my own wounds and seek inner and outer help for them, I am taking steps that I believe my father wished on some level to take, and yet shrank back from. When I work to integrate my healing and consciousness on deeper and wider levels of my being, I like to think I am holding a torch my father bequeathed to me and carrying it further, shining it brighter, than he could—at least in this lifetime.

As our healing and growth continue, our level of emotional reactivity to our families gradually decreases. Once we are able to fully feel all of the grief, rage, confusion and other emotions our families trigger within us, they can pass through us the way rainstorms pass over a landscape, making way for the sun to shine again. Eventually we become able to see our parents and siblings as people completely distinct and apart from us, people with their own wounds, gifts and trajectories that exist completely apart from our own. They didn't intentionally fail us; in fact, whatever they did or didn't do to or for us had nothing to do with *us* at all. We were actors in their drama just as they have been actors in ours. And just like them, we too have "failed" many people, and failed ourselves. Yet from another standpoint, the concept of failure doesn't even exist; the mistakes we and others have made are simply threads that help make up a much larger pattern, necessary and even beautiful parts of the tapestry of human learning and development.

33
Right and Wrong

The most distressing thing that can happen to a prophet is to be proven wrong. The next most distressing thing is to be proven right.

– Aldous Huxley

Most of us feel a need to be "right"—to have our perspectives and experiences recognized and reflected back to us by others as correct or valid. The need to be right—to be affirmed and validated—is a healthy, appropriate need at certain stages of our development, and if this need is not met during those stages, our sense of self, others and world will suffer. In fact, as a result of that suffering, many of us have also developed some level of need to be "wrong," as well—or at least a belief that we *are* wrong, or an expectation that we will be found to be wrong. Of course, this only reflects the shadow side of the need to be right.

On the human level, there are situations that appear cut and dried, times when one person or stance is truly correct and another incorrect. For instance, if you are buying something that costs 75 cents and give the cashier a dollar, it is right for you to expect and receive 25 cents in change. If the cashier insists otherwise—for instance, if he says that you are due only 5 cents in change—he is wrong. If you point out to the cashier that he has given you an incorrect amount of change, and he realizes his error and corrects it, your ego receives reassurance and calibration of a kind that is necessary and valuable on the human level.

If, on the other hand, the cashier argues with you and continues to insist that you are only due five cents in change—and there is no one else present to support your claim or challenge the claim of the cashier—then you are likely to experience disorientation and even ego damage, particularly if you are still at a vulnerable stage of your own development. Depending on your personality, there are myriad ways in which you might respond, each its own kind of effort to metabolize the discord and give you a way to move forward, and each its own kind of distortion. For example, you might develop a posture of self-doubt and self-negation; you might inwardly collapse and become depressed or ashamed; you might develop a generalized anger, suspicion and mistrust toward others (perhaps toward people of whatever gender, race, age group or body type the cashier happened to be; toward this particular store, toward stores in general, or toward capitalism); you might adopt a generally aggressive stance; you might become hypervigilant, paranoid, excessively anxious or fearful; you might develop agoraphobia which keeps you from going to stores at all; you might deny the importance of money and develop energy leaks that would prevent you from appropriately accumulating financial or other resources—and so on.

Most of us have experienced some amount of this kind of disorientation with our parents or other early caretakers, whether mild or extreme. It is important to heal these wounds, strengthen this aspect of our egos, and recalibrate our sense of self before we proceed further on the larger spiritual arc of releasing the need to be right or wrong. In other words, we need to be standing on firm ground on the human level before climbing higher.

It's easy to see that if you run into a mistaken cashier once you have already formed a strong, healthy sense of self, others and the world, it will not cause damage. In that case you might leave the store with your five cents' change in hand, shaking your head with bemusement, yet still feeling fundamentally clear, oriented and whole. A healthy sense of self and a humanly appropriate ego-strength would enable you to assimilate the "wrong" done to you by the cashier, and the loss of the twenty extra cents owed to you, with relative ease and grace, and with no need to blame, attack or defend yourself or him.

This same ego-strength enables us to tolerate the times when we ourselves are in the wrong. For instance, let's imagine that you miscalculated and believed you were due 45 cents in change, rather than 25, and that you browbeat the cashier until he became confused or weary enough to give you your 45 cents. If you realize your error after leaving the store, a healthy sense of self enables you to assimilate your own mistake and redress it without requiring you to blame, attack or defend yourself or anyone else.

If you find your internal equilibrium and sense of well-being overly impacted by situations in which others have made mistakes *or* in which you yourself have made mistakes, it's a sign that you need this kind of egoic healing and recalibration. Yet if you find yourself too easily able to shrug off all wrongs you or others have committed, that is *also* a sign of a need for this kind of recalibration. In other words, over-reactivity and under-reactivity are both evidence of underlying imbalance. Human emotional and spiritual maturity require us to develop the ability to accept and tolerate our own and others' mistakes, and also to correct such mistakes where possible, while still maintaining our inner balance. Yet few of us have yet developed that degree of maturity; most of us habitually over- or undercompensate in our responses to our own errors or the errors of others.

Here are a few questions that can help us identify such distortions in our responses, and achieve appropriate balance:

"How would I see this situation differently if I loved myself, and knew without any doubt that I am loved?"

"What would I do in this situation if I knew for sure that I have intrinsic value and worth, and am worthy of love, no matter what?"

"How would I respond if I was certain that I am safe and whole, no matter what happens?"

The knowledge that we are loved, worthy of love, and safe generally exerts a medicinal effect on us. Filled up with such medicine, we become able to relinquish our need to be "right" (or wrong), and even the need to have others avoid wrong in their dealing with us. This allows us to experience new levels of calm and openness.

Years ago, before studying healing work, I was involved with Joanne, a sweet, smart, self-aware woman with a committed Buddhist meditation practice. She told me frankly that she had been raised in an abusive, alcoholic household in which her father terrorized her and her siblings; the children never knew when something they said or did would provoke verbal abuse or a beating. Even worse were the times when her father would rouse Joanne and her sisters in the middle of night, then force them to watch as he beat up their mother.

I didn't fully realize how deeply all this had affected Joanne until our first camping trip. On a day hike one afternoon, we decided to part ways for an hour, then meet at a particular hot springs pool at 6:00. I was there right on time, but Joanne was nowhere to be found. Ten minutes passed; the mosquitoes were beginning to get fierce, and I had no idea what to do. Should I walk in one direction or another, or simply wait? Had something happened to Joanne? I peered anxiously up and down the path, then waited ten more minutes. Finally, at 6:20, I began to walk toward another hot springs pool someone had told us about. At 6:30, when I arrived, Joanne was there.

"Where were you? We agreed to meet at that other pool at 6:00!"

"I figured you'd think of coming here. I wanted to see this pool," Joanne explained.

Having waited, worried and been bitten by mosquitoes for a full half-hour, I didn't let go of the issue right away. "But we agreed to meet at that other pool. Why would I have thought of coming here instead?"

"Well, it's just logical. I figured that when you didn't see me at the first pool, you would know that I had gone to the second pool," Joanne repeated.

"But that doesn't make any sense. We agreed to meet at the other pool. I waited there for you for a long time."

As we hiked silently back to our tent, Joanne withdrew into herself, going further and further away. That night, she curled into a ball, shaking, unable or unwilling to talk to me. I realized that admitting that she had been wrong was impossible for her. In her childhood, acknowledging a mistake would have brought devastating consequences. Yet not acknowledging a mistake was terrifying, too.

Belatedly, my sense of self-righteousness drained from me and I tried to reach out to Joanne. "It's really okay," I told her softly. "It's not a big deal that I waited half an hour. Maybe you're right—maybe I should have thought of looking for you at that other pool. I mean, eventually I did think of it. Anyway, we did find each other. That's all that matters." But nothing I did or said could reach her.

In the days that followed, things seemed to normalize between us. But Joanne was never able to talk about what had happened that night. Less than a year later, after many other times when our communication had completely broken down, I ended the relationship and found myself tempted to construct a story about it. Initially, that story focused on Joanne's damage. In my version of events, I had tried my best, but Joanne was so wounded and traumatized by her childhood that there was no way our relationship could work.

Yet something about that story made me uneasy. Sure, I could amass plenty of evidence to support that version of events. But what about my own wounds? One day I had gotten very anxious when Joanne drove fast, passing every car on the road. Instead of addressing the issue directly, I had tried to get Joanne to let me drive. That had prompted a fight between us, too. It had taken me days to realize that my anxiety was a holdover from my own past, from all the times in my childhood that my father had driven recklessly. What if I had been more self-aware—would things have gone differently? What if I could have said, "You know, you're not doing anything wrong, this is just making me nervous because of how my father used to drive?" Might that have avoided a fight? Or what if I could have recognized the source of my anxiety and comforted my younger self without even having to say anything at all to Joanne? Could I really know for sure that her *damage was the reason we couldn't be together?*

My relationship with Joanne was a significant turning point for me. Perhaps it was because she had truly touched my heart. Maybe it was all the conversations we'd had about meditation and self-awareness, in our better moments, and the times when she had pushed me to be more vulnerable. Or maybe it's just that I had finally tired of the narrative in which my relationship troubles were always the other person's fault. In any case, I stopped telling the story in which I knew exactly what had happened and why Joanne and I couldn't be together, and started giving a much more honest, self-implicating and uncertain answer to the question of why we'd broken up. I believe this inner change readied me to find the teacher and healer who helped me go much deeper on my own healing path.

At some point in our souls' journey, continued growth requires us to go beyond releasing the need to be right or wrong. Although simple mathematics enables us to calculate the correct change we should receive from a store clerk, most human circumstances are far more complex and nuanced. Given the vastness and multidimensionality of the tapestry of reality, any stance that appears right or correct from one distance or angle is bound to look very different when viewed from another. Ultimately, as we become able to hold multiple conflicting points of view at once, our notions of right and wrong will have to shift, stretching so far and in so many directions as to become almost unrecognizable. This work of stretching is often uncomfortable for us as human beings, but it is deeply nourishing to our souls. It brings us closer to the actual elephant, rather than keeping us tied to one leg or tusk.

Many spiritual teachers emphasize the importance of deconstructing our habitual stories. Thich Naht Hanh suggests writing a note to ourselves that says, "Are you sure?" and taping it up in places where we'll see it multiple times each day. Byron Katie uses three main questions in her work: "Is this really true? How can I know that this is true? Who would I be if this weren't true?"

As Rumi wrote many centuries ago,

There is a field beyond right and wrong.
I'll meet you there.

34

Intimate Relationships

If life is a school, relationship is its university.

— Judith Saly

From the soul's point of view, we are here on earth to fulfill our inner design. In that process, it doesn't really matter whether we remain in one intimate relationship for an entire lifetime, have many intimate relationships, or even have none at all. We will, of course, always be in relationships; the very essence of human life is interdependent and relational. And whatever our specific relational circumstances may be, our real work is the work of becoming more fully ourselves.

And yet most of us have a very strong drive toward intimate relationships—or at least, toward pair-bonding, a process we hope will provide us with the feelings of safety and security that we often confuse with intimacy. In fact, true intimacy rarely creates what the human personality self experiences as safety, and the kind of safety that seems desirable to some parts of the personality actually leads to stagnation of other parts of us, and of our soul. This is one reason why so many of us experience romantic relationships as a source of great confusion and suffering.

True intimacy is an experience of deep contact in which one consciousness appreciatively encounters another. Since each of us contains many levels and aspects of consciousness, we can experience intimacy (or lack thereof) within ourselves, or with any other living thing. Although intimacy may be present with people whom we know very well, a sudden flash of intimacy can also occur in a brief exchange between strangers.

Intimacy takes place on the level of consciousness, the level where the soul resides. Therefore, it both requires and facilitates authenticity, the

219

dropping-away of social masks. This is one reason why many people find it easiest to experience intimacy with animals, who neither wear social masks nor respond to such masks in us. It's also why so many of us find it surprisingly difficult to actually be intimate with our lovers or partners. Very often, people in designated "intimate relationships" fall into patterns which are destructive to intimacy—for instance, when we attempt to require certain feelings or behaviors from each other or from ourselves, or when fear leads us to hide aspects of ourselves. Ironically, the intimacy in most "intimate relationships" has a very short life-span, if it is ever present at all.

Many of us hold particular visions or ideals for romantic relationships. We may believe that our partners should or must have particular physical and emotional characteristics, live their lives in certain ways, and be with us in ways our human selves find pleasurable or comforting. While there is nothing "wrong" with any of these beliefs or desires, they have absolutely nothing to do with love or intimacy. They are based on a transactional model of relationship, a model which is appropriate in a market context ("I'll give you one dollar, you'll give me one avocado") but is irrelevant, even antithetical, to authentic connection.

"But having a partner who is X or who does X would bring me joy," part of us may protest. Actually, that's not exactly true. Our human selves have many preferences, and as we've discussed, it is harmonious for us to arrange our lives in accordance to those preferences, rather than in opposition to them. Yet the exclusive goal of creating a life that meets our preferences leads to a never-ending search—since no matter what we choose, our deeper work will always present itself to be done, often in ways that bring challenge or discomfort. And joy is an inner soul movement that can and does often arise regardless of whether our preferences have been met, or completely subverted. For instance, no parent would prefer to have a child with Down syndrome or severe disabilities, yet many parents of children born with such conditions report that their children bring them enormous joy.

The belief that we must have things a certain way in order to be happy emerges from a part of the self that has not released life on its own recognizance, has not said *Yes* to ourselves and our world as it is. All of us have such parts, but allowing them to dominate our relationships is a recipe for pain, both for ourselves and whoever we attempt to love. Love does not dictate conditions; love embraces conditions exactly as they are.

Eckhart Tolle says matter-of-factly, "In case you haven't noticed, relationships are not here to make us happy." Yet even when we *have* noticed this, we may continue to hope blindly that it's simply because we haven't yet found the "right" relationship, the partner who will give us everything we want and believe we need.

Practicing the rewarding and demanding work of intimacy is an important part of the inner design of most people. Yet this work, when properly understood and engaged, looks little like the "happily ever after" myth we grew up with. In fact, the ability to develop and sustain true intimacy with self and others depends upon the willingness to wonder about ourselves and each other, to stretch, explore and inquire in an atmosphere of open, compassionate curiosity. In his book *Soul Mates,* Thomas Moore describes this well: "I am not referring to endless analysis and introspection, which can dry out a relationship with the drive toward understanding. Wonder and open discussion are more moist. They keep people close to their experience, while at the same time they offer a degree of imagination, an element sorely needed in every intimate relationship."

Truly intimate relationships require us to be willing to see and know our partners, and also to tolerate being seen and known. At the same time, they require us to bear those ways and times when it appears that our partners cannot or will not see or know us, and those times when we ourselves fall short of that difficult work.

Relationships that are genuinely intimate also require us to take responsibility both for our own pain, and our own needs. In fact, relationships of all kinds are ideal places for practicing the challenge of self-responsibility. We can start by remembering that other people, including our romantic partners, are never the cause of any pain we experience. All other people can do is illuminate the collapsed places in our own beings—places of soul loss, damaging imprints, shame or self-hatred, victim consciousness or problematic emotional postures. Because of the spotlight they shine on these hurt places within us, relationships can be great catalysts for growth and healing when we allow them to be—and when we can accept the messages they bring us without blaming the messenger.

Full self-responsibility requires us to remain clear that it is never our partner's job to meet our emotional needs (nor, of course, is it ever our job to meet our partner's needs). Of course, if none of our emotional needs are ever met within a given relationship, we may decide to discontinue that relationship, or to change its form. But in most cases, those whom we attempt to love do meet *some* of our needs, some of the time. Strangely, the fact that some but not all of our needs are met often causes us great pain. Faced with this situation, most of us either try to exert pressure on our partner to meet more of our needs, or begin to punish our partners or to emotionally withdraw from the relationship. Rather than reacting in this way, we would be better served to inquire into these things we experience as "needs," and the real source of the pain we feel when they are not met. Generally this process of inquiry can lead us toward healing processes that have little to do with our current relationships, and much to do with ways we have separated ourselves from ourselves, from compassion, and from life.

Of course, this doesn't mean that we should remain in relationships that we don't want to be in. It simply means that whether we choose to end a given relationship or stay within it, we recognize that the pain, fear or other challenging emotions that have been brought up in us are *ours*—ours to work with, heal and dismantle. In fact, the most painful relationships of all are those in which people refuse this self-responsibility, and instead persist in endless power struggles and unsatisfying negotiations with each other, all in an effort to flee from difficult emotions. In contrast, the most rewarding relationships are those in which both partners recognize their own responsibility, and work side by side on their own growth and healing—including those areas in need of healing that are continuously brought to their attention by the relationship.

Sometimes people attempt to support one another by taking over the emotional work our partners find most difficult, but this is a risky approach. For instance, Person A has trouble allowing herself to be vulnerable; Person B provides a safe space for her to do that. Person B has trouble valuing herself; Person A continually reflects her value back to her. Although this type of dynamic can be supportive if it leads to Person A becoming more able to tolerate her own vulnerability and Person B becoming more able to value herself, all too often this is not what occurs. Emotional support, like physical crutches, can be used in ways that facilitate healing, or in ways that keep us from that healing.

The purpose of a crutch is to support an injured leg by allowing us to keep weight off it for long enough that it can heal, so that it can then bear weight once again. Yet if we use the crutch improperly, we may become so accustomed to leaning on it that our injured limb never regains its strength;

instead it becomes weaker, even atrophies. Sometimes well-intentioned intimate partners provide exactly this sort of unhealthy crutch to one another. They may not realize until too late—when either or both partners are feeling stifled, stagnant, or desperate to regain her own power—that they have "outsourced" skills they truly needed to develop for themselves.

Another soul posture crucial for the experience of true intimacy is the ability to embrace change. Because human beings are living, growing, changing organisms, change in our relationships is not just likely, but certain. Yet, although the soul is tuned to follow joy through a constant series of movements and calibrations, our human selves often fall prey to the erroneous belief that our personal happiness will come about by achieving and maintaining a fixed, unchanging state. When we do experience happiness, some part of us reflexively assumes that it will continue if only we can find a way to maintain the exact conditions present in that moment. Of course, this is impossible; we can never maintain a fixed, unchanging state—not within ourselves, not within our partners, and certainly not between two living, growing people in a relationship that must also grow if it is to survive.

The truth—as many people have already discovered—is that if we want an easy, predictable and relatively unchanging long-term relationship, we would do better to adopt a dog. The stable companionship available from "man's best friend" is simply not possible with human beings, nor should it be. Human intimacy offers us something entirely different: a kind of love that is far more challenging, and also offers us much deeper possibilities for transformation. Thomas Moore describes this kind of partnership as a sacred marriage, "a union at a far deeper or higher level than personalities and lives." The deepest commitment we can make to one another is a commitment to supporting the growth of our own and each other's souls, even while knowing that this support may require difficult labor on the human personality level.

In fact, since our primary responsibility is to the project of our own soul's development, any relationships we form with other human beings are rightfully subordinate to the needs and signals of our souls. This subordination does not mean that we cannot truly love others, or receive their love. Rather, it means we must expand our notion of what it means to love others, and to receive their love. Many people attempt to conduct intimate relationships in a manner that has nothing to do with genuine love, requiring instead that each member of the partnership attempt to constrict and control herself or her partner. Such partnerships require compromise and sacrifice at every turn; in this scenario, where people disallow real contact with themselves and each other, there is no alternative.

Of course, there is nothing "wrong" with compromise or sacrifice. The soul actually welcomes these experiences, too, if they come about in a context that brings joy. Something that appears to be a sacrifice when viewed from the outside may have a wholly different meaning to the person or people involved. For instance, all parents make numerous sacrifices, yet if having children is a genuine part of their inner design, the meaning of what they must "give up" in the process is transformed. If an apparent "sacrifice" represents a fulfillment of someone's inner design, it is not truly a sacrifice at all; it would, in fact, be more of a sacrifice to forego that fulfillment. Once again, only our own experience of joy—or our lack of joy—can help us discern what is and is not in alignment with our inner design.

Like every other aspect of life, we, our partners, and our relationships constantly change, morph and transform. If we are able to welcome this natural process of reconfiguration, it will energize us and deepen our ability to love and be loved. If not—if we respond to changes in our partners or ourselves with fear, grief, judgment or anger, or with an attempt to manipulate or suppress ourselves or the other person—then we will find ourselves working against the movement of love within us and outside of us.

Again, this doesn't mean that we should remain in partnerships in which we or our partners have changed in ways that make us deeply incompatible. At times real love requires us to release ourselves or our partners with well wishes and blessings. When properly understood, this kind of parting can be deeply intimate and loving. At other times, love can help us re-shape our relationships in ways that continue to suit our partners and ourselves as we change.

Few of us have been exposed to the kind of love that is able to encompass growth and change. Instead, we are told that if we love someone, we will make pledges like these:

"I will love you forever."
"I will never hurt you."
"I will never leave you."
"My feelings for you will never change."

This misunderstanding of love pits our "love" for another person against our soul's deep need for growth. And, since our lover's soul contains the very same need, this misguided attempt at love leaves us working against his or her deepest well-being, too. If part of us still subscribes to the transactional model of relationships, we may feel angry and bitter when these promises inevitably get broken. "I kept giving you dollars, but you stopped giving me avocadoes," or "I gave you good avocadoes, but I see now that your dollars were counterfeit all along" would be reasonable complaints to make in a marketplace, but since love and intimacy are soul-movements rather than transactions, these kinds of protestations only take us further from real love.

In order for relationships to serve us on a soul level, we must revise our understanding of the nature of commitment. Commitments like "I will stay with you forever" are inherently limiting to the full flowering and expression of the soul. Perhaps staying together "forever" will produce conditions under which both people can thrive and fulfill their inner design; perhaps it will not. Since there is truly no way to know or predict whether this will be so, it is misguided to make such vows. If it turns out that the soul's fullest growth is not being served by these conditions, joy will depart, resentment will set in, and the vows will be eventually be broken, whether emotionally, physically, or both.

Yet there is a very different kind of commitment we can and should make with those whom we love, or wish to love. In place of commitments which attempt to predict or mandate a specific outcome, we can instead commit ourselves to a loving, conscious process. Here are some examples of such commitments:

"I commit to allowing my higher self and my soul to work through me in all aspects of my life, including this relationship."

"I commit to the effort of loving both you and myself as fully as I can."

"I commit myself wholeheartedly to my own growth and development, and to using this relationship in the service of that commitment."

"I commit to doing my best to remain present with you as we learn together about the nature of love."

When made with deep feeling, these commitments are actually far more challenging than more traditional commitments, because they require so much more consciousness, attention and presence. They are commitments to ways of being, to energy flows, as well as to actions. The soul rejoices at these sorts of commitments; they facilitate true intimacy with both self and other, thus supporting the fulfillment of our inner design.

Author and aviator Anne Morrow Lindbergh offers a poetic description of this process: "Security in a relationship lies neither in looking back to what it was, nor forward to what it might be, but living in the present and accepting it as it is now. For relationships, too, must be like islands. One must accept them for what they are here and now, within their limits—islands surrounded and interrupted by the sea, continuously visited and abandoned by the tides. One must accept the serenity of the winged life, of ebb and flow, of intermittency." And poet Rainer Maria Rilke concurs, "Love consists in this… two solitudes that border and protect and salute one another."

It is the deepest expression of love to support another on her or his growth path, wherever it may lead. If you cultivate the ability to give and receive that kind of support, your relationships will become truly intimate, durable and nourishing.

The most joyful and sustaining relationship in my life has undergone numerous metamorphoses on the level of form. From the beginning, Michelle and I recognized that we were on similar growth paths, even though her primary spiritual framework was Christian and Buddhist, while mine was shamanic and mystical. We agreed early on that our commitment was to process, not outcome.

Initially, our sense of rapport was so strong that we entered into a partnership more traditional than either of us had imagined for herself at that point in our lives; we moved cross-country, bought a house, and lived together. Yet I didn't thrive in that context. Less than a year later, when I decided to move back to California on my own, Michelle accepted my decision with love and support; when she expressed her desire to remain in Massachusetts indefinitely, I did the same. But I was overjoyed when, seven months later, she changed her mind and came back to California, too.

Over the years we have moved through many forms of relationship. We have lived together as partners alone, in a group house, and in neighboring apartments; we have lived apart as partners; we have lived apart as friends, or, in a term we came up with to describe the depth of our connection, as "soul kin;" we have explored being sexual as loving friends, rather than re-entering the frame of partnership. Michelle was my loving witness when I entered into another relationship, journeyed through the challenges and healing it brought me, and then journeyed out the other side. I have been her loving witness through her own explorations of sexuality and gender. Of course, we have also supported and challenged each other through growth and healing in many other aspects of our lives. Through it all, we have remained deeply open both to ourselves and to each other.

Yet very early on, before Michelle and I had developed the depth of connection that has sustained us through these many changes, I almost aborted that process. When we had been dating for just a couple of months, I felt attractions to several other people, and wondered whether or not to pursue them. When I asked my guide for advice, here is what he said:

Allowing sexual energy to flow toward more than one person—for you, at this point in your development—is a way of anchoring yourself closer to the surface. It may look or feel like "freedom" on a superficial level, but it arises from resistance to the depths—to your own depths, and to the depths of intimacy. The world is full of intriguing possibilities, intriguing rivers, yet to think of Rivers B or C while you are canoeing down River A is to miss the boat, so to speak. You can only, and always, learn from where you are. If at some point where you are ceases to feel tenable, desirable, satisfactory, you can go somewhere else, and learn there. But what you are learning most importantly right now is to open. And you are opening in ways that surprise and enrich you—so it is freeing, not constricting, to keep your focus there, uncluttered and unobstructed and undiluted, for now.

You fear this opening because it is bringing you into uncharted waters within yourself. This is because you are being reached in ways you had not thought you would be reached; you are being held in ways you had despaired of being held. Your being is like a honeycomb, and there were many rooms or cells closed within it. What you are experiencing now is the sensation of more of those doors popping open each day. You are still not really loving, however. It will take you a long time to learn to love, and a long time to allow yourself to be—and to believe yourself to be—truly loved. But the person in question does have the capacity for that. You too have the capacity, though in the past you have worshipped many false gods in this arena. This is why it is so important to continue canoeing down one river—because it is so hard for you, as humans, to truly love. Very few ever achieve it, particularly in a specific, personal, one-on-one relationship.

The path of one-on-one relationship is a path into the self, and into the world. In some ways it will appear to "slow down" your spiritual development, but it will also deepen you in ways that another path would not. You each have an opportunity to learn to allow the other's feelings for you—and yours for her—to become a source of strength and freedom, rather than a force that drains and binds, as you have each previously experienced in partnership. It is this understanding that can help you learn to actually love.

Right now the river is very broad and wide, and there is much scenery on both sides. At other points it will twist more; at other points you will encounter rapids. At times you may tie the canoe and get out to picnic on the banks. It is important to understand that this is always the river—that the river in all its different aspects is still the same river—and not to become dismayed, or confused, or bored, or to think that something is wrong or that you have been misled. Steadiness has not been your strong suit up till now. You have achieved some measure of it externally, but have fluctuated wildly internally. In the past, on other rivers, you have often removed yourself energetically or emotionally from the canoe, while physically remaining in it—or, at times, you have physically removed yourself, while emotionally and energetically remaining in it. You have the opportunity to practice something very different now, a very different level of internal alignment. You know, of course, that I do not suggest that you suppress or ignore any feelings, but that you remain in the canoe while you work with them (unless at some point you decide to exit the canoe, of course—but if that occurs, let that be a conscious choice, not a partial fleeing.) Again, it is important to understand that what I am describing is not a movement of constriction, but one of focusing and aligning your intention and the levels of your being.

As always, what matters most isn't what we do, but why or how we do it. It seems clear to me that my guide is not advocating monogamy in all circumstances; rather, he is indicating that for me at that moment, giving attention to other relationships would have diluted the transformative potential of my relationship with Michelle. I am enormously grateful that I recognized the truth in his words, turned away from my other attractions, and continued to deeply explore what was possible between Michelle and me.

In hindsight, I can clearly see times over the years when one or the other of us emotionally exited the canoe or even walked away from the river for a little while. Yet in spite of our human confusions and wounds, we have always found a way to deeply re-engage with one another. I know that through this process, I am learning what it truly is to love and be loved. I am deeply grateful.

35
Sexuality and Gender

Eros is the nearest thing to love the undeveloped spirit can experience. It lifts the soul out of sluggishness, out of mere contentment and vegetation. It causes the soul to surge, to go out of itself... Eros gives the soul a foretaste of unity, and teaches the fearful psyche the longing for it. The more strongly one has experienced eros, the less contentment will the soul find in the pseudo-security of separateness.

— The Pathwork

The human sexual experience both touches upon and emerges from every part of the self—and since we are not truly a single self, but a braided strand of various levels of consciousness, it's no surprise that this touch brings us both bliss and torment, crystalline clarity and stinking, stagnant murk.

Each of us contains a limited, wounded human personality—made up, itself, of many different components—and a timeless, vast, eternal soul. Each of us is both a physical, biological creature and a non-physical, non-local mass of shifting energies. Therefore, by definition there is a mismatch or misalignment between our biological, animal sexual inclinations, and the states of higher consciousness to which our sexual energies can be a portal. This does not mean that our biological, animal sexual inclinations are bad, wrong, or even lesser than our higher states of sexual consciousness; they are simply dimensionally different. The challenge of working within the various dimensions and aspects we contain is part of what we are here to experience.

The spiritual purpose of sexuality is far larger than pleasure. Sexuality can offer us doorways into the places of our deepest fears and wounding, and also into the places of our greatest passion, aliveness and potential. The catch is that the doorways are sequential; we cannot reach our greatest aliveness without traveling through our fears, distortions and wounds. Fortunately, our biological and hormonal draw toward sexual expression generally compels us to remain engaged with this field of learning; unfortunately, the power of those physiological and chemical impulses can also work against mindful, conscious engagement with sexuality.

At its essence, sexual energy is the energy of life itself. As such, sexuality is neither bad nor good, just as wind, rain and sun are neither bad nor good. But in the individual manifestation of most peoples' sexuality, there is a combination of currents, some more "pure," essential, unwounded, connected to self and life, and others more distorted, polluted or cut off from self and life. A "pure" current is simply the full, natural, unhindered sexual expression of any aspect of the being. A distorted current results from the tangling of such pure currents with socially-constructed or wound-based imprints, such as the desire to have power-over or to be disempowered, to prove oneself as a lover, to exhibit only "male" or only "female" characteristics, or to maintain control and resist vulnerability and exposure. Of course, these distortions can and do present themselves in many other aspects of our lives, as well. Yet our sexual desires and lives play an important role in revealing these currents to us, so that we can recognize what is stuck, awry or wounded within us, and work toward healing.

It is common for whatever damage we have experienced to become erotically imprinted on us. For instance, many women who were sexually abused as children find that dynamics from that abuse persist within us, whether in our actual relationships or our erotic fantasies. The Pathwork explains that we often eroticize what we find most unbearable, in an attempt to metabolize or assimilate it. Obviously, however, this can negatively impact our sexual lives.

A client named Sarah came to me with this dilemma. After having been both verbally and sexually abused as a child, she had gone on to have verbally and physically abusive relationships as an adult. After much effort, she had externally extricated herself from those relationships. Yet, although she very much wanted a healthy, loving connection, many of her sexual fantasies involved being raped or otherwise mistreated, and she found herself consistently unattracted to men whom she could see might make good partners. Here is the counsel my guide provided to her.

When Sarah asks what would be necessary for her to open her heart and her sexuality, what she is really asking is, what would be necessary for her to open the core of her being? The answer is simple. *Trust* is what would be necessary. Without trust, one cannot open. One can only be forced open, which is essentially what has occurred in Sarah's life and what occurs in her fantasies. But the true openness she yearns to experience cannot come about as a result of force—neither force exerted from "outside," nor force exerted by Sarah herself. It can only be invited, promoted, facilitated, call forth by an atmosphere of inner nourishment, patience, gentleness and love. When the inner conditions are right, a wholesome and full-being openness naturally results. When they are not, it cannot. So this is an inner project that requires ongoing tender attention from Sarah, as well as an attitude of relaxed confidence.

This process is something like the gestation period of a human infant. Much must occur on many levels to nourish the process and prepare for "birth." It is a natural unfolding, yet it is also delicate, and requires care. A woman pregnant with a baby—or with a healing process—must treat herself with respect for what she is carrying, and must listen to the signals of her inner being and of her body, in order that she may be the best vessel possible for what she wishes to bring forth.

Sarah must remember that she is working to transform the accumulated psychic residue not only of this lifetime, but of many others. The task is large—not too large for her, but certainly worthy of her, her passionate spirit and her dedicated attention. Her intention keeps her moving forward, but her impatience actually slows down progress. Impatience, too, is born of lack of trust. It would be helpful for Sarah to let go of attachment to a certain outcome within a certain time frame, and just keep her focus on the inner work to be done, which is continually revealing itself to her—knowing that each piece she accomplishes does unfailingly bring her closer to the opening she desires.

Although each reader of these words has his or her own personal configuration of sexual currents, my guide's words apply to all of us. Each of us will benefit from cultivating a posture of relaxed openness to whatever needs to occur within us as we move toward wholeness and healing. If we are to develop the ability to live in harmony with ourselves and with our sexuality, we must avoid falling prey to a sense of hierarchy ("good/bad" "better/ worse" "more evolved/less evolved"), or standing in judgment of any aspect of our sexual selves. Any such notion or judgment is misaligned with the larger vision of the tapestry of which we are part, the level Buddhists call "ultimate reality." And in sexuality, as in all other spheres, our purpose here on earth is actually to experience the entire spectrum of being. It is only in this way that we can grow toward our own fullest expression, including our fullest expression of sexual energy.

Yet at the same time it is important to recognize and acknowledge currents within our sexuality, as well as within other aspects of our being, that have been distorted by our wounding and that do not currently enjoy the state of wholeness and health we wish for them and for ourselves. The challenge before us is how to work to transform such currents, to heal our sexuality and ourselves, without ever passing judgment on ourselves or on one another. An attitude of tender acceptance will open channels within us, making possible our continued growth and development.

Most of us remain largely or completely ignorant about the true magnificence of our sexual potential—the depths and heights to which our sexual responses can bring us, both in terms of intimacy with other human beings, and intimacy and alignment with the universe itself. Few of us are ready to access that level of experience at this time. We must, instead, heal our way toward it. In the meantime, we would do well to stop expecting our bodies to respond like pleasure-providing automatons while we wade through the valleys of our wounds and confusions. If we intend to use sexuality as a vehicle for our growth, we should accept the possibility of not having any recognizable form of "good sex" for some time; in fact, we would be well-served to abandon our notion of "good sex" altogether, and instead dare to be fully authentic in our sexual and sensual contact. Our bodies are less capable of dissimulation than our minds, so they cannot fail to help us enter into the terrain that scares us, and that our minds would therefore avoid.

Our bodies are highly sensitive instruments; we do not nourish ourselves by having mechanical sex, sex which neither satisfies us, nor brings us closer to others or to ourselves. That kind of sex will neither ease our distress, nor further our evolution. It is more harmonious to treat both our own and each others' bodies as the sacred vessels they are, containers of our hopes and fears, our wounds and resilience. In that way we can enter into a kind of "sex therapy" that aids in our healing and clearing process. We can consciously use our bodies and our sexual arousal as vehicles of presence; we can maintain awareness of what we are communicating through our touch, and what we are and are not able to give and receive in any given moment. Throughout this process we may even experience a tender kind of amusement as we witness the gaps between our consciousness, and our sexual response. It can be as if we are witnessing the first fumbling steps of a child just learning to walk. As we watch, we know that the child will eventually become proficient at walking, even at running. But we also know that the process of learning to walk involves continued effort, clumsiness, holding onto physical supports, fumbling, and even falling.

It is this way with our own sexual and spiritual development. If we critique or judge ourselves in our states of clumsiness and falling, we effectively arrest our own development. Fumbling and falling are necessary stages in development. Judgment is not! This point cannot be overemphasized, as the pattern of self-judgment is so deeply embedded in most of us. And it is *that* which interferes with our growth, not any one of the tangles, knots or confusions we may currently encounter within ourselves.

We can and must also hold what our partner is or is not able to give— or to receive –in each moment, with the utmost gentleness and respect. In other words, we can make a practice of holding no expectations or demands of ourselves or of each other in the realm of touch and sexuality. If we let go of our attachments to specific sexual outcomes, our bodies can serve both as our teachers, and as conduits which help us contact wounded parts of ourselves which need our compassionate attention.

As we proceed with this process of development and healing, we should even consider whether it serves us to spend nights in the same bed as our lovers. People sensitive to energy know that much energetic mingling takes place during a night's sleep, and this mingling does not always serve our efforts toward greater clarity and wholeness.

People often wonder about the spiritual value of choosing monogamy— pledging to engage sexually with only one partner—versus various forms of polyamory, in which partners are either open to, or committed to, maintaining multiple intimate and sexual relationships. The simplest answer is that here, as elsewhere, it doesn't matter so much what we choose, but why and how we are choosing it. It's possible to adhere to monogamy from a place of insecurity, rigidity and fear, a terror that either you or your partner might find another person so attractive as to nullify your own connection. It's also possible to choose monogamy as a way of focusing one's sexual energies in order to achieve the deepest possible connection.

Some people gravitate toward polyamory as an outgrowth of a deep soul-level openness to life. For them, experiencing intimate sexual love with numerous partners is a joyful way of fulfilling their inner design. Yet other people are drawn to polyamory in a misguided attempt to avoid childhood imprints of neglect or abandonment, hoping on some level that having multiple intimate partners, rather than one, will help them avoid the pain that intimacy inevitably brings to the surface.

In fact, no form of relationship can keep us safe from pain, nor should it. Healing is equally possible—and equally necessary—in any relational context. Whichever model of relationships you are drawn to, the path of growth requires you to look honestly at your motivations and fears.

The same principles apply in the areas of sexual orientation and gender. Learning, growth and healing are available to us whether we engage our sexuality in heterosexual, homosexual or bisexual directions, or in no outward direction at all. If we discover, through a process of inner inquiry, that our sexual orientations have been shaped by trauma—that we are either drawn or not drawn to certain people or genders because of damaging imprints or soul loss—then it is, of course, harmonious to work to heal that damage. In fact, it is necessary for our well-being, because any damage present will find ways to surface in our lives, regardless of how hard we may try to avoid it.

Although society prescribes certain characteristics for men and for women, we are all, as previously discussed, braided selves. If we are truly sensitive to our inner design, none of us can perfectly fit into socially-constructed notions of gender. What we choose to do about that is up to us. Increasing numbers of people are declaring themselves "transgender," and undergoing lengthy medical procedures to transition from one gender to the other. Others name themselves "genderqueer," reject traditional notions of maleness and femaleness, and attempt to forge new gender identities in a liminal zone in between, or beyond, those binary categories. Either of these movements can represent acts of healing and liberation—or can become a diversion from necessary healing, depending on the energies that fuel them.

Human beings have the freedom to choose the contexts in which we will work with our traumatic residue and pain, but the option of avoiding it entirely is not available. So if we believe that we will escape our wounds by choosing monogamy or polyamory, by being heterosexual, gay, lesbian or bisexual, or by adopting a new gender identity, we are bound to be disappointed. But if we allow our relational, sexual and gender choices to give us a strengthening, joyful context in which to approach the work of growth and healing, we will, as always, be supported both by our inner teachers, and by life.

I had romantic relationships with men for the first seven years of my sexual life, and then spent more than twenty years having relationships with women. Being with women was enormously freeing for me; it helped me release the oppressive notions of femininity that I'd absorbed from my mother and my culture, feel comfortable in my own body, and own my own sexual power. Yet once I embarked on a more conscious healing process, I realized that there were things I needed to learn by being with men again. Dating men brought up wounded places in my psyche and sexuality that simply didn't come up with women.

For several months I was involved with Jon, a man who shared my passion for spiritual and emotional growth. Our relationship gave me an ideal arena in which to identify and clear old imprints. For instance, one afternoon when Jon and I were sexual, neither of us had an orgasm. Although I didn't mind not having an orgasm myself, part of me felt very anxious that Jon hadn't come. When we talked about it, he assured me that he didn't need anything from me; he added that if he needed to have an orgasm, he could always masturbate. In other words, he released me from any responsibility for his sexual satisfaction.

Later that day, while I was out doing errands, I realized I was feeling a strange sense of panic. Intellectually I knew there was nothing wrong; in fact, I felt liberated by what Jon had said. I wrote in my journal:

"Something in my emotional body was totally flipped out, but I didn't know why, and could see no reason for it. Yet the disconnect was so deep that I had a real feeling of cognitive dissonance hearing my normal-sounding voice come out of my mouth... I realized that a tremendous anxiety got set off in me precisely by Jon's statement that he didn't need anything from me...Part of me believes I am only worthy of living, I earn my right to live, by giving others what they need from me. With Dad, it was my job to make him feel good—I really, deeply believed he wouldn't love me if I didn't. So Jon has taken away my job, which means the walls, floor and ceiling are all gone—I've collapsed into total formlessness. I don't know what my job is, what I am for, what sex is for, what a relationship is for, what

anything is, if it's not about my taking responsibility for the other person's wants and needs."

I found that all I needed to do to clear this response was allow it to fully emerge in my body, recognize its distortions and untruth, and ask for divine help in clearing it. Later, I wrote:

"What if Jon and I could just come together as two self-sufficient, happy beings—not projecting, pulling, pushing, poking, prodding, blaming, manipulating...? What if? It's such a radical new paradigm—I get lost in it..."

After several months, Jon and I discontinued our lover relationship, though we remained friends. About a year later, I met Michelle, and we became partners, even though I had expected that my next relationship would be with a man. When I asked my guide about the question of my "sexual orientation," he responded:

As you are aware, you have opened things up. That was what needed to happen. On a higher level there is no gender, so issues of sexual orientation are irrelevant. What is relevant is the presence of states of rigidity or fixation. Such states always indicate the presence of distortion in the being. Where there is no distortion, there is a relaxed outflowing of energies. This does not mean that everyone is necessarily bisexual—there are always individual variations in the types of frequencies that most attract. The rigidity and fixedness of complete homosexuality does indeed indicate a distortion, but there are many distortions present in most manifestations of heterosexuality and bisexuality as well.

In your own case, there is a fairly equal outflowing toward persons of both genders. You fixated on women for many years, due to distortions of which you have since become aware. Then, in a compensatory movement, for a time you fixated on men. But in fact there is no either/or, no need to choose, except in a given moment. Your recent experiences with men have illuminated, exposed and healed much of what needed resolution in that arena. Beyond that, the work of being with another human being is simply that, regardless of gender.

Several years later, when Michelle and I had shifted from partnership to friendship, I figured that my next sexual relationship would be with another woman. I was wrong again. To my great surprise, a man I had loved nearly thirty years before returned to my life. Craig and I spent fifteen months together, and were able to do a lot of healing for our younger selves as well as learn from and enjoy each other in the present. Then we, too, shifted into friendship. At this point I would lay odds on only one thing: my sexual growth path will continue to confound my expectations. Or then again, maybe it won't...

36
Physical Pain

Pain insists upon being attended to. God whispers to us in our pleasures, speaks in our consciences, but shouts in our pains. It is His megaphone to rouse a deaf world.

- C.S. Lewis

Physical and emotional pain are similar phenomena manifesting on different levels of our being. Emotional pain, as we have discussed, emerges from and reflects postures of imbalance and separation within the non-physical part of the self, and is therefore most effectively addressed through non-physical means. Since physical pain affects us physically, we might assume that it would be best addressed through physical means; however, this is not always the case. Often what we experience on a physical level is actually the end result of a severe, long-standing non-physical imbalance; in these instances, non-physical means are necessary to heal the source of the pain at its root. And even when pain has a clear physical source, the posture we take toward it can profoundly impact its resolution.

Of course, most of us are aware that the experiences of emotional and physical pain are not wholly distinct, but frequently interwoven. When not addressed, emotional pain can actually produce physical pain. Physical pain can also produce emotional pain—for instance, when it causes us to feel shame or self-loathing.

Although physical responses to physical phenomena may be necessary and appropriate, the inner, non-physical stance we take toward our physical pain is more important than any physical action. For instance, it can be useful to take the pills commonly known as "pain killers" to alleviate physical pain—as long as our inner focus is directed toward allowing the pills to work, and to help us work, in harmony with the larger flow of life. In fact, rather than calling these pills "killers of pain," we would do well to think of them as "servers of life;" that would make our ideal relationship to them more clear. If we take such pills with an inner posture of love and respect for life, for ourselves, and for our bodies, they will probably serve us well—although it is also true that if we can cultivate such a posture of love and respect for life, ourselves and our bodies, our pain may diminish on its own, without need of pills. If, on the other hand, we take "pain killers" in an attempt to kill off, silence or numb the part of ourselves that is feeling pain, or in order to force ourselves into a level of functioning or artificial "well-being" not in concert with our inner experience, we are removing ourselves from the stream of life's compassion. In this case, while the pills may or may not do their job on a surface level, our inner attitude will move us further from, rather than closer to, true healing.

Although they may seem subtle, these distinctions are profound. When we look at these questions more closely, we see again that *what* we do matters far less than why and how we do it. For instance, if we take analgesic pills as an act of compassion for our body–which is working so hard on our behalf, which is suffering and manifesting the physical effects of all our inner confusions and distortions, and which needs our tender attention and our focused work in order to become more able to manifest the *true* state of well-being which would represent the fulfillment of its inner design—then the pills can actually serve as emissaries of the universe, assisting us in our larger project. If instead we refrain from taking such pills as a means of withholding compassion from ourselves and our bodies, forcing ourselves to "tough it out," then the pain we experience will become magnified and amplified—reflecting not only the original processes which led to its manifestation, but also the secondary processes by which we fracture and divide ourselves from ourselves, and separate ourselves from the universal flow.

On the physical plane, sometimes physical actions are necessary or appropriate to aid in the transformation of physically-manifested phenomena. Yet our reasons for taking those actions, and the emotions and energies with which we undertake them, are always more impactful than the presence or absence of the physical intervention itself.

It's also true that sometimes energies must move through our bodies and take shape on the physical level as part of the process of being transformed.

Our wish to "kill" the pain or banish its source often stems from a misunderstanding of this larger process—a belief that pain or illness means that we have done something "wrong," or failed to do something right, or that pain indicates that there is something "wrong" with *us*. In fact, any instance of physical pain or illness is simply the natural result of a particular energetic process. While it may be true that this result could have been avoided if different internal actions had been taken, that understanding cannot help us now, and is not really the point—just as berating ourselves now for having denied ourselves compassion in the past is not the point, and cannot possibly help.

The most common human response to pain is to attempt to push it away. This reaction is so strong and immediate that I suspect it is instinctual. Certainly it would have been a useful response much earlier in human history, when we were running away from saber-toothed tigers and had to ignore our wounds in order to survive. However, at this point in time, unless we are in immediate physical danger, we can usually afford to turn toward our pain rather than away from it. Compassionate attention is the one medication which is *always* indicated; if we are willing to open to that healing energy, align ourselves with it, and allow it to work with us and within us and on our behalf, we will be more able to heal on both physical and non-physical levels.

Even after years of consciously working with physical pain, I notice that my first response to a minor injury is an inner cut-off, as if whatever part of me that's hurting is an annoyance which is better ignored. Within a second or two, though, I catch this response and turn it around, reorienting myself toward connection with the part of myself in pain. Then, using a technique called Focusing, I stop whatever else I'm doing and actively try to "listen" to the part in pain, making myself available to really "hear" (or feel) its ache, pulse, burn, or whatever other sensations are present. This generally makes those sensations grow stronger for a moment, but if I stay present and keep listening, the pain then rapidly decreases. I've found that using this technique for just a few minutes often brings about very rapid healing of injuries that would otherwise have caused pain for hours or even days. Of course, what I am actually doing with this "listening" is applying the medication of compassion—which inevitably supports and activates my body's ability to heal.

I've also used non-physical healing methods to help resolve much more major pain. Years ago, I donated a kidney to my then-partner, Ana. After the surgery, once the morphine wore off, I found myself in a lot of pain. Fortunately, I had just begun to learn about how to work with non-physical reality. Before going into the operating room, I had used my powers of visualization to bring my body to a safe place in non-ordinary reality, leaving it in the crook of a tree that I loved—so when I woke up with pain, it reminded me that I needed to retrieve my body and comfort it. I went to the tree where I had left my body in non-ordinary reality, picked up my body and held it close for a long time while it shook and cried. After that, my pain began to lessen, but I sensed that something else remained to be done. I realized that my body needed to understand why *I had put it through such pain. So, still working in non-physical reality, I took my body to visit with Ana, who, in my vision, was lying on a gurney underneath a different tree. My body and I held and kissed Ana, and all of us cried together with sadness, relief, gratitude and love. Then I left Ana and returned with my body to my own hospital bed—where I found that my physical pain was gone. After that, my surgical wound healed quickly and without discomfort.*

37
Illness, Healing and Death

Much of your pain is the bitter potion by which the physician within you heals your sick self.

– Khalil Gibran

Severe health problems generally occur as part of a larger process designed to get our attention, to show us where and how we have separated ourselves from ourselves or from life. When illness brings us to a point of crisis, it offers us a powerful gift—the opportunity to stop avoiding the message that various parts of our being have likely been attempting to communicate for a long time: *We cannot go on living as we have been living. Change is necessary. It is time to choose on behalf of ourselves, and on behalf of life.* It is important to find ways to hear and to heed the messages contained in our illnesses, never blaming ourselves—as we have seen elsewhere, blame is always a fruitless loop—but being willing to take responsibility both for our present physical circumstances, and for the deeper underlying patterns which have created them.

In many illnesses, part of the pattern at work involves a movement toward our own life force, and a counter-movement against or away from it. When both movements are very strong, it can feel as if we are standing between two very strong winds, each blowing in an opposite direction. These winds work inside us like magnetic poles; unless we have dismantled the underlying energetic phenomenon at work, strengthening one pole will also cause the other pole to experience an increase in strength. This is why sometimes an illness may continue to progress, despite or in some cases even *because* of our having accomplished a significant amount of healing.

Painful emotional states play a major role in the genesis of most illnesses. This is because the energetic misalignment that creates illness—the separation between a person and his or her own life force—both emerges from, and leads to, states of emotional pain. Self-hatred and self-rejection, in particular, are commonly involved. When we are very knotted-up by self-loathing, we can actually come to perceive a movement against our own life force as being in favor of life. We may believe on some level that our very existence and needs are somehow anti-life, and that these must be suppressed or negated in order for life to be served. Of course, this is not and cannot ever be true. We are a part of life, and life is therefore served by our well-being. But there are many paths by which we can come to believe otherwise. For instance, if we felt unloved or disliked by one or both of our parents, we may have perceived that in order to align with them, we had to turn against ourselves. In this way it may have seemed as if we needed to create an anti-love, anti-life current within ourselves *in order to stay alive and receive love.* Yet because there is no way for us to hate or reject "ourselves" without also hating and rejecting life, this pattern will invariably lead to physical illness.

Another pathway to this particular distortion is an acute awareness of the suffering of others, and an early misperception regarding its cause. As infants or very young children, we may have perceived our existence as burdensome for our mother or other caretaker, and concluded that life—in this case, our mother's life—would be better served if we did not exist, or did not *fully* exist. Over the years, this sort of misperception can remain with us and even seem to acquire layers of "proof," because our experience of reality will so often manage to "prove" whatever we already believe. If we become and remain ill, it may indeed seem as if we are burdening others around us, which will make it even harder to heal the original misconception. The result may be that the part of ourselves that is determined to serve life by eliminating us grows quite frantic to make this occur, while the part that wants to choose on behalf of our well-being becomes equally frantic in response.

To heal these kinds of distortions, we must work at their source. For instance, we must directly examine the conviction that our own full existence is somehow inappropriate, undesirable, or damaging to life. We must expose all of the distorted beliefs that have been running us from underground, so that we can clearly see their distortions. Only in this way can we become able to develop a clear and fully aligned intention to heal.

The following exercise, developed by Leslie Temple Thurston, can be very useful in helping us to identify and clear out some of the internal matter that may be at work in our illness:

◎ Identifying and Clearing Distortions

Begin by taking a piece of paper and drawing two lines across it, one horizontal and one vertical, to create four equal squares. Then, give each of your squares a title. This exercise can be done with any pair of opposites—for instance, Happiness vs. Depression, or Powerful vs. Powerless. In the following example, the opposites are Alive vs. Dead. Your four squares will address your desires and fears in relation to both conditions. So, your titles for this example will be:

1. Why I desire to be alive

2. Why I fear being alive

3. Why I desire death

4. Why I fear death

Now, fill in as much as you can within each of the four squares. You *must* write something in every square; if at first it seems as if one or more of the four squares does not apply to you, look more deeply. Dedicated attention to these four questions will almost certainly yield some surprises.

This is a powerful energetic process, and should not be misunderstood as merely a mental exercise. You may find it impossible to do the entire process in a single sitting. You may also find you need to do it more than once. If you scour yourself deeply enough, you will find at least some degree of distortion and "charge" in your answers for each of the four squares.

Once you have identified the distorted attitudes or postures at work within you, you can turn them over to your inner teachers, the universe or God. You can also use the tools of intention and prayer to untangle, clear, correct or release the erroneous beliefs. Remember, these attitudes, postures and beliefs are "real"—they are actual, though non-physical, structures inside your being. But they are not true, not Truth. And just as you have the power to transform or release physical structures in your life, you can transform or remove these beliefs.

All roads lead back to the relationship with the self; healing can only occur through a process of full self-embrace. And yet at times we may have carried so many misconceptions about ourselves, so many currents of self-rejection and self-negation, for so long that they have braided, knotted and massed together, forming the equivalent of an "inner destroyer"—a dark force or energy which actively works to push us away from wholeness and from life. As we grow in consciousness and strength, the Destroyer grows, too, fed by the underground currents of our self-loathing, and a tremendous strain results. When both forces within us, that which seeks to heal us and that which seeks to destroy us, grow strong enough, the internal tension produces an implosion, and a crisis on the physical level is a likely result.

The problem is that even spiritual growth can serve to deepen existing fault lines and ruptures within us, if it is not fully and evenly integrated on all levels of our being. The more contact we have with the beauty of higher consciousness, the more fervently the distorted parts of ourselves may struggle to hold themselves—and us—away from that light. Meanwhile, for those parts of ourselves that have glimpsed Truth, the fact that so much of our being is still segregated and held apart from that Truth can feel increasingly intolerable. So both the light-aware, light-seeking part of us, and the shame-filled inner destroyer then work harder and harder, causing more of what we experience as pain and illness, in order to get our attention.

When this occurs, the solution, as usual, is love. Specifically, we must work to love and value ourselves as never before; we must commit to recognizing our own true goodness and beauty, our intrinsic worth and value, our inextricable connectedness to life. We must call upon all of our external and internal allies, friends and teachers, and ask them to join us in flooding our being with love in order that the balance may shift in favor of our continued physical existence, rather than against.

We may also carry within us old angers which have formed hard knots in our being. Over time we may develop the misconception that our lives depend on those knots, as if they held us together with their bitterness and bile. In fact, however, they prevent the natural upwelling of gratitude in us, and separate us from the flow of life. In order to heal this pattern, we must open the knots and allow their venom to drain out—but within an internal environment so filled with higher knowing that the venom simply burns up, and becomes transformed into particles of light.

In other cases, part of the spiritual purpose of an illness or other grave challenge may be to soften us. This is particularly true for those of us who have confused softness with weakness, and who have struggled to be strong at all costs. The problem, or rather, the inharmonious posture, is our attempt to be stronger than the universe. This effort is destined to fail; the truth is that the universe is far stronger than us, or at least, far stronger than our small personality selves, which is the only part of us that would engage in this type of power struggle. In essence, life is like a masseur which holds us in its hands; depending on the strength of our resistance, it can either massage us into softness, or it can break us. The choice is ours. Healing can never be brought about through sheer force of will, although strong-willed people often attempt to heal in this way. This is simply another manifestation of the belief that we can be stronger than the universe itself, so this effort is doomed to fail. Instead we must become able to shift in such a way that we stop trying to dominate the universe, to *force* it to heal us, while also opening more fully in order to *allow* it to heal us.

As we begin to open in these ways, the question of forgiveness may arise. We may have to forgive those from whom we first learned to be so "tough;" we may also have to forgive ourselves for the harm our "toughness" has caused, both to ourselves and to others. Fortunately, forgiving ourselves will help us to forgive others, and forgiving others will also help us with the ongoing work of self-forgiveness. As this new energetic pattern gains momentum, the feeling of having been wronged or having done wrong will inevitably wither, and gratitude will arise organically in its place.

Of course, all of these shifts are parts of a much larger process of realignment, in which we are likely to develop a very different understanding of strength and weakness. We may come to understand that the posture we have held and taken as strength has actually made us weak, and that the postures parts of us still see as weak—the postures of forgiveness, receptivity and gratitude—actually represent great strength. As we incorporate these new understandings more fully and deeply, the life energy in our bodies will redistribute itself in such a way as to facilitate our healing.

Quite simply, the crisis of serious illness asks us to *decide to live*, to embrace our own life force wholeheartedly, to stand openly and forcefully in our own being—and also to directly confront, heal or release those internal configurations which prevent us from doing so. All of our own life force waits to embrace us and work toward helping us heal, if we will only turn ourselves decisively in the direction of choosing that, allowing it, directing our wills toward that natural process rather than toward suppressing ourselves. This cannot fail to be the case because at the deepest level life is not, and can never be, opposed to life. Our life-force is not truly being contested by anyone other than ourselves, and we have turned against ourselves only because of ancient errors in perception. All that is really required to begin to reverse this is a conscious and full-hearted decision to do so, a clear setting of a new intention.

It's important to acknowledge that although healing is always available to us, survival is not. At times, inner work can bring about seemingly miraculous changes on the physical level. Spontaneous remissions of advanced cancers and other illnesses do occur. Yet at other times, certain anti-life physical processes may have progressed so far within us that even deep non-physical healing cannot turn them around. It's also possible that our soul may simply be ready to continue its journey in a new form. Therefore, we should never imagine that death represents a failure of any kind. In the big picture of our souls' development, we can never lose our way or go astray; we are part of life, and carriers of life, and life does not ever prefer any circumstance or situation over any other. Whatever we experience—even death—can be used by our souls as fodder for growth, and will, in that sense, help us to fulfill our inner design.

When my good friend and shamanic colleague Eddie was diagnosed with lung cancer, I emailed him:

Wow. On a human level, of course, I am so sorry that you're dealing with this rotten and scary condition. But on other levels way beyond that, I am moved and even excited for you. I know that you know way too much to succumb to traditional or conventional ways of viewing this crisis/opportunity... you have been studying, learning, transforming so directly in order to be able to confront this, it seems to me...

But after pushing "send," I got nervous. Although I knew Eddie's understanding of illness was similar to mine, a more conventional part of me wondered, What kind of person tells a friend that they're "excited" about their diagnosis with lung cancer? Would Eddie think I was a heartless bitch? *I wrote him again, expressing my fear. Soon after that, I got his response.*

Dear Ruth, Heartless Bitch,

I soooo found your attitude genuine and supportive—I'm sorry you had a twinge. You know I love you and it's so great to hear from someone with a shared perspective. I've avoided telling certain circles of colleagues and friends to avoid the long sad looks and the (well-meant but unhelpful) stories.

Shortly after that, Eddie asked for a reading from my guide, and I gave him several single-spaced pages of challenging information and suggestions. Eddie's patterns included the attempt to be stronger than life, and the confusion of softness with weakness. He received the information non-defensively, saying that it felt true to him on a deep level, and scheduled several intensive healing sessions with a close friend of his in order to work on those patterns. He also asked a third friend to be his "witness" as he allowed the full range of his feelings and aspects to surface.

Eddie engaged deeply, courageously and sincerely in his healing process for the next two years. During that time, I moved to the other side of the country. On the night that he died, not realizing that he was already gone, I began wondering whether I should fly to California for a visit, and did a journey to check in with him. I immediately got the sense that there was no need for me to come; in fact, I sensed that that his spirit was joyful, practically jumping up and down with excitement as it prepared to embark on its next adventure in consciousness. This fit with the Eddie I had known. He loved life and had put tremendous energy into trying to stay alive; yet, when it became clear that things weren't going that way, he turned to embrace what came.

At Eddie's request, I officiated at his memorial service. That morning, I had a conversation with his spirit, and asked what he would like to communicate to the more than 100 people who would gather to mourn his passing. Here is what he told me to say:

It's all so beautiful. The place of stillness and peace and compassion that took so much effort to reach when I was alive—it's effortless now. It's all right here —it's an earthly paradise. Paradise is made of what's inside of you, not what's outside. Push less—allow more. All you really have to do is hold your intention and allow.

I'm not gone—I'm right here. I'm here for anyone to talk to. I've shed what I didn't need any more. There is nothing to grieve— it's all so beautiful. You have a beautiful life to live, and then you get to come here.

As the great German novelist Herman Hesse said, "The call of death is a call of love. Death can be sweet if we answer it in the affirmative, if we accept it as one of the great eternal forms of life and transformation."

38
Understanding Karma

Situations seem to happen to people, but in reality, they unfold from deeper karmic causes. The universe unfolds to itself, bringing to bear any cause that needs to be included. Don't take this process personally. The working out of cause and effect is eternal. You are part of this rising and falling that never ends, and only by riding the wave can you ensure that the waves don't drown you.

– Deepak Chopra

"Karma" is a Sanskrit word that refers to "the natural laws of causation"—in other words, the process by which certain things are caused to happen in a given human lifetime, rather than others. Although karma is sometimes mistakenly thought of as a system of reward and punishment, it, like all other phenomena, is actually neutral. My favorite definition of karma is this one: If you plant an apple seed, you may or may not get an apple tree, but you can be certain that you *won't* get an orange tree. In other words, while it is impossible to predict the exact results of our actions, there *is* a relationship between the actions we take, and what occurs.

Each of us has our own karma, produced by the intersection of our wounds and distortions, our inner design, and the dynamic impact of each and every choice we make. We might also understand karma as the combination of the soul's chosen curriculum with the human personality's exercise of free will. Either way, certain aspects of our karma are "set"—the lessons or paths chosen by our souls—and others are mutable, shaped by our own actions and decisions, and continually available to be transformed.

Saying that each of us has our own karma is simply another way of saying that we each have our own life to live, our own metaphorical garden to tend. It is not our place to change the karma of others, just as it is not our place to garden in other peoples' yards. Actually, it is impossible for us to change the karma of another—or at least, it is impossible for us to do so by an act of will. Because of the synergistic nature of life, our presence in others' lives will indeed impact them, and in this way may influence the ways in which their karma plays out. But because each person has her own set of lessons to learn, his own set of inner obstacles to overcome in the fulfillment of his inner design, our relationship to the life processes of others can only impact the specific forms in which those lessons come, rather than affecting the lessons themselves.

When I donated my kidney to Ana, I understood much less than I do now about physical illness and karma; I truly hoped that the transplant would restore her good health. However, although the transplant itself was successful, Ana went on to suffer from many other health problems—some caused by her long history of diabetes, others caused by the post-transplant medications. In the years since then she has been through many surgeries, and has spent a great deal of time in the hospital. Recently, 17 years post-transplant, she was diagnosed with a form of lymphoma caused by the immune suppressant medications she takes to keep her body from rejecting my kidney. Once again, Ana is fighting for her life.

With the understandings I now have, I imagine that Ana's spirit must be trying to learn important lessons through the experience of chronic and life-threatening illness. Although I can't know the exact nature of her spirit's curriculum, I can better understand now why I couldn't save her from ongoing health difficulties. (Of course, if I had somehow been able to restore Ana's health, her lessons would simply have had to take a different form.)

By giving a kidney to Ana, I did change the form in which her karma played out. She loathed dialysis and did badly with it, so the transplant did probably extend her life by many years. Yet it could not remove the karmic imprint which had created her diabetes and kidney failure to begin with. When someone's relationship to herself or to life is distorted, the work of unknotting is hers and hers alone. No one else can do it for her, no matter how hard they try. And whatever she leaves undone in this lifetime will simply await her in the next.

In the bigger picture, did my gift of a kidney help Ana, or harm her? In one way, it helped her by giving her a longer time period in which to work at her karma in a single lifetime. In another way, it may have made her path more difficult, since living longer has allowed more time for other medical problems to develop. Ultimately, I believe that my actions neither helped nor harmed; they simply reconfigured the stage set, the outer forms through which Ana would have to work. On a soul level, her work remained unchanged.

Knowing what I now know, would I still donate my kidney? I suspect that I would, because she needed it, and I was able to provide it. But I would do so with a very different understanding of my role and its limitations.

If we fear "interfering" with someone else's karma—or if we imagine we can change their karma to achieve a more positive outcome—we are in error. There is actually no way to "interfere," for good or for ill. It is impossible. As Ana's story shows, each person's karma will simply reshape itself around the new relationship or circumstance. We can circumvent or influence a specific occurrence, but not the overall movement of what will occur—what *must* occur, according to spiritual law.

And just as we cannot change the karma of others, we cannot escape our own. Our choices on the human level are limited to the outer circumstances in which our karma will play out. It is not that we are "stuck" with our karma, but rather that, in the oft-quoted words of the twelfth-century Indian poet Akka Mahadevi, "The only way out is through." Instead of recognizing this, we often dig our wheels deeper into the mud of our karma by trying to change it from the outside, rather than addressing it at its root.

This does not mean that we cannot or should not change the outer form of our lives. If a given circumstance, say, a job or relationship or physical location, does not have or has ceased to have a deep resonance and compatibility for us, we can change or exchange it, "trade it in," just as in a game of Scrabble we can choose to skip a turn and trade in our letters for other letters. However, just as in Scrabble, the new "letters" provided to us by life will offer new challenges—or, more accurately, the same challenges in a different form. Ana's story is a clear demonstration of this; her physical challenges continued, albeit in different forms, after the kidney transplant. Our underlying lessons are provided to us as a given, just as with Scrabble, the board, rules, and specific letters are provided. We get to choose the words we will spell out within that structure, just as we choose the forms in which we will play out the karma we have created or inherited from other lifetimes—but there are truly no shortcuts in the process of learning. Sometimes, in fact, we must change not only the circumstances in our lives, but our lives themselves—in other words, we must physically die—in order to continue our learning.

Again, it's important to understand that this does not ever mean we are being "punished." The concept of punishment does not even exist on higher levels of being; it cannot possibly exist, because from that level, there are no mistakes, and nothing is wrong or right. Yet the places where we have separated from ourselves, others or life will and must be continually revealed to us, because the work of healing those separations is intrinsic to our inner design as a human species. From the standpoint of our larger selves, death doesn't mean we have done something wrong; in fact, it can be better understood as a major hit of the re-set button, a chance to begin life all over again with a new set of circumstances, and an even better-informed soul.

39
Living with Fear

Courage is not the absence of fear, but rather the judgment that something else is more important than fear.

— Meg Cabot

Fear is an inevitable part of the human experience, just as having skin—a vulnerable, breachable barrier—is an inevitable part of the experience of having a human physical form. Just as we would not strive to have physically unbreachable skin while in a human form, neither should we strive to eliminate fear, or even imagine that it would be desirable to do so. Our experiences of vulnerability, our limits, are part of being human; they are an essential part of what we are here to work with and within.

Some human beings identify strongly with their fear, feel it often, and go through life alert to the possibility of harm around every external or internal corner. Others attempt to banish their fear and identify instead with a constructed "invincible" persona. Both of these approaches offer gifts and challenges; the beings who adopt them might be compared to a violet, a delicate flower that grows only in moist shade, and a prickly pear, a robust cactus that can handle much harsher conditions, and protects itself with thorns. Each life form is beautiful; each has its own integrity and purpose; each is sturdy, in its own way, and yet also vulnerable. And each offers a different vantage point from which to learn about and experience life.

Although we often attempt to sort and label our fears, distinguishing between those that are "justified" and "unjustified," that is a misguided effort. In our internal landscapes, fear simply *is,* just as, in our outer landscape, rain simply *is*. The question, therefore, is not whether rain is "justified," but how we will respond to its existence. Will we go outdoors anyway, or will we stay home? Will we wear boots, coats, hats, and use umbrellas, or don bathing suits instead, and go splashing through puddles—or, perhaps, wear regular clothes and then complain about getting wet? All of these options and more are available to us, because fear, at its base, is just another phenomenon to be explored and engaged with. As always, there are no wrong choices and no right ones, although some choices will bring us into deeper harmony with ourselves and with life, while others—like the choice to ignore what we feel—will tend to separate us.

As we grow spiritually and emotionally, some of us become argumentative or frustrated with our fear, or with the aspects of our being that experience fear. We may begin to see fear as somehow problematic, a circumstance to be healed or remedied. In truth, however, fear is neutral, as all energetic phenomena are neutral—neither bad nor good, neither right nor wrong. It is an illusion to think that fear must be overcome in order that more interesting landscapes may be explored. The internal landscape and its complex mix and interaction of "weather patterns" is the terrain we are given, and there is none more interesting. So we do not need to fear (!) being "held up" by our attention to whatever is within us; that attention is necessary and actually part of, not merely precursor to, our further explorations. Fear can be a pathway to light; we hew to this path by honoring, not disregarding, what we find on the way.

At the same time, it is also true that on one level there is never anything to fear—there are no real dangers—because our essence cannot be harmed. When we sense this truth, we may become frustrated that our human selves persist in feeling fear. Yet on the human level, harm *is* possible. In this, as in all other aspects of life, we straddle multiple realities. Depending on the distance from which we view the tapestry, very different things are true at once.

In most cases, for instance, contact with hot coals will burn human skin. Yet in the context of fire-walks, thousands of people have experienced states which enable them to walk barefoot on burning coals without injury. This shows us something about what is *possible*. It is useful for how it challenges our sense of immutable laws. Yet it does not mean that we should cease to use pot-holders while cooking.

As human beings, we carry fear within us because all of us have experienced fearsome things in our physical lives. This fear has created structures in our internal landscapes which render us vulnerable. So, although it is the presence of fear that makes danger into danger, rather than the reverse, the danger is still real. Cultivating an attitude of bluffing or bravado—attempting to hide our fear from others, and most especially from ourselves—actually leaves us more open to being "harmed."

We might understand fear as a kind of porousness in the being. All human beings have this porousness, though in different locations and to different extents. When a child scrapes her knee and the skin barrier is broken, pathogens can enter her bloodstream. When a human being has fear, his energetic barrier is broken, and pathogens can enter his energy field. It is fear itself that creates the opening, fear that renders us vulnerable to intrusion or harm—and yet the vulnerability, once present, cannot usefully be ignored, denied, or argued with. If we wish to heal that vulnerability and soothe the fear, we must instead use the medicines of compassion and love. By working with our inner teachers we can become less identified with the parts of ourselves that feel fear, and thus more able to offer them support and tenderness. Over time we can cultivate the kind of relationship with our fear that a loving parent has with a very young infant. Such a parent would not attempt to reason with the child or to talk him out of whatever was distressing him; clearly such an approach would be useless, and would only make him cry harder. Instead, the parent would hold her child lovingly, gently soothing and rocking him to sleep. As we become able to respond to our fear with this kind of tenderness, our perception of danger will decrease—and in fact, the actual possibility of harm will decrease as well.

40
Working with Anger

Just like our organs, our anger is part of us. When we are angry, we have to go back to ourselves and take good care of our anger. We cannot say, 'Go away, anger, I don't want you.' When you have a stomachache, you don't say, 'I don't want you, stomach, go away.' No, you take care of it. In the same way, we have to embrace and take good care of our anger.

– Thich Naht Hanh

Anger is a reflexive, protective response which emerges, at least initially, from a primitive part of our being—"primitive" only in the sense that anger has been with us for as long as we have been embodied. It can flare up in an instant at the sight or sound of a threat; then, if inner and outer conditions allow, it can dissipate just as quickly. Anger that has not been distorted by other wounds and confusions is like a guard dog who can bark, snarl and growl very fiercely in the presence of perceived danger, then flop down on the floor and roll on its back to let its belly be petted a few moments later.

Because we live as separate beings in a world of other beings who also perceive themselves as separate, anger is a necessary response to circumstances in which we are encroached-upon or deprived. Of course, in a state of unity consciousness, anger would not exist; in fact, it could not even be conceived of. But in our human lives anger is natural and appropriate, when we can allow it to serve its purpose—the laying-down of a boundary—without emotional complication. It serves a function as basic as the functions of hunger, thirst and sleepiness, all of which exist to ensure that we attend to important needs.

The problem is that in most human beings, anger is no longer an elemental, uncomplicated state. Instead, it has become enormously entangled with other emotions, patterns and imprints: for instance, the pattern of turning against and negating ourselves, which then requires a compensatory lashing-out at others; the pattern of suppressing ourselves and our natural responses, which produces unsustainable states of pressure in the being; the pattern of allowing others to mistreat us, which creates free-floating anger that can poison us and others with its invisible time-release action—and so on.

Most of us, therefore, have some sort of "anger problem." In some of us, that manifests as what appears to be too much anger. We may operate on high alert, responding with instant fury to even the smallest threat, and have great difficulty relaxing our inner being into conditions of ease. This pattern can lead to other patterns; for instance, we might become angry at ourselves for feeling and expressing so much anger toward others. This would then add another step to the dance: 1) Perceived threat, 2) Instant fury at the perceived source of the threat, 3) Immediate fury at the self for experiencing instant fury. Obviously, step three does nothing to facilitate the state of calm openness in which we are most able to contact universal sources of love and compassion; in fact, it locks us even more firmly into the physiological and emotional hyperarousal of anger. This is a very common pattern among survivors of physical trauma, and is often classified in mainstream psychology as Post-Traumatic Stress Disorder (PTSD).

On the other hand, some of us manifest what appears to be too little anger, failing to react even when others blatantly invade or violate us. Some people even imagine that this is a spiritually advanced way to be. While it is probably true that an enlightened being would be non-reactive in this way, it's safe to say that few if any readers of this book have achieved that degree of enlightenment. Instead, what is usually at work in this response is a different pattern of dance steps: 1) Perceived threat, 2) Instant fury at the perceived source of the threat, 3) Immediate suppression of fury. This anger dance generally leads to states of resignation, depression and internal collapse—and sometimes also to physical illness. While the person who is frequently angry lives in a state of chronic energetic hyperarousal, those who are rarely or never angry live in similar discomfort at the opposite end of the energetic spectrum: chronic hypoarousal, usually experienced as emotional or physical weakness or malaise. This, too, is a very common pattern among trauma survivors.

Of course, there are infinite variations on these patterns and intricate complications that can ensue—for instance, a pattern of using drugs or alcohol to medicate either the hyper- or hypoaroused states; a pattern of passive-aggressiveness, in which the anger we have attempted to suppress leaks out indirectly; a pattern of perseveration, in which we find ourselves drawn to endlessly revisit or talk about the situations that have produced the anger; a pattern of withdrawal, in which the hyperarousal of anger so frightens or disturbs us that we isolate ourselves in an attempt to avoid it; a pattern of displacement, in which our fear of our own anger leads us to develop phobias, allergies, physical symptoms or other diversionary responses in its place—and many others.

If you ask your guides for help in dispassionately exploring your own response to perceived threats or actual violations, you will easily be able to map out your own most common dance or dances of anger. In and of itself, this mapping can be very helpful in diffusing the emotional charge most of us feel around the topic of anger. When we examine the vast number of ways human beings have twisted and tangled ourselves and each other into painful, angry knots, we can start to take our own relationship to anger less personally.

Beyond that, the work of harmoniously realigning our relationship to anger is the same work described throughout this book. Assuming full responsibility for our own anger, no matter what others may have done or failed to do, is the stance that enables us to begin this process. Soon we will become able to see that beneath each step in our own personal anger dances, some healing, clearing or energetic correction is needed—perhaps one or many soul retrievals, releasing of imprints, straightening-out of our non-physical posture, or the removal of energetic interference. Thich Naht Hanh advises, "When you are angry, and you suffer, please go back and inspect very deeply the content, the nature of your perceptions. If you are capable of removing the wrong perception, peace and happiness will be restored in you, and you will be able to love the other person again."

The following notes describe a sequence of four shamanic journeys I took a number of years ago, which helped me dismantle the anger I felt in a specific circumstance, and begin the very necessary healing process which lay beneath it. More often I do only one or two journeys at a time, but as you'll see, in this case, all four were necessary. The entire process of taking the four journeys and writing them down took less than an hour in ordinary-reality time.

Journey #1: I felt angry at a human mentor who I believed was using me. My journey question was, What do I need to understand or heal in relation to that anger?

I found myself having to squeeze through a very thin tunnel, and also being strained through a sieve, on my way to the upper world. When I finally got there, I asked my guide what to do with the anger. He said, What anger? I explained. He said it made no more sense to be angry at my mentor than at myself, and made no more sense to be angry at myself than to have any other reaction. Yes, people will "take advantage" if you walk around in the world with the kind of weak spot I've had, but it's like water rushing through a wall that is weak, or has a hole in it. Does it make sense to be angry at the water? Does it make sense to be angry at the wall? Or does it just make sense to see what has occurred, and fix the hole and/or make the wall stronger?

Although I could see the truth of what my guide was saying, I was kind of pissed-off by not being able to hold anyone else responsible, even a little bit. I felt resistance and kept getting distracted. Finally, by following the distraction, I could see that the "wall" is really more like vapor in me, no clear boundary at all. I got that it's because I've given so much of myself away to practically everyone. So I focused on getting more of myself back from all the different sources—family members, ex-lovers, friends. I could feel myself getting stronger, yet I still kept feeling resistance to the process.

Journey #2—What's all this resistance about, and what needs to happen with it?

I found myself in a cave in the lower world, surrounded by a circle of guides who were praying for me. I felt uncomfortable and thought, Why are they praying for me? Then I realized that my difficulty accepting their attention was part of the problem (i.e. difficulty in receiving,) so I relaxed and let them pray for me. After that, it seemed I needed to have layers of skin peeled off of me by a giant carrot-scraper-type apparatus. As they got peeled off, blue and lavender light got sent in. Then I was taken to a room where I could convalesce. There was a skylight in the room, and again, the bluish and lavender light was streaming in. In the physical world, I started drumming harder, and directly over my body. It felt like something related to the resistance needed to leave me, so that I could really embrace taking full responsibility for myself.

Journey #3—Check in with the anger, resistance and self-responsibility now.

I went back to the room where part of me was convalescing. She now seemed like a girl of about twelve. She was kind of feverish and writhing around in the bed, not doing too well. I sat down on the side of the bed and just kept her company. At one point I called my guide in to ask if there was anything else that needed to be happening, but I got the message that there wasn't. So I just sat there with her. Images came of different ways she/I had betrayed her/myself—all the times I had sex I didn't want to have, or gave or lent people things or money which I never got back. I felt no judgment toward her or myself, just held these images. Eventually she calmed down; I lay down beside her in the bed and we just looked up at the skylight together. Then we merged—she came into my body—and then it was just me lying there and looking up at the skylight. Then I brought in images of the ways I've been with my mentor—how hard I was trying to cater to her, how eager and in a way desperate I was. I was able to look at that without judgment, as well. That way of being was so deeply imprinted in me, and with her I justified it to myself by saying it was because she was such a force of good in the world, etc., so didn't it make sense to just turn myself over to her needs and wishes and pleasures? But of course it didn't—I could see that now, and stop blaming her for the compulsive way I'd been with her, and also stop blaming her for accepting it. Sure, she was the water that flowed in through the hole in my wall (or the vapors where a wall should have been), and if she were completely healed, she would not have done that. But she isn't, and I'm not, and there's no point in blaming either one of us—the point is just to make a wall, not a fortress, but a sea-wall, where there needs to be one.

Journey #4–Check in on the status of all of these issues now—wholeness, boundaries, giving, and my relationship to my mentor.

I went to the convalescent room to check on myself there, but my guide came and playfully dragged me out to the edge of the cliff, where we took turns diving and jumping off the cliff, landing on the bottom, then going back up to dive or jump again. Then at some point we were jumping into a deep pool of water instead, and the message seemed to be that all the different kinds of shattering—for instance, the shattering of the water, when we hit it—were necessary. Then I was swimming in the water like an eel and realizing that "boundaries" could operate just the way my skin does in the water. It's not that the water is bad or that I need to "protect myself" from it, it's just that it's not appropriate for it to come inside me, because I have my own chemical makeup which is different from the chemical composition of the water. The boundary of the skin is easy and natural. I can learn to emulate that with my emotional and energetic boundaries.

This series of journeys illustrates many of the healing and teaching methods commonly found in shamanic journeys. In Journey #1, my guide used a metaphor—the image of a wall with a hole in it—to help me see my situation more impersonally, release anger at my mentor and at myself, and move beyond the impulse to blame either one of us. Yet although I was able to begin that process in this journey, my resistance showed that more energetic work was needed.

In Journey #2, my guides initiated several kinds of healing. The first came about as my guides prayed for me, and as I made the internal shift needed in order to receive the healing energy of their prayers. The second healing, in which I was peeled by the giant carrot scraper, is an example of a shamanic healing technique known as dismemberment. Although dismemberment can sometimes appear brutal—this was a relatively mild dismemberment, but even in this one, layers of skin were removed from me—guides use it as part of a compassionate process of energetic cleansing and reconfiguration. My sense is that the energy I called "resistance" was buried beneath my skin, so the "peeling" was necessary in order for me to release it.

The third form of healing in Journey #2 involved the use of blue and lavender light. Each color carries its own healing frequency, and evidently these were the frequencies I needed at this time. My sense is that this light was used both to purify my energy, and then to help me recover from the dismemberment. I believe that my urge to drum over my body in physical reality also came as a directive from my guides; the vibrations of the drum further cleansed me, offering a fourth kind of healing and completing the process of releasing the "resistance" energy.

In Journey #3, it became clear that in addition to the clearing and dis-memberment I had experienced in Journey #2, a soul retrieval was taking place. The journey suggests that I experienced some significant soul loss at around age twelve which led to an inability to set or maintain healthy boundaries. Although it was painful to see the ways that that soul loss had led me to betray myself, I was able to maintain compassion both for my younger self and my present-day self, which enabled the lost soul part (the "girl") and I to reunite and become one again. With that part of my soul restored, I was even more able to accept what had occurred with my mentor, and release both her and myself from anger or blame.

Journey #4 suggests that since the necessary healing for this cycle had been completed, it was now time to play! Guides generally have great senses of humor, and journeys often offer teachings in playful forms. In this case, my guide used the experience of jumping and diving into a pool of water to provide me with more understanding about the nature of damage ("shattering,") and the nature of healthy boundaries.

I encourage you to do your own series of journeys to clarify and heal your relationship to anger. You may also want to develop your own prayers and statements of intention on this theme. Here is one example.

Prayer for Healing Anger

Guides, universal sources of deep love and wisdom, please help me to recognize and embrace the valuable role anger plays in my life, while also helping me to work skillfully with that anger so as not to harm others or myself.

Please help me heed the messages of my anger and respond swiftly, appropriately and effectively to protect myself and my boundaries when necessary, while also allowing my anger to dissipate completely as soon as the need for it has passed.

I affirm that I have the right and the responsibility to protect the borders of my apparently separate self, and I thank my anger for helping me do so. I also affirm my connection to life and to all of the benevolent and compassionate forces in existence, and declare my intention and willingness to feel and to trust that connection more fully, so that the painful sense of separation at the root of much of my anger may dissolve and heal.

Please help me to love and honor all of the parts of myself, including my anger, while also helping me to heal and make amends for any damage my anger may have caused, both internal and external. I acknowledge that I may also have caused damage to myself and to others by withholding or suppressing my anger, and I ask for help in allowing myself to embody that anger as fully as I need to, in order to harmoniously release it when the time is right.

I decide, choose, intend and desire to release all blame, whether of myself or of others. Please help me move through the world with ever-increasing clarity, integrity and grace, so that I may more fully love and be loved in ways that both respect and transcend the boundaries of my separate self.

41

The Uses of Doubt

The more we actually progress in our practice, the more things become unsure, evasive and difficult to implement; the more they become slippery and even unstable... It is actually a progress and not a failure, it is a gift and not a problem—a sign and indicator for being on the right way and path.

— Yoav

Human beings contain a multitude of states of faith and states of doubt, knowing and not-knowing, all at the very same time. This is so because, as we've previously discussed, there are so many different layers and levels of what we consider to be "us." Our larger selves dwell in a place where doubt does not exist—where doubt is not even possible, so complete is the sense of knowing and of being held. Yet other parts of us are trapped in states of confusion and desolation, where faith and knowing are entirely inaccessible. Other parts of ourselves access the entire spectrum that exists between these two poles. And all of this is real; all of it is "us." We are like pianos with keys spanning the full range, from the very highest to the very lowest notes. The lower notes on the piano are not "worse," nor even "less evolved;" they are simply sounded by strings of a different length. Each key produces the only sound it can make, based on its distance from or proximity to the center—that is, the higher self.

It can be disconcerting to experience such extremes within ourselves—to ricochet, for instance, between states of calm assuredness and abject terror, particularly when both emotions exist in response to the same external or internal circumstance. Yet it is very human.

Of course, as the doubt-filled parts of ourselves have more contact with the larger self, they evolve and heal—and when that happens, our entire keyboard moves upward. We have access to many more "high" keys, and their highs grow progressively higher. Even our lowest keys do not go as low as they used to, although they never disappear entirely. It is not possible to eliminate *all* doubt or fear on our plane, because it is impossible for human beings to hold a completely accurate perception of the nature of reality. Dimensionally, it simply cannot occur. Our minds, our senses, our apparatuses of perception cannot expand that far. Trying to see the entire tapestry with our human eyes is something like a mouse trying to open its jaws wide enough to eat an alligator. The mouse can see the alligator; it can even scamper the length of the alligator's body and get to know it piece by piece, taking tiny nibbles here and there—but it cannot possibly eat the entire beast in one bite.

So, since an entirely accurate and comprehensive perception of the universe is not available to us as human beings, some degree of doubt or confusion must always remain within us. It does no good to fight that; of course, as we have seen, it does no good to fight *anything*. Yet doubt is not actually a single phenomenon; there are many kinds, layers and levels of doubt—and some specific doubts that arise do point to aspects of our being that are in need of healing and clarification. For instance, if you feel persistent doubt regarding the pursuit of a path that other aspects of your being deeply *know* to be correct, that doubt bears further attention. On the other hand, doubt sometimes comes as a messenger regarding something that another part of your being is attempting to avoid seeing—something which must, in fact, be seen. In that case, the healing movement involves allow the message carried by the doubt to be received more fully within you, so that you can consciously explore the issues involved.

Doubt serves as a useful challenge to the part of each of us that wants to insist that things be black or white, completely one way or completely another. Doubt interrupts that thinking by upholding an opposing point of view: when we think something is *this,* doubt asserts that it may be *that,* or vice versa. However, doubt doesn't actually help us transcend the binary framework; it only assists us in moving more freely between its poles. Since in actuality all things are *simultaneously* this and that, and also *neither* this nor that—"both and neither," as the Buddhists say—doubt ultimately falls short as a tool. The doubting parts of us cannot help us conceive the full complexity of life; only our larger selves can do that, and they are completely free of doubt. In truth, nothing is truly "right" or "wrong," "bad" or "good;" we ourselves, the perceivers of things, are also neither bad nor good. Everything in our loves is an amalgam of many twisted and braided currents of darkness and light.

Take, for example, a case in which we have been cultivating a generous or positive view of a particular person or endeavor. When doubt arises, it can swing us back toward a more negative perception of that person or thing. Most likely, all of the evidence our doubt can mount for that negative case is true. Yet it is likely that the evidence with which we had been assembling the positive case is also true. Furthermore, there are many additional true perceptions that we have not yet had, and may never have. It is difficult for us to stand in the fullness of what *is;* we tend to think we need to narrow, simplify and judge reality in order to reach a conclusion, form a stance and interpretation, make a decision, and so on. But all of these assumptions rely on our limited human perceptions as the determinants of our actions, and on our human will as both motor and rudder.

This is not "wrong," but there are alternative approaches which can bring us into closer relationship with the true, multidimensional nature of reality. Instead of making judgments and decisions and thereby fixing our gaze on a particular outcome on the horizon, we can cultivate the ability to allow all of the different factors, perspectives, perceptions, and levels of being to exist simultaneously (as, in fact, they actually do—regardless of whether or not we "allow" them to!) From this greater vantage point, we can see that we do not and cannot know what is "right" or "best"—in fact, those concepts actually cease to hold meaning at all. Once we realize this, doubt ceases to hold a positive function for us, and becomes instead a state to be healed—or to be tenderly accepted, just as we accept our other human limitations.

42

The Dilemma of Power

Power is of two kinds. One is obtained by the fear of punishment and the other by acts of love. Power based on love is a thousand times more effective and permanent than power derived from fear of punishment.

— Mahatma Gandhi

As a species, human beings have often used our personal power to do great harm to one another, to animals, and to the earth itself. A review of human history might lead us to conclude that being human—or using human power—is the problem. Unfortunately, this incorrect conclusion can lead us to starve ourselves of our rightful life energy, thereby stunting our ability to manifest and create in the world.

What *is* power, anyway? Power is actually just another name for life energy. Plants use their power when they push themselves up through soil, or through cracks in concrete, in order to grow. And we, too, must use our power if we are to become fully ourselves and fulfill our inner design.

Power is inherent to, and the birthright of, all living things. Even those things which human beings do not generally recognize as living have their own power. Fire, wind, water, sun—the power of these forces arises directly from their *beingness,* their nature. Power, in other words, is the mechanism by which things express their nature fully into the world. As such, it is clearly neither "good" nor "bad," and it certainly cannot be eradicated; without power, nothing could exist.

The problem, as seen from the human level, arises when one thing's active nature leads it to interfere with another's. We could take the exuberant life force of the morning glory plant as an example. The nature of the morning glory's power, the full expression of its morning glory-ness, leads it to twine around and grow over whatever it encounters—whether it's a fence that might eventually be pried apart by the morning glory's strong tendrils, or a rosebush that will no longer receive the sun it needs once the morning glory has twined on top of it. The morning glory does not care about these things; however, it does not *not* care, either. Neither caring nor not-caring, it simply expresses its beingness by growing as vibrantly as it can, wherever it can.

Because human beings have individuated consciousness, which leads us to perceive ourselves as separate from all other beings and things, our relationship to our own power is appropriately more complex. A morning glory's consciousness does not enable it to consider the other life forms it might harm by expressing its beingness. Our consciousness, however, does enable such considerations; in fact, it requires them—if we are to live in accordance with our true nature, the nature within which we know ourselves connected to all that is.

In the final analysis, life itself doesn't care how the balance of power works out—whether the yard ends up being filled with morning glories, roses, roses choked out by morning glories, or even concrete. Life understands that power "lost" from one place or form is always "gained" by another; since all forms are life, life cannot possibly prefer one over another. When trees grow tall, they are life, exercising their power. When fire comes and burns trees to the ground, it, too, is life, and it, too, is exercising its power. When men come and cut the trees down, they, too, are life. When tsunamis wash over the land and sweep men away, they are life too. Life is endlessly interfering with itself, recycling itself, and shifting its own balances and forms, all without judgment, blame, recrimination, "villains" or "victims." Regardless of what happens on the physical plane, all phenomena are harmonious when viewed from the point of view of the larger tapestry.

And yet, from the human level, a given phenomenon can appear grossly inharmonious or even tragic in its particulars—for instance, when one person assaults or abuses another. A tall tree may prevent a smaller tree from growing and bear no moral responsibility in the matter; it is simply being itself, allowing life to move through it. But when an adult harms or kills a child, there *is* moral responsibility involved. The adult perceives herself as separate; she has choices about how to use her power, in ways that a tree or morning glory does not. And so when she uses it to harm what she perceives as "another" being, she is betraying her responsibility to life. (In fact, although she may not realize it, she is also betraying her responsibility to herself. Because we perceive ourselves as separate, we are able to choose to act in ways that cause harm to others; however, because we are truly *not* separate from others, or from the earth, causing harm to "them" also inevitably harms us.)

So how can a human being responsibly hold and express his power? This is a question of great importance to our species at this point in time. For that reason, the work each of us does with this issue is not ours alone; it is of direct benefit to the entire collective.

Given the complexity of this issue, it is natural that some of us long to back away from the whole arena. Yet backing away from our power also separates us from our nature, our energized life force. This damages us and negates the current of life; it also represents an evasion of our responsibility, the responsibility with which we have been blessed. Moreover, our own disowned power will continually attempt to return to us from the "outside," usually in the form of externalized bullies and tyrants who have no compunction about taking, using, exerting, or even "stealing" our power. If we don't want it, someone else will! In short, when we suppress or constrict our own power, we harm ourselves, we shirk our sacred duty, and we also render ourselves inappropriately vulnerable to others.

If we as conscientious human beings wish to embrace and express our own power in a manner harmonious both with the forces and flow of the universe, and with our own role and nature, we must begin by clearing away the cobwebs, prejudices and myths which have grown up around the subject of power within our beings—so that we can approach this topic with open eyes and with full intelligence, with clarity of purpose, intention, and trust in the support of the benevolent universe. Yes, it is an enormous responsibility to be powerful, but in essence it is no different from the responsibility inherent in simply being alive: that is, the work of fulfilling our own inner design. If we truly wish to serve life, we must face and clear the impurities and distortions within ourselves, both so that we can grow stronger, and so that we can remain in alignment with that increasing strength.

In this process of "self-facing," as the Pathwork calls it, we may discover that we are afraid of exploiting or damaging someone or something because of the aspects of ourselves that remain unhealed, and thus distort us. On the human level, this is a valid and appropriate fear, but it is *not* a valid reason to shrink back from full development of our power. Rather, it is a reason to actively continue developing our power, while also working to resolve and heal what is unhealed within us at the same time. Developing our power will aid and motivate us in our healing process, and as we heal more, we will access even greater power.

In relation to power, as in all other aspects of our lives, what matters most is not *what* we do, but the energy and intention we bring to the effort. Given the enormity of the tapestry we are part of, in one sense it might seem hardly to matter how we might damage ourselves by suppressing our power, or how we might damage others by expressing it. And yet because of the energetic principles by which reality operates, our smallest efforts matter far more than we can understand.

The morning glory exists without a differentiated ego, without individual desire or will or intention—other than the intention shared by all living things: to live, to grow, to express its beingness as fully as possible. In this, there is nothing "wrong;" there cannot possibly be anything wrong. On the largest level of the tapestry, the level Buddhism calls "ultimate reality," wrong does not exist. No one would accuse a morning glory of being morally corrupt for harming the plants it had twined itself around, or try a cat for murder because it had eaten a mouse. Because the morning glory and cat are simply being true to their own natures, what they do cannot be seen as "wrong." Throughout nature, life forms kill other life forms, or interfere with their full expression and growth—and where there is no separate consciousness involved, concepts like "abuse," "genocide," and "tragedy" do not exist. From that perspective, the actions of a human being like Hitler are not really different than the actions of a rapacious morning glory vine, or a powerful tsunami. Yet on the level of human consciousness, where a vast experiment in the illusion of separation is being played out, it is necessary and appropriate to apply an entirely different set of frameworks.

It is the differentiation of the human ego, the human structure of consciousness, that creates the possibility of intention—including the intention to align ourselves with the larger flow of life, or to separate ourselves from it. If humans, like morning glories, did not perceive ourselves as separate, there would be no "wrong" in one human killing another. Yet without the concept of the separate self, there would also be no possibility of any person harboring a desire to kill another.

Since humans are not truly separate from the rest of creation, on one level it does not matter what damage we may appear to cause in expressing our humanness. Yet, since humans *believe ourselves* to be separate from the rest of creation and from each other, we are capable of harboring an *intent* to cause damage in a way that no other entity can. It is this *intent* that is the problem—and therefore, it is with this intention that we must, as conscientious human beings, do our work.

If humans truly came to understand that we are not separate from creation or from other humans, there would be none of the distorted suppression of power that currently exists, because to suppress "oneself" would be clearly understood as no better than, and in fact, no different from, suppressing "another." At the same time, there would be none of the distorted expression of power that currently exists—because to suppress "another" would be understood to be no more desirable than, and in fact no different from, suppressing "oneself." Yet since most human beings do not deeply hold this understanding—since our consciousness predisposes us to the illusion of separateness—how can we ever reach a responsible relationship to our power?

The answer, unsurprisingly, is love—though what is required is a deeper, broader, wider, more enveloping love than any we have yet known.

Precisely because humans live with the illusion of separateness, we are capable of feeling love for one another *as* "other." Although this capacity for love is often misunderstood, misused and distorted, it alone offers humans the possibility of experiencing harmony. Love by its nature transcends the state of duality and separation, precisely because it does not discriminate. It offers itself equally and in abundance to the morning glory and the rose, the tall tree and the small, the fire and the wood-cutter, the cat and the mouse—and yes, to every human being, too. All things and beings are held equally within love's embrace; none are preferred or rejected.

When human beings try to emulate this phenomenon, we almost invariably distort it by loving "ourselves" in a way that removes love from others, or by loving "others" in a way that strips love from the self. Most commonly we alternate between these two patterns, with myriad intricate variations on the theme. In the thousands of years since Christ first instructed us to love our neighbors as ourselves, we have generally managed either to love our neighbors *instead of* ourselves, or vice versa, but not to hold ourselves *and* all others within the same great, abiding and generous flow.

Loving ourselves and others fully would dissolve the illusion that loving the self requires harm to others, *or* that loving others necessitates harm to the self. Once this illusion is dissolved, there is no real meaning left to the concept of the "separate" self. In this case the self would remain separate on the level of *form*, but in *essence* be understood as undifferentiated, simply one of the billions of individual manifestations emerging from the great pool of life. With this understanding, the possibility of *desiring* to cause harm to another or to the self would be eliminated, and with that shift, the game of separation would end.

Without the illusion of separateness, there is no need for a concept like "integrity." Within the framework of the human, separate self, the development of integrity and responsibility is our contribution to make. Yet the truest integrity or wholeness comes from or with that kind of non-discriminating love which is only to be found beyond the veil of separation. So humans who wish to play out their humanness in as conscious a manner as possible must in essence exist both within, and beyond, our notion of separation. When we achieve too much awareness of unity, we leave humanness behind; when we have too little awareness of unity, we cannot access the transformative potential inherent in the structure of our consciousness.

All of this may seem to make theoretical sense—yet on the level of form, cats *do* kill mice, tall trees *do* block the growth of small ones, and the morning glory *does* harm the other plants it twines itself on. So how is it possible within the "separate state"—or even beyond it—for one human not to harm another?

It is possible only when we remember that on the level of ultimate reality, harm does not exist. There is merely a constant flux of shifting forms and expressions, like that in a kaleidoscope. No pattern truly destroys another; each new pattern simply replaces the last, and then in its own turn is replaced. Yet on the level of physical form—which is also the level of human consciousness—harm not only exists, but is inevitable. There is no way for humans to live, breathe, eat, drink and eliminate on this planet, without causing harm. This seemingly doomed configuration is necessary for the transformation of our consciousness. We must believe that harm is possible, so that we may be motivated to avoid causing harm; therefore, it is the apparent reality of the plane on which we live. We must strive to untangle the distortions that lead us to *wish* to cause harm to ourselves or to another—regardless of the fact that on the human level such harm is often unavoidable, and on the larger level, such harm does not even exist.

Our challenge, then, is to heal the wounds and confusions that distort our relationship to power, to fully embrace our power—and then to use that power in the service of love, a love that fully encompasses both "ourselves," and all other beings.

Some years ago, when I found myself internally blocked in relation to moving ahead as a shamanic healer and teacher, I did a series of shamanic journeys to explore my obstacles to standing in my power. Here are the notes from those journeys.

Journey #1: What are my obstacles to standing in my power?

My guide told me that I was resisting my power, and that I needed to know why. He pointed to two glowing balls on either side of my solar plexus [the site of the third chakra, generally considered to be the "power chakra."]. I could see that these balls were like radioactive isotopes, releasing a slow poison. The message contained in the left ball was, "No one else can be trusted, I can only trust myself to hold the power," and the message of the ball on the right was, "I can't be trusted to hold the power, so someone else will have to do it." Obviously these two messages conflicted with each other, causing a logjam in which I neither fully inhabited my own power, nor fully turned power over to anyone else.

When I asked what to do, my guide drained the ball on the left, the one that said "No one else can be trusted." I understood that that ball was ready to be drained because I had recently been doing a lot of internal work on my mistrust of others. However, I still needed to work more with the other ball, the one holding my mistrust of myself.

My guide showed me that much of that mistrust came from my relationship with my father. Some of it was because of ways in which that relationship had led me to turn against myself; for instance, I had learned to cope with my father's sexual violations by experiencing his feelings as if they were my own. Of course, since this was an act of self-betrayal, when I was doing this I truly wasn't worthy of my own trust.

275

I also saw that I had imported my father's template, or constellation of imprints, around power. My guide showed me that my father hadn't really wanted to hold his own power, either, but also hadn't wanted anyone else to hold it for him. He didn't trust other "authorities," yet didn't truly feel large enough to be his own authority; that was part of why he began using drugs, in order to make himself feel larger. Yet because he also felt regret, shame, confusion and embarassment about using drugs, his drug use rendered him even more unsuitable for holding power, and his shame rendered him even less able to hold it well, even as the drugs also gave him the illusion of being more powerful. In this way, as is typical with addictive patterns, my father's drug addiction worsened the internal split he had attempted to medicate.

As I saw all of this and began disentangling the strands of belief that made up the "ball" on the right, I realized that they contained several very different kinds of mistrust of my own power:

- I can't be trusted because my father has turned me against myself so I can serve him.

- I can't be trusted because my father doesn't trust himself, and then actually does things that make him even less trustworthy in an effort to medicate his feeling of untrustworthiness.

- I can't be trusted because I have energetically imported my father's beliefs about himself, and held them as beliefs about myself.

Journey #2: *My guide instructed me to give all the beliefs that belonged to my father back to him. As I did so, my ball of self-mistrust shrank until it was just a tight hard knot. When I traveled inside that knot, I found that it was made of grief—grief that I had felt so desperate for my father's love that I had turned against myself in order to get it. There was also some anger at myself for having done that. The image of a close friend came to mind, and I realized it was because she, too, had turned against herself in this way—yet I noticed that when I think of her, I feel only tenderness and compassion for her little-girl self. I recognized that feeling this for her could help me learn how to feel it for myself.*

Journey #3: *The next day, I did another journey to check in on the status of the balls and my relationship to my power. This time I found myself in the ocean, swimming toward an island, where I found another version of myself lying on the beach. I merged with that part of myself, and became larger and stronger than my body is in physical reality. Then I walked all around the island naked,*

exploring its circumference. I felt totally unashamed of my body and my naked-
ness, and the whole island felt as if it was mine. I climbed a tree and sat in it; I
found food to eat, and ate it. No one else was around. Then I found a little hut
which was comfortably furnished; it seemed to be mine. I went inside, feeling
completely trusting of myself.

Obviously, this series of journeys is only part of the process of healing my relationship to my own power. That, like most acts of healing, will take a lifetime, or perhaps many more. But the journey did help me understand one source of my fear of power, and also helped me glimpse the joy and possibility available to me—and, by extension, to all of us—as we shift our distorted imprints and embrace our strength.

Ways to Excavate, Heal and Clear Your Relationship To Power

1. Ask your guides for help in a shamanic journey. You may find yourself experiencing one or more soul retrievals, or a process of energetic clearing.

2. Use the exercise on p. 243, "Identifying and Clearing Distortions," with the following four statements:

   - Why I desire to be powerful

   - Why I fear being powerful

   - Why I desire to be powerless

   - Why I fear being powerless

3. Develop prayers and statements of intention in relation to your power. For instance, you might pray:

   Please help me heal my fear of my own power. Please help me release any
   and all distortions, from all sources, that would make my use of power unsafe
   or inharmonious for me or for others. I choose, decide, desire and intend to wel-
   come and honor my own power, on my own behalf and on behalf of life. I affirm
   that I wish and choose to use my power with full love, consciousness and in-
   tegrity, and I ask for the help of my guides in doing so. Please help me retrieve
   any parts of my own soul that are necessary for the full and harmonious use of

my power, and the release of fear, confusion and distorted beliefs related to my power. Please help me clear my energy field of all energies not my own, so that I may more fully know, feel, experience and trust my power as mine. I affirm my desire to live my life in power and integrity, and I ask for help from all of the larger compassionate forces in doing so.

43
Limits and Encumbrances

Choose your love. Love your choice.

- Thomas S. Monson

Life on the physical earth, in physical bodies, is an experience of working within limits. The part of us that remembers or senses another way of being—the vast freedom available to us beyond form—may struggle against this reality of the earth plane. Yet if we use our (limited!) energy to fight and resist the existence of limits, we miss out on the opportunity to engage creatively with those limits, and with the richness of experience they can produce.

The well-known architect Frank Lloyd Wright famously asserted, "Limits are an architect's best friend." He explained that if he gave an architect an unlimited budget and told her to build the most beautiful house in the world, it would be an impossible task. Yet if he gave the same architect a predetermined site and a set budget and asked her to build the most beautiful house possible *within those constraints,* she would be able to do so. Limits work the same way in our lives. We are given our "sites" and our "budgets"— our histories, our bodies, our temperaments, our circumstances—and with them have the opportunity to create the lives that will be most beautiful to us, the lives that will best fulfill our inner design.

When we resist limits, we are resisting physical life itself. Each physical thing or being must have limits; that is what creates its reality as a separate thing. For instance, a cup has contours, limits, to define what is cup and not-cup. If it had no limits, it could not be a cup—it would have to be the entire world. And on the physical plane this would be very problematic, since we cannot lift the entire world to our mouths to drink our tea!

Although we sometimes experience limits as curses rather than blessings, we are actually as gifted by what we cannot have and do as by what we can. These two streams—the inner stream of "can," of capability, and the outer stream or defining contour of "cannot," of non-capability, together create the terrain in which we live.

Of course, it is possible for us to change the specific contours of certain limits. If we run for twenty minutes every day, we will soon find ourselves able to run further within the same time frame. But this broadening of terrain occurs most effectively when we cultivate a stretchy, dynamic relationship with limits, a kind of dance which simultaneously respects limits as they are *and* explores conditions under which they may expand. Otherwise, we will either cause harm to ourselves by running too far and too fast, or we will be unnecessarily hampered by current limits and rob ourselves of the chance to experience their possible expansion.

Many human beings have confused limitlessness with freedom. We may hold an image of "casting off the chains" of limits, or of limiting beliefs. It *is* true that many people are limited by beliefs about themselves or the world which are inaccurate, and therefore unnecessarily or distortedly limiting—so it is harmonious to cultivate an exacting degree of discernment in relation to all of the limits we perceive in our inner and outer lives. With that discernment, we can recognize and embrace those limits which give our physical lives shape and contour, while also unmasking and dissolving the false limits that distort and hobble us.

Like limits, encumbrances—things that "weight us down," physically, emotionally and energetically—are a necessary and inevitable feature of life on the earth plane. Some of us gravitate toward encumbrance, or certain types of encumbrance; for instance, we may take pleasure in owning many possessions, or having many close relationships. Others tend to resist encumbrance, taking pleasure in emotional and/or material simplicity. Neither state is "better;" encumbrance and unencumbrance are like weight and weightlessness, each necessary and each freeing in its own way, and each of us is bound to prefer and create different configurations—all of which is appropriate in the process of fulfilling our inner design.

Each of us yearns to feel connected to ourselves, and to life. Some of us locate the access to that feeling in our relationships with other people, or even with material objects; others locate that access more individually and non-physically. For instance, some people thrive on a great deal of contact with friends and extended families; they may own houses that continually need work, actively enjoy doing favors for others, do a lot of volunteer work, or otherwise involve themselves closely in interdependent, cooperative communities. All of these are examples of encumbrance which can, if freely chosen and maintained in alignment with the soul, contribute to the fulfillment of one's inner design.

Other people feel more connected to life and to themselves when they exist in a relatively less encumbered state. They may thrive on solitude; they may choose to remain unmarried and/or childless; they may prefer to rent an apartment, or just a room, rather than own a house; they may actively work to keep their lives simple and their possessions few. And this, too, is a valid path to fulfillment of one's inner design.

Of course, many of us vacillate between forms of encumbrance and unencumbrance. We may choose greater or lesser encumbrance at different points in our lives, or in different aspects of our lives, and this, too, can be harmonious—as long as it is freely chosen, and brings us joy.

All of us came to the earth plane to be limited and to be encumbered. Those are the conditions of life on earth. Yet it is harmonious for us to choose our encumbrances carefully and consciously. We make our inner work far more difficult when we choose encumbrances that do not truly suit us, or take on encumbrances without fully acknowledging that we have chosen them. Once we have chosen encumbrances, it is most conducive to joy if we can either 1) Embrace the ways these encumbrances weight us, the gravity they exert in our lives, or 2) Unchoose them. Choosing them and then resisting and resenting them is also an option, of course, but it is far less likely to bring us joy, and is therefore less harmonious.

All relationships and circumstances do create a certain amount of energetic encumbrance, yet that need not interfere with our sense of connection to our own depths. If we find that our connection to ourselves feels impeded by our encumbrances, we may have chosen ill-fitting encumbrances, or we may have outgrown them. It's also possible that we are misunderstanding the nature of the encumbrance. For instance, some of us feel unnecessarily and inappropriately weighted-down by our encumbrances because we internally take on responsibilities that are not ours, and, often, are not even possible—for instance, when someone thinks his role is to "make things okay" for everyone else, or to maintain a house full of children and pets in spotless condition.

Our relationship to specific encumbrances is highly individual. One person with a houseful of children and pets may thrive on the lively chaos; another might feel continually drained and overwhelmed. One person might relish a great deal of solitude, while another would feel desperately isolated under the same circumstances. If our relationships or other encumbrances feel burdensome, we would do well to ask ourselves: *Is this an encumbrance that brings me joy? If so, how can I accept its terms and release my resistance to it? And if not, how can I harmoniously shift my relationship to it, or release it?* Similarly, if our lack of encumbrance leaves us feeling empty and fulfilled, we can ask: *Is this sense of emptiness emerging from a place in my being that needs healing? If so, how can I do that healing? And if it is bringing me a genuine message to change my life in ways that further encumber me, then how can I harmoniously create those encumbrances?*

Recently, my friend Jasmine had her first child. It has been beautiful to witness her joy at taking on this "encumbrance," and to see how consciously and fully she has given herself to every aspect of motherhood. From the outside, it might appear that Jasmine's world has shrunk; she has gone from being a busy, active business owner and entrepreneur who salsa-danced or rock-climbed several times a week, to being a single mother in a small basement apartment, spending 24 hours a day caring for an infant. Yet Jasmine actively chose and is thriving on her new life; in fact, she extended her original four-month leave from work to six months instead, buying herself more time with her child. What might appear narrowing to some has clearly been deepening for Jasmine.

I, on the other hand, feel grateful every day not to have had children. It brings me joy to have vast spaces of time to devote to inner work, writing and other forms of creativity. When I'm not working, I choose to spend the majority of my time alone—yet I feel very much in contact with my non-physical teachers and with the energies of the natural world, which are harder for me to sense while in the presence of most other human beings. When I'm working, I spend hours in astonishingly intimate contact with people, hearing many unimaginably painful stories, witnessing the after-effects of trauma and damage, and also witnessing the tremendous light available to help people heal. These sessions often move me to tears; it feels to me as if they bring me into direct contact with both the difficulty and the joy of being human.

As I contemplate the very different lives that Jasmine and I have chosen, I see clearly why joy is our best navigational aid. Many of my clients wrestle with the question of whether or not to have children; recently, one woman told me that while she doesn't actually feel a desire *to have a child, she is afraid that if she doesn't have children, she will be "missing out on the richest experience life can offer." As I see it, having children is* not *the richest experience life can offer—and, of course, neither is remaining childless. Both paths—all paths—offer potential riches. As always, it is our task to determine which of those riches call most strongly to us.*

Of course, there are also limits and encumbrances that we do not consciously choose—for example, physical disability. It's important to remember that our lives are co-creations; even when the universe introduces variables we would never have wished for, we always have a choice about how to respond—and our choice either further connects us to, or further disconnects us from, the larger flow of universal energy in which our lives are held. As the Roman emperor Marcus Aurelius wisely observed almost two thousand years ago, "If you are distressed by anything external, the pain is not due to the thing itself, but to your estimate of it; and this you have the power to revoke at any moment."

My friend Soraya's life has been upended by chronic illness over the past several years. When she first became sick, she was working full-time in a business she co-owned, had taken on a leadership role in her church, and was involved in many activities. Over several months' time, she came to the difficult realization that her health would no longer allow that level of activity. She exited her business partnership, resigned from her position in the church, and arranged to work only 20 hours each week—and work at a level much lower than her capabilities or her previous role. Of course, she also makes much less money.

Although many people would experience this as disaster, Soraya has found ways to thrive in her new life. She has much more time now for quiet and contemplation, and as a result her emotional and spiritual growth have greatly accelerated. Since her stress levels are greatly reduced, she has found herself much more able to do her own creative work, and has written and self-published several novels. Although there are things she misses about her old life, she fully recognizes the many gifts her new life has given her—gifts that were able to come because she chose to embrace an encumbrance she would never have wished for.

As poet and activist Audre Lorde, who lived with breast cancer for more than a decade, said simply, "There is nothing I cannot use, somehow, in my living, even if I would never have chosen it on my own."

44

Money and Abundance

Not what we have but what we enjoy, constitutes our abundance.

– Epicurus

Regardless of how much or how little material wealth we have, our relationship to money is likely to be distorted. Because money plays such an oversized role in our outer and inner landscapes, it is a powerful metaphor and magnet for our confusions and wounds. And since material resources are generally closely linked to our sense of personal power, freedom, and worth, exploring the distortions in our relationship to money is a fruitful way to uncover energetic leakages or blocks that also distort other aspects of our lives. In fact, Brad Laughlin, executive director of the spiritual organization Corelight, suggests that if we simply focus on clearing every aspect of our relationship to money, by the end of our work we will find ourselves nearly enlightened!

Money has a way of pointing us toward our internal contradictions, where we will invariably find imprints and parts of ourselves in need of attention. Few readers of this book would consciously equate someone's financial status with his or her human worth or value—and it's obvious that such an equation would make no sense to our larger selves, since no person could possibly have any more or less worth than any other. Yet even when we consciously reject the equation between money and worth, we remain subject to its influence on subtle levels, and often this creates discord between different parts of the self—for instance, when one part of the self envies wealthy people and longs for more material privilege, while another part rebels against that value system, resents wealthy people and glorifies downward mobility.

In some spiritual circles, it has become popular to focus attention on peoples' fear of money or abundance, and promote magical thinking about what could occur if we freed ourselves of such fears. It's certainly true that many of us do have resistance to receiving what we want or need, and where such fears or imprints exist, it's important to heal and release them as part of our larger process of opening to universal support. However, the implication that this kind of healing will, could or should lead to material wealth for everyone who does it, is absurd. Attachment to wealth and fear of poverty is just as much a distortion as fear of wealth and attachment to conditions of lack. A truly aligned relationship with money is free of this kind of inner pushing and pulling in either, or in any, direction.

Many spiritually-oriented people misunderstand the Law of Attraction, interpreting it to mean that as we connect to our spiritual power, we are released from limits and therefore become able to create or attract unlimited quantities of material wealth. This misinterpretation conflates two different realms of being: the non-physical realm, which *is* limitless, and the physical realm in which limits are necessary and inevitable. It also reflects confusion about the nature of spiritual power. True spiritual power comes to us through aligning ourselves with the larger synergistic flow, trusting and resting within that flow, and opening to it—not dominating or manipulating it to try to grab a larger share of goodies for ourselves. In fact, the more connected we are to our spiritual power, the less likely we are to care so much about "ourselves" in the narrow sense of that word.)

The physical universe cannot exist without limits, so the concept of "unlimited abundance" on this plane is necessarily a fairy tale and a distortion. A more appropriate understanding of abundance is the one offered by Leslie Temple-Thurston, who says simply, "Abundance is having what you need, when you need it."

On the spiritual level, all of us have access—*abundant* access!—to this kind of abundance. We *can*, in the non-physical realm, have exactly what we need, whenever we need it. Yet on the physical plane this is clearly not the case; vast numbers of people do not have the money or material privilege they need, while a very small number of people have wealth so great that it renders the concept of "need" obscene or absurd. This is no coincidence; our human economic systems have been deliberately designed—and/or manipulated—to maintain this kind of inequality. They actively require most people to have less so that others can have much more. It is simply not true, under current conditions, that everyone can have as much as they need—at least not while our sense of "need" is structured by a consciousness of separation, which is, of course, the only consciousness in which greed could possibly exist.

Therefore, it is not only our limiting beliefs and our wounds that keep people from having enough money or resources. We live within a system which actively creates and maintains unequal access to wealth. Yet it is also true that even within the constraints and biases of that external system, our beliefs and wounds do shape our experience, just as they do in all other spheres of life. How, then, are we to understand and work with the highly charged issue of money?

We can begin by remembering that even here, there is a very important locus of power within us. Although we do not singlehandedly have the power to change the larger economic system, we *do* have the power to define our relationship to that system. For instance, we have complete power over the beliefs and imprints alive within us, including those beliefs linking our material wealth with our sense of value or worth. When we bring these beliefs to conscious awareness and recognize that they are not Truth, we can dissolve them. Spiritual and social justice activist Nichola Torbett founded a group called "Recovery from the Dominant Culture," modeled on 12-step programs, as a way to help people do precisely this kind of work.

We can also retrieve the parts of our souls that may have been wounded by lack of access to money—or by inconsistent access, manipulated or distorted access, or even excessive access to money (for instance, parents who gave us expensive gifts in place of time, love and presence, or relatives who abused us and then bought our silence with money.) We can release the imprints that make us see ourselves or others as unworthy or "less than" for *any* reason, including reasons having to do with money—and also those imprints that make us see ourselves or others as "better than" for any reason, or that inflate us with false pride.

It's also useful to dive beneath the surface of the issue and work directly with the many deeper issues with which money becomes entangled. By removing our blocks to, or our misconceptions about, freedom, support, receiving, deserving, love and related topics, we clear the pathways by which what we need can reach us—not only in the form of money, but in all other forms, as well. And as always, our inner teachers can help.

Here are some questions that can help you begin that process.

 **Self-Inquiry Related to Money—and More**

Justice

How do I feel about living amid human injustice? Where there are "haves" and "have-nots," do I feel a need or obligation to be in one camp or the other—or a fear of being in one camp or the other? What is my right relationship to the financial injustice in the human world?

Freedom

How do I feel about having the freedom to do what I most want to do? Do I believe that I deserve it? Do I trust myself to use it in ways that serve my larger self?

Receiving Support

How do I feel about receiving my full complement of support from the benevolent universe? Do I believe that I deserve it? Can I be trusted with it? Do I have fears about what I might do—or fail to do—if I were fully supported? Do I believe that there would be a cost to receiving such support?—and if so, what do I believe that cost would be?

Intrinsic Worth

Do I know, with every fiber of my being, that I have intrinsic worth—that I belong in this world and am valued, accepted and cherished by this world, exactly as I am?

Safety

Am I willing to allow myself to feel safe? What does or would safety mean to me? Are there structures in my being which constrict against the possibility of relaxing into safety? Am I able to receive what comes to me without fear or hoarding, and let it go with confidence that more will come?

Abundance

How do I feel about having abundance—having all that I need, when I need it? Do I feel comfortable with that state of being? Why or why not? Would it feel safe to me to have all that I needed? What fears do I have about what might happen—within me, or outside of me—if I had abundance?

Love

Do I know, beyond a shadow of a doubt, that I am loved—by the universe, my larger self and my guides, at the very least? Am I able to fully open to and take in that love? If not, what prevents that opening? Do I believe that others love me for myself, just as I am, or do I fear "hidden agendas," costs, conditions or requirements?

Working with these questions—and doing whatever healing work is revealed to be necessary by your answers—may well be a lengthy process. But as you do so, you will clear up whatever distortions are present in your financial life, as well as open inner pathways for receiving and experiencing more safety, love and freedom.

45

Forces and Counter-Forces

Knowledge of the self is the mother of all knowledge. So it is incumbent on me to know my self, to know it completely, to know its minutiae, its characteristics, its subtleties, and its very atoms.

— Khalil Gibran

The physical plane is a realm of duality, a plane on which we experience many seeming "opposites"—rich and poor, day and night, wet and dry, hot and cold. When we can glimpse the tapestry of existence from a bit further away, it becomes clear that these "opposites" are not truly in opposition to each other at all, but are, instead, different points on a continuum, or different aspects of one larger thing. Yet on the human level, because we are given to binary perception, we often experience another pair of seeming opposites: forces and counter-forces.

If you've ever made a serious, firm decision to start going to the gym every day, and then found yourself not only staying home but also upping your junk food consumption in response, you have experienced forces and counter-forces at work. In this case, the "force" was your intention to go to the gym more often, and the "counter-force" was produced by other parts of you that hadn't agreed to that plan—hadn't, in fact, even been consulted or acknowledged.

The concept of "self-sabotage" has been bandied about so much in self-help circles that many people now believe they house an inner saboteur who is trying hard to prevent them from making positive changes. Some spiritual literature even posits that this inner enemy is the ego itself. In this interpretation, the ego or small self feels threatened by our emotional and spiritual development, and therefore tries every trick at its disposal to trip us up.

Although sometimes, as discussed in Chapter 37, the energetic equivalent of an "inner destroyer" does form within us, most often what we experience is simply the play of forces and counter-forces within us. In most cases, none of these forces is actually opposed to our well-being; they simply hold opposing notions of what would constitute such well-being. And it is an integral part of our growth and development—not a distraction, obstacle or diversion from it—to become responsive to, and able to cooperate with, these forces and counter-forces within us. Of course, as we do so, we may learn that some of them are in error, or in need of healing. In that case we can be grateful to have that need brought to our attention, so that we can work toward greater integration and wholeness.

Balance is necessary for our well-being on the earth plane, where we experience so many "opposites" and extremes. In order to achieve emotional and spiritual health, we must learn to live much of our lives between these extremes, incorporating the strengths of each. For many of us, this is difficult; we tend to prefer one side or the other of any given spectrum. Some of us might prefer it to be sunny every day, and never rain; or to be daylight all day, every day, and never get dark; or to be winter all year round, and never get warm. And yet these conditions, which each represent only one half of the duality, would not actually work well in sustaining our physical lives on earth. We *need* both the force of the sun and the counter-force of the rain, the force of the day and the counter-force of the night, the warmer weather and the cold. The interplay of forces and counter-forces regulates and supports all of the interconnected life forms with which we interact, and on which we depend.

For instance, we know that on the earth plane, we are subject to the force of gravity. If we leap from a plane or a bridge, we fall to earth. If a cup slips out of our hand, it falls to the floor. Gravity is a physical law which is always with us. And yet, despite this physical law, if we are able-bodied we can still move our limbs up and down, run, jump and dance. We do this by using the counter-force of our own life energy, in concert with the force of gravity. If gravity were the *only* force, if there were no counter-force, then we would be like stones, unable to move at all. Yet if there were no gravity, life as we know it would be completely impossible. We, and every other physical object in existence, would be floating through air rather than being steadily held here on earth. So it is both the force of gravity, *and* the counter-force of our own life energy, that make possible the lives we live.

Within each of us, too, forces and counter-forces are constantly arising. It is part of their nature, their inner design, to dance with each other, and to teach us balance by ensuring that we dance with both or all of them. Yet many of us misunderstand this principle, and believe that the dance of our inner forces and counter-forces represents "self-sabotage." If that were the case, then night would also represent the "sabotage" of daylight! And yet in truth night is daylight's complement; the two depend upon one another, and work in tandem.

So, how are we to respond when we set an intention, and then find a counter-force in us producing a behavior that appears to be in direct opposition to that intention? Rather than becoming angry and frustrated with ourselves, if we step back a few inches from the tapestry we will see that this interplay of force and counter-force is actually preventing us from creating too large a gap between the different aspects of self. In this way it can serve our wholeness, particularly if we are able to recognize what's going on and respond with understanding and respect for all of the parts of ourselves.

In order to achieve the kind of inner unification which enables us to move forward with our entire being, we need to consciously work to bring all aspects of self, all forces *and* counter-forces within us, into alignment. Because *what* we do is less important than *why* or *how* we do it, trying to leap-frog over any part of ourselves will never serve our health or wholeness. Any attempt to avoid, evade or deny those parts of ourselves that are not in agreement with planned changes will inevitably trigger a response from our counter-forces. Yet when we recognize why this is occurring and bring whatever we had been avoiding or denying into the light of our awareness, the dance of force and counter-force can serve our growth and our internal balance, and help us enter into greater harmony with life itself.

A few years ago, I became uncomfortably aware that I was spending most of my energy on the surface of my life, in ways that weren't truly satisfying me. Although I believed that I wanted to journey and connect frequently with my guides, in practice, my time seemed to go elsewhere. That was how it felt to me— my time "went elsewhere," as if of its own accord. I realized that I needed to talk to my guide about this. Here is the conversation we had.

Me: *Where have I been? Lost to myself, in some ways. But why? Why has it been so hard for me to make/take the time to daily set and reaffirm intentions, connect with you…? I really don't understand what keeps me from it. Even now, I feel distracted by the physical—thoughts of food, sex. And those things are fine; I'm glad I have this body. But there is a deeper place where I live, that I'm having such trouble getting to—that it feels like a part of me is refusing to go to.*

Guide: First of all, this struggle is not yours alone. It is valuable that you deeply experience it and engage with it so you can know it from the inside out. Within the human collective there is a strong movement toward consciousness, *and* a strong movement against it. The relative strength of each movement differs among individuals and at different times in individuals' lives, but all people experience both. The movement against or away from consciousness is what many religions have personified as "Satan," and the desire for money, sex, food, material possessions, etc., has been vilified precisely because the energy of desiring those things easily aligns with the counter-consciousness force, and they mutually strengthen one another. This is what you are experiencing. But yes, the counter-force can align with many other things, too—for instance, in your case, email.

Me: *Why does this counter-force exist? What is its purpose? I can see why it has been viewed as evil… but I assume that it isn't?*

Guide: Asking why it exists is like asking why both hot and cold exist. Your plane is a plane of dualities. If a movement toward consciousness is to exist, then a movement away from consciousness must also exist. It is not even that this has been "planned" or "designed," exactly, it is more akin to a magnetic principle. In the world of form, forces have mirror- or negative images, "opposites." That simply *is*.

Me: *Okay, then. So what I am experiencing is my own piece of this larger phenomenon, as usual. So what do I do with it?*

Guide: Call in your guides, which is to say, the forces of consciousness with which you are best acquainted, and ask for their help. It will take steady, consistent requests and intention to turn this phenomenon around within you, as you have been "feeding" the counter-force for months now. It will feel abrupt and difficult, almost like breaking an addiction, to change that. But you will, if you ask for it, have a lot of help. It would also help to remember why you *want* to turn back toward consciousness. What does it give you, or allow in you, that the counter-movement does not?

Me: *Joy. A sense of deep rightness. A sense of flow on every level of my being. What I experience in my other self is pleasurable (sometimes), but thinner, less dimensional.*

Guide: Yes. So it will help you to remember that you are not choosing consciousness because it is "better" in some moral sense—because thinking of it in that way sets up a power struggle within you, which is not the point at all. If you choose consciousness it is because it is the fullest expression, the fullest embodiment of your *self,* your being. *That* is what you are choosing, that fullness over, as you call it, the "thinness." It may even help you to phrase it that way as you realign yourself and ask for your guides' help. "I choose fullness of being." "Please help me choose and open to my own fullness of being, and joy." That may help to dismantle the rebel dynamic.

Me: *Okay—that helps, to have the larger context, and to have the construct of moral "rightness" removed. But—isn't it better for people to choose consciousness, rather than against it? Better for us as a species, better for the planet, etc.?*

Guide: The concept of "better" presupposes a particular agenda—for instance, the survival of the species, the survival of the planet in its current form, or at least not a radically reconfigured form. You must remember that from another level, this outcome is not desirable. Neither is it undesirable! It is simply one possible outcome. Yes, if many more people more consistently choose consciousness, that outcome becomes more likely. Yes, if more people choose consciousness, there will be more joy and less suffering. But from a soul level that outcome, too, is not "better," only different. An integral part of the human experience is having preferences and opinions about outcomes—trying to choose between and influence outcomes, etc. This is not "wrong," as it is an important learning tool on your level of being. But it simply does not exist on other levels. So it is a "confusion of levels" to apply that kind of thinking to the realm of consciousness—it makes no sense, since when you are *in* consciousness it can be easily experienced that there are truly no better—or worse—outcomes. It is only from outside the place of consciousness that those things can appear to be so.

It is as if you are offered a magnificent banquet, but also various trays of food that are rotten or simply not nourishing. As you already know, on a literal level, many people will choose the "junk food" over what truly nourishes. From the standpoint of public health, this is problematic. From the point of view of the manufacturers of junk food, it is desirable. And from the level of ultimate reality, it is simply interesting. How many ways there are for human beings to choose against their own best interests, and what a fascinating conundrum the human species faces at this time! How easy it is, given so much choice to play with, to choose against oneself without even realizing it. It's like that expression, "giving someone enough rope to hang themselves with." Of course many other things can be done with that quantity of rope—hanging oneself is far from the only option! Yet that is in fact what many people are doing.

Some people spend years or decades or lifetimes doing the equivalent of what you have been doing for a few months now. It is simply a way of running in place, running on a treadmill rather than covering actual ground. For instance, email, for the most part, is a treadmill. It accepts your life energy and gives you little back in return. So if you do not know, or have not decided, what to do with your life energy, it is very appealing! These kinds of treadmills (including the literal ones) are everywhere in your culture right now. Choosing your relationship to them is part of choosing a "thin" or a "full" experience of being. Nothing is wrong—on the level of ultimate reality—with any choice you make. It is simply interesting to notice whether and when and to what extent you are able to make the choices that truly delight and nourish you, versus those that do not.

46

Attachment to Outcome

It is a timeless spiritual truth: release attachment to outcomes, and deep inside yourself you'll feel good no matter what. You'll feel good because you are connected to, one with, the energy of the universe, the beauty and power of creation itself.

— Jim Dreaver

Many religions teach the principles of surrender and non-attachment. It is a central tenet of Buddhism that attachment brings suffering. Christianity advocates surrender to God's will, which might be broadly understood as a synonym for the larger tapestry of reality. And it is true that releasing our attachments, including our attachments to our own will—our own strong convictions and preferences concerning what should happen, when, and how—can profoundly open us to the love, magic and wonder available in the universe.

And yet this principle of surrender is complex, and subject to considerable misinterpretation and misapplication. That's because *the emotions and energies that we carry into our surrender* determine what it is that we surrender *to,* and also what is born of that surrender. If our self-surrender emerges from an internal posture of fear, dependence, and need—or from a sense of unworthiness, self-negation and separation—then whoever or whatever we surrender to will be a tyrant to us. This is the phenomenon we see in cults of all kinds, whether cultural, religious or military.

Harmonious surrender is an act of self-affirmation, not self-negation. Surrendering our personal attachments, including our attachments to specific outcomes, *can* bring about deep relaxation and joy—but only if it follows from the realization that we are supported at every step by forces and energies far wiser and more benevolent than our human personalities. When we know ourselves to be held within the arms of a loving universe, relinquishing our self-will allows that universe to use us for its own purposes—which are actually identical to the purposes of our souls. Yet since so few people fully know or trust in the love that surrounds us, most acts of surrender of the personal will are more like offering up the contents of our wallet to the first taker. Although it's possible that someone wise and compassionate would be first in line, it's more likely that our "money"—our life energy—will be taken and used by confused, needy, destructive human beings, in ways that cause harm both to them, and to us. Therefore, before we can entertain the idea of such surrender, we must cultivate our ability to sense, know and trust the larger compassionate forces around us and within us, and also to distinguish between those forces and their imitators or pretenders, the "wolves in sheeps' clothing" described in the Bible.

When we feel and know ourselves to be in the loving hands of the universe, we can safely remember that our individual human perspective leaves us unable to see or understand the big picture. We can also remind ourselves that everything we encounter, both on the levels of external and internal matter, is only a temporary form or manifestation. Everything—including us—is in a continuous state of flux. For this reason, it is misguided to become attached to any particular outcome. It suggests that we know more than we can possibly know, and relies on circumstances to remain as they are—or as they appear to us to be—rather than changing. Since our attachments to outcome, our sense of what is "right" or preferable, inevitably emerge from our limited perspective, they cannot possibly be accurate or complete.

There's a well-known Buddhist story which is often used to illustrate this point.

One day a farmer's horse ran away. Upon hearing the news, his neighbors came to visit. "Such bad luck," they said sympathetically. "We'll see," the farmer replied.

The next morning the horse returned, bringing with it three other wild horses. "How wonderful," the neighbors exclaimed. "We'll see," replied the old man.

The following day, his son tried to ride one of the untamed horses, was thrown, and broke his leg. The neighbors again came to offer their sympathy on his misfortune. "We'll see," answered the farmer.

The next day, military officials came to the village to draft young men into the army. Seeing that the son's leg was broken, they passed him by. The neighbors congratulated the farmer on how well things had turned out. "We'll see," said the farmer.

In this story, the farmer represents the wiser part of ourselves, the part aware that we can't know in any given moment whether something is "good" or "bad" in the larger picture of our lives, much less in the vast picture of the cosmos. If we attempt to judge each thing that happens, we find ourselves, like the farmer's neighbors, on a continuous roller-coaster of emotion; what looks good one day may appear bad the next, and vice versa. Of course, all of it is likely to look very different a year, five years, or a decade down the line. Since we cannot ever know what each event will bring or make possible, much less what is "right" or "best," we can save ourselves a lot of emotional energy by cultivating the farmer's non-reactive posture: "We'll see."

Attachment to outcome is, by its nature, a manipulative energetic current. In essence, when we are strongly attached to one outcome over another, it is as if we are trying to say to the universe, *I must have things* this *way, and not that,* or *You must do things* this *way, and not that.* Yet addressing the universe in such a way implies that we know more than it does about what would be most harmonious, or even what would bring us most joy—which, in fact, we cannot know. When our attachment is directed toward maintaining things as they are, we are resisting the dynamism of life. When we are attached to an outcome which is not yet manifest, we are placing ourselves in resistance to life's creativity. All of these states of attachment create a tension in the being, and pit us against the universe in a struggle which is erroneous, unnecessary, and counter-productive.

And of course, the universe always wins! This does not necessarily mean that the outcome to which we are attached will not manifest; sometimes the person who is sick *will* recover, or we *will* get the job or the house or the lover we so desperately want. The universe neither rewards nor punishes us; we neither induce a specific outcome, nor prevent it, through our attachment to it. Yet our attachment does negatively influence our own ability to live in a state of peace, harmony and trust with the larger currents of life.

In addition, when we do have a strong attachment to outcome and that outcome manifests, it fosters within us an unwholesome relationship to life.

If we feel vindicated or rewarded, our attachment to the next set of conditions or outcomes we believe is best may grow even stronger. If that next outcome doesn't manifest, we are likely to feel even more deflated, resentful, angry and betrayed by life, the universe, or God, as if a contract we thought had been signed has now been broken. All of these energetic loops result in a squandering of the energy which we might otherwise use in full and joyful cooperation with larger forces, those weavers of the tapestry whose design is so much bigger than we can see.

It is very difficult to grasp the operating principle of these larger forces from a human perspective. That's why we often imagine God as a judgmental, even punitive parental figure—someone rather like us, only much bigger and more powerful. In truth, assigning a form to "God," or to the active life principle in the universe, is like assigning a form to love. Love could, and does, take *any* form. Its essence is formless, yet we know with certainty when we are in contact with it. Its formlessness is not powerlessness; rather, its formlessness gives it the ability to inhabit, imbue and work through any form in the universe—and so it does, when we do not block it from doing so.

Not only do our attachments emerge from an inaccurate or incomplete vantage point, waste our energy, and fail to influence the direction of the universe; they also invariably create confusion and suffering both for us and for others. The only way to alleviate that suffering is by making a deep inner commitment, setting a new intention at the deepest levels of our being, to accept whatever *is,* whatever circumstances our lives bring. The poet Galway Kinnell says it beautifully:

> *Whatever* is *is what I want*
> *to want. Only that.*
> *But that.*

This acceptance of what *is* doesn't mean that we cannot also work toward change. What *is* is dynamic, not static; it changes constantly even if we do nothing—and we do have the ability to influence its change. The path to greatest influence involves saying *yes* to what is, rather than fighting it. This kind of surrender does not mean subjugation to inner or outer tyrants; it does not mean abandoning our own wills, our powers of discernment, our sources of joy—or even our own preferences. It simply means acknowledging and remembering that we are working within, and held by, a larger field of intelligence and compassion that is available to guide us, that knows and sees more than we do, and that is powered by love. The country-western song "I Thank God for Unanswered Prayers" makes this point in a humorous way, as the singer thanks God for not having given him the woman he wanted long ago—since he now recognizes that the woman he married has been a much better partner for him.

There is a fine art to acting in accordance with our own preferences and navigating by joy—while also accepting and trusting what comes, and remembering that we cannot truly know what is "best" for us, much less for anyone else. But all of us have experienced states of being in which we know ourselves to be both active and receptive, times we can feel "the wind at our back"—can feel life's energetic currents supporting our chosen movements, even as we also feel our movements being shaped by that wind. Our inner teachers can help us cultivate this posture, and as we do so, a new relationship of trust can grow between us and life. As Pema Chödrön says, "To lead to a life that goes beyond pettiness and prejudice and always wanting to make sure that everything turns out on our own terms, to lead a more passionate, full, and delightful life than that, we must realize that we can endure a lot of pain and pleasure for the sake of finding out who we are and what this world is, how we tick and how our world ticks, how the whole thing just *is.*"

47

The Role of Crisis

Any deep crisis is an opportunity to make your life extraordinary in some way.

—Martha Beck

Human beings tend to become attached to things as they are or have been, and to fear change—even when "things as they are" are profoundly misaligned with our inner design as individuals or as a species, and change is absolutely necessary. Most of us do everything in our power to avoid crises, yet a crisis is simply a point at which a certain pattern or energy movement becomes unsustainable, and must, therefore, give way to a different pattern. Crisis is therefore a gift to be welcomed, a blessing capable of bringing about a profound reconfiguration. When crises are allowed to do their work, or not prevented from doing their work, they make it possible for what we know as polarities to reverse, for darkness to turn itself inside out and reveal its facets of light.

Many years ago when I worked as an AIDS educator, I met a man whose story offers a poignant example of this principle. Jack told me that after his AIDS diagnosis he had felt increasingly embittered and alone; finally, after many months of depression, he decided that life was no longer worth living, and decided to kill himself after attending one last Gay Pride parade.

Then, on his way home from that parade, Jack got gay-bashed, beaten and robbed. When he woke up in a hospital bed covered with bruises, his state of consciousness had completely changed. He realized that he wanted to live—and to dedicate the rest of his life to helping other people with AIDS who felt as alone as he had. The very next day, still bandaged and black and blue, Jack hobbled into the San Francisco AIDS Foundation and volunteered to help start a support hotline specifically for people with AIDS.

The Chinese language recognizes the role of crisis in the strokes which are combined to form the word—characters which represent both "danger" and "opportunity." But the true danger lies in *not allowing the crisis to do its work*, thus preventing it from having the effect it is designed to have, in accordance with its own deep internal structure. Most often, when we manage to avert or short-circuit a crisis, we simply prolong cycles of darkness—thereby creating conditions in which the crisis, when it comes, will need to be even bigger on the level of form in order to accomplish its mission.

This is why it is impossible for us to know what should or should not happen. For instance, in the story above, would it have been better if a bystander had intervened before Jack got severely beaten? It's possible that the bystander's caring would have moved Jack so deeply that he would still have chosen to live—but it's also possible that, had he not been beaten so severely, he would simply have gone home and fulfilled his plan to kill himself. We cannot know what will result when we try to "help" someone.

Yet the tapestry of reality is vast—and each thread on it is important. If a bystander did witness a savage beating, and did nothing in response, what effect would that have on her? Would the guilt of that turn her against herself, and against life? Or would it transform him? Whose crisis is this, anyway? In a sense, a crisis belongs to each person who is touched by it, however peripherally. The possibility of transformation exists in and for each one of us, always ready to be activated when we allow it to be.

While the solution does not lie in "helping" others, it does not lie in "not helping," either. In fact, there is no solution, because on the highest level of being, there is no problem—there are simply myriad opportunities and choice-points in each of our lives. Only we can determine in a given situation what it means for us to choose love. And yet choosing love, whatever that looks like *to us*, is the only movement that can align us with the larger compassionate forces of the universe. Although we cannot know what specific impact we will have or "should" have, we can choose the energies we let ourselves be fueled by.

Until the mission of a crisis has been accomplished—that is, until the darkness inside a person or circumstance reverses into light—no real shift can take place. And yet each circumstance and individual is distinct, with its own uniquely calibrated tipping-point. Again and again that tipping brings us from darkness to light, both individually and collectively. How ironic, then, that most of us do everything we can to avoid reaching this point, or to forestall it in the lives of those we love. We may be forestalling the changes our spirits or theirs most deeply need.

This does *not* mean we should refrain from acting when we see someone in need. As a species with individuated consciousness, a species capable of harboring an intent to harm, it is harmonious for us to establish and maintain rules, laws and guidelines to try to enforce civil behavior. Yet whatever we do, acting from a feeling of duty, rage or self-righteousness will not create greater harmony; only acting from love can have that effect.

Everything in the universe exists on a multidimensional, constantly fluctuating spectrum of light and darkness. The exact nature of the relationship between this light and darkness is complex; they are not opposed to one another or in contradiction to each other, as is often supposed. Rather, they are aspects of one another, as is graphically depicted in the yin-yang symbol—which shows darkness and light nestled together, and each containing a portion of the other. On the level of the larger tapestry, neither is "better" or "worse;" each has its functions, as do literal night and literal daytime on our planet. Although we are accustomed to thinking of light as "good," and can therefore easily begin to imagine that darkness is "bad," it would be more accurate (though still an oversimplification) to think of darkness is being akin to the season we know as winter. Although there are crops that cannot grow in cold weather, many others actually require a time of cold in order to fully develop.

As a species, this is true of us, as well. In order to fulfill our inner design, we need to interact extensively with both darkness and light. And because we are designed to perceive phenomena within the framework of duality, we cannot truly recognize or choose light without also experiencing darkness.

On the level of the larger tapestry, there is nothing wrong. There is only what *is,* and since it *is,* it cannot possibly be wrong. There are no enemies and there is nothing that needs to be judged, eliminated, or vanquished, including darkness. Yet it is also true that there is an evolutionary process at work in our species in which what we know as "darkness" is primed to undergo a metamorphosis into what we know as "light." Because of this, wherever there is too much darkness within a given individual or circumstance, light is eventually created though a kind of alchemical, reverse polarity process. This takes place on both the macrocosmic and microcosmic levels.

We can observe this phenomenon in individuals who "hit bottom" with addictions or other destructive patterns, and afterward become able to make wholly different movements. We can see it in the stories of spiritual teachers who awaken into enlightenment after being ravaged by severe depression. And we can see it in the larger society in events such as the dismantling of the Berlin Wall, the fall of apartheid, and the replacement of a United States government that espoused simplistic "us against them" messages with one whose platform was based on unity. In each of these examples, the beneficial effects of crisis are at work.

And so, if a crisis looms in your own life, how can you respond? In one of his famous "Letters to a Young Poet," the great poet Rainer Maria Rilke had this to say: "So you mustn't be frightened…if a sadness rises in front of you, larger than any you have ever seen; if an anxiety, like light and cloud-shadows, moves over your hands and over everything you do. You must realize that something is happening to you, that life has not forgotten you, that it holds you in its hand and will not let you fall. Why do you want to shut out of your life any uneasiness, any misery, any depression, since after all you don't know what work these conditions are doing inside you? Why do you want to persecute yourself with the question of where all this is coming from and where it is going? Since you know, after all, that you are in the midst of transitions and you wished for nothing so much as to change…"

And elsewhere, Rilke also wrote: "Let life happen to you. Believe me, life is in the right—always."

Working With Crisis

When you experience a sense of crisis, when your human resources are exhausted, ask for help. Remember, your guides, higher self or God are ready and able to assist you in making the leap that will allow you to reap the healing benefits of this crisis, whatever they may be.

Times of crisis are ideal times to pray. Your prayer might be something like this:

Guides, I need and ask for your help. Please help me open myself to your support and assistance. Please allow me to feel, trust in and experience your love, compassion, wisdom and guidance. May I learn what I need to learn, see what I need to see, heal what I need to heal and transform what I need to transform through this challenging experience. May I act with love for myself, and love for others. I affirm that I am strong enough to make use of this crisis for my highest good, and I ask for help from you, and from all of the larger benevolent forces, in doing so.

I choose, decide and intend to allow this crisis to propel me forward, to help me grow in wisdom, integrity and strength. May this crisis help me more deeply connect with the core of light within my own being, and also serve as a vessel of light for others who are also in crisis.

Guides, please help me know, deep in my heart, that this crisis is a necessary step in my own evolution. May that knowledge replace my sense of overwhelm and despair with a deep faith in the larger workings of the compassionate universe, however mysterious those may seem to me in this moment. I ask for your help and your guidance, that I may I be supported and healed—whatever that may look like on the level of form. I am deeply grateful for your assistance, for the knowledge that you are larger, wiser, more loving and compassionate than I am, and that you hold me in your hands and bless me with your light. Thank you.

48

When There is No Solution
on the Human Level

Love is the only reality and it is not a mere sentiment. It is the ultimate truth that lies at the heart of creation.

— Rabindranath Tagore

We may understand, in the abstract, the importance of allowing crises to do their work. We may even believe, at least theoretically, that, as Rilke says, "Life holds us in its hand. It will not let us fall." And yet each of us experiences times in which it feels nearly impossible to hold onto those larger truths. When things occur that appear terrible and tragic on the human level—particularly when they directly affect us, or people whom we love—we may be plunged into a different sort of crisis, a crisis of faith in life itself. No matter how much wisdom we have cultivated, we may find ourselves entirely shaken, even despairing. Of course, like all crises, this experience can be transformational for us, if we can allow it to be.

When you encounter a problem or circumstance for which there truly seems to be no good human solution, the answer is love, and there is no answer. On one level, there is no problem. On another, there is no solution, and there is an insoluble problem. Love seems an "impractical" or non-specific solution, yet where there is sufficient love, it renders all other questions irrelevant. The answer—and the challenge—lies in removing our resistance to this plane so we can live our human lives ever more completely, while also remembering that our human perceptions are fragmented and distorted, that we can never see much with our eyes pressed so close to such a large tapestry.

309

Essentially, when we wrestle with a problem for which there *is no solution* at our current level of consciousness, we have two options: run or transform. To "run" means to flee from the level of consciousness on which we perceive the problem, or perceive it as unsolvable. There are many ways to run—denial, legal or illegal drugs, "insanity," sudden illness or injury, and even suicide—but they all amount to the same thing: an act of escape from perceptions we feel we cannot bear. The other option is to transform—to dissolve the level of consciousness on which there appears to exist no solution, or to allow that level of consciousness to dissolve so fully within us that we can simply step out of it, as from a husk.

Therefore, when life presents us with a dilemma for which there truly is no good human remedy, we face both a dead end and a portal. As a result of the distortion and inversion currently present in human consciousness, this is true of a great many human circumstances at this time. And yet when a circumstance touches us so deeply that our consciousness simply cannot, at its current level, abide it—and when we are committed to refusing any of the ways "out"—then we may instead receive access to the way "up." When this occurs, we are catapulted out of the limited frame in which we had perceived the dilemma, and into a much higher, deeper and wider point of view.

When this soul movement takes place, we may open to an entirely transformed experience of love. Rather than continuing to ask what to *do* or which action to take, we can allow ourselves to actually enter into the field of love—or allow the field of love to enter into *us*, which is, of course, the same thing. Love does not discriminate or differentiate; it rushes out equally and constantly to all things and beings, all forms and phenomena. It always has, and always will. It cannot do otherwise.

On a human level, when you confront an insoluble problem, it truly makes no difference what action you take. And yet when you allow the fullness of love—or of God, which is the same thing by another name—into yourself, into every nook and cranny and crevice of your situation, *or your perception of your situation*, then love becomes the solution that dissolves both the current problem and all other apparent problems. This love is a force like the sun: the sun that is always there, even when it cannot be seen from our earth because it is nighttime, or foggy, or raining. Where does the sun go at night, or when the day is foggy or rainy? Has it vanished? Has it left the earth behind, abandoned it? Has it ceased to exist, or ceased to shine? We know, of course, that the answer to all of these questions is No. We must remind ourselves that love works with us, within us and upon us in just the same way.

When there is confusion and torment within us, we can bring those emotions to the field of love—where they can simply be held just as a crying baby is held by a loving parent. When that happens, the illusion of separation, which was, of course, the source of the pain, dissolves. As Marianne Williamson says, "A miracle is a change in perception." By allowing the universe to change our perceptions—by allowing the force of love to bring us into contact with deeper levels of truth—we create the conditions for miraculous lives.

IV

Prayers and Intentions

Recently a client came to me and said simply, "I want to learn how to pray." She had been raised Catholic, and the prayers she'd memorized and recited as a child no longer held meaning for her—but no one had ever taught her how to develop her own form of dynamic, present-day communication with the Divine. Although she sensed that it was both possible and necessary, she simply didn't know where to begin. It is my hope that the 21 prayers that follow will show her—and you—how to engage the powerful tool of prayer in your own way. Although you are welcome to use the topics and words I've provided, the prayers will be even more powerful if you change and adapt them so that they are truly the words of your own heart and soul.

One way to understand the practice of prayer is to imagine that someone whom you trust deeply and absolutely—someone whom you know loves you completely, unconditionally and eternally—has asked you, "How are you? No, really, how are you? What do you most want and need? How can I help alleviate your confusion or suffering right now?" In fact, the larger benevolent universe—God, our guides, our higher selves—are actually beholding us with that kind of love, and listening to us with that kind of heartfelt receptivity, in each and every moment. Yet all too often we don't recognize their presence, and don't answer them—and when we don't communicate directly with them, their ability to help us is far more limited. Because they respect our free will, they rarely intervene in our lives unless and until we specifically ask them to. That's why prayer is so powerful; by requesting the kinds of help we most deeply want and need, we open doorways between our human selves and higher consciousness, creating channels through which that help can come.

Chapter 5, "Intention and Prayer: Inner Technologies of Change," describes guidelines for effective use of prayer, and outlines four major prayer styles. If you reread that chapter before reading the prayers that follow, you'll see the way I've combined those styles and made use of those principles. Again, these 21 prayers are just a jumping-off point. Each one of us could compose a new prayer, or many, every day. There are so many circumstances in our inner and outer lives which confound us, and in which we'd benefit from higher levels of assistance—why not ask for it?

Statement of Intention to Connect with Others and with Life

I decide, desire, wish, intend, to allow myself to feel deeply, to connect profoundly to others and to life, in every way possible. I accept what my personality sees as the risks involved in this, and welcome the pain and confusion and difficulty that may ensue, as well as the delight, joy and harmony; I ask for help in remembering that the risks are false, that what I truly am can never be harmed or destroyed. I ask for help in allowing that truth to bring me courage and I declare my willingness to stand naked and unprotected in this world, to experience all its forces and seasons.

I determine to facilitate, foster and nurture the permeability of my heart—so that others may more easily and completely feel me, and so that I may take others more fully into myself, not haphazardly, accidentally or compulsively, but with consciousness and with active willingness to allow myself to touch and be touched, engage and be engaged.

I ask for the willingness to be as fully present as possible, wherever and whenever and with whomever I can. I decide, desire, request, and intend to allow these changes for the sake of my own highest spiritual and emotional well-being, and to further my evolutionary progress, regardless of how it may look or feel moment by moment on the human level.

I affirm that by opening more fully to the forms and phenomena of this world, I am opening more fully to God, since God resides in each form and phenomenon. By opening more fully to other people, I open more fully to God. I open more fully to God, and to life itself. By opening more fully to myself, I open more fully to God, and to life itself. I affirm my desire, my intention and my willingness to further my openness to God in all of these as well as in all other ways, so that I may live more fully, and life may also live itself more fully through me.

⟲ *Prayer to Facilitate Internal Transformation*

I ask for help in remembering that I am fully capable of changing my internal matter, including all of those thoughts, feelings, beliefs and emotional patterns I have thought of as "mine." I acknowledge that on the human personality level, there are confusions and distortions within me, as there are within everyone, and I acknowledge, affirm and embrace my own ability to shift, heal or release those distortions. May the larger compassionate forces help me recognize and clear, soften, loosen, untangle, unblock and unknot all those places in my being that keep me apart from life, compassion and love.

I ask for help in releasing my sense of identification with my thoughts, feelings, beliefs and emotional patterns, and in remembering that who and what I truly am exists apart from these temporary configurations of internal matter. I ask for help in fully knowing and remembering that I am not my internal matter, and that therefore I can change that matter—just as I know that I am not my clothing, and can change my clothes as I choose.

I remind myself, and ask for help in remembering, that the locus of power is within me. I ask for help from God, my guides, and all the benevolent forces, that they may assist me in feeling that power and in skillfully using it on behalf of my own transformation of consciousness—so that I may change, transform, heal and evolve in ways that serve my highest good.

⟲ *Prayer for Healing and Releasing Illness*

I acknowledge the higher truth that every level of my own healing—physical, mental, emotional and spiritual—is entirely my own responsibility, and no one else's. I declare my intention and willingness to completely claim, acknowledge and accept this responsibility, and I ask for help from the larger compassionate forces in fully doing so, so that I may restore my knowledge of my own power, inner and outer, physical and non-physical, even as I co-create my life and health with forces larger than myself.

I affirm that it is only by accepting full and complete responsibility both for my own illness or imbalance, and for my own healing, that I can actually heal. I also acknowledge that "healing" and "cure" are not the same. If I have physical illness, I ask for help in generating sufficient non-physical energy to transform my physical condition; if physically irreversible injuries or disease processes have taken place, I ask for help in releasing judgment and expectation, notions of failure and success, so that I may enter more fully into the work of whatever healing is available to me at this time.

I ask for help from my higher self, guides and God in fully and completely accepting responsibility for my own healing, while also deeply opening myself to receive their help.

May I receive assistance in continually making the subtle yet profound distinction, on every level of my being, which enables me both to accept full responsibility for my own healing *and* to be fully open to receiving help from all truly compassionate sources inside and outside of me. May I be shown whatever imbalances, distortions or wounds are present within me, on any level of my being; may I cultivate and be given the strength, the courage, the clarity and the will to more fully allow the light, the forces of greater love, to work on and in me, rebalancing, untangling, clearing and healing me in every layer, part and aspect of myself.

If I work with a doctor, healer, therapist, chiropractor or other healing practitioner, I ask that the larger realms help me become receptive to all that that practitioner gives, shows or teaches me, and help in using those gifts in the service of my highest good and my most profound healing—while still remembering that my healing is my own responsibility.

I also ask for help in removing any projections I may have placed on anyone whose assistance I have sought, in any healing capacity, including

319

physical, energetic and mental health practitioners, as well as family members, friends, spiritual leaders and teachers. I affirm my intention to accept any and all gifts from these outer sources which can truly support me in my healing process, and also to gently relinquish any efforts or energies from these outer sources which do *not* serve me at the highest levels. I acknowledge that all human practitioners are simply that—human, and that each is on her or his own path; I ask that our teaching and learning, our receiving and giving be harmonious and fruitful.

I affirm the wisdom and discernment of my body, mind, heart and spirit, and ask for full participation of every level of my being in taking from others only that which truly serves my healing, and releasing that which does not. I affirm that just as my body is capable of wisely excreting vitamins and minerals in excess of what it needs, my heart, mind and spirit can also wisely and harmlessly excrete any energies, thoughts, beliefs, suggestions or projections that come from others in relation to my healing process, and that do not serve me.

I affirm that I, and only I—not my small personality-level I, but my larger I, my soul, my spirit, my Higher Self I—am capable of discerning what physical and non-physical methods and approaches best serve my healing, and I ask for help from that larger I. I ask that my larger self partner with my human self so that I can more easily and quickly recognize the approaches that hold benefit for me, and those that do not. May my higher self, guides and God give me the strength and determination to fully participate in the healing approaches that truly serve me, and fully withdraw myself and my energies from those that do not. And may I find and cultivate within myself the ability to fully embrace, to fully say *Yes,* to myself and my life, knowing that that *Yes,* that embrace, is healing in itself, and will also contribute immeasureably to further healing.

◎ Prayer for Releasing Someone on Their Own Recognizance

Note: this prayer is equally helpful and appropriate in relationships that are ongoing, as well as those that appear, on the level of form, to have ended.

I resolve, now, with all my heart, mind, body and spirit, with all the cells of my body and all the energies of my being, to let go of [say full name and relationship here: e.g., "John David Jones, my father"], to send him on his way—whatever that way may look like, on the level of form—with pure, undiluted currents of blessings, love, gratitude and appreciation.

I thank _____ for all the gifts he has given me, all the lessons s/he both taught and brought me, all of the ways in which those lessons came—including and especially those lessons I found painful or enraging. I honor the path of my own soul, and the ability of my soul to make use of and transmute each one of these teachings in ways that serve my highest intentions, and my highest good.

I affirm my intention to release _____ to his own karma, his own soul path and destiny. I release him on his own recognizance. I release him gladly, and with love and thanks. I honor all that he gave me, and also all that it appears, on the limited human level, that he took from me. I choose to relinquish any thoughts, feelings or beliefs that anything _____ did, or anything that occurred between us, was wrong in any way. In fact, I affirm my deep knowing that there *is* no wrong on the highest levels of being, and that the role of _____ in my life has been that of a teacher bearing gifts. I affirm my desire, my willingness and my ability to accept those gifts, to use them as fully and as harmoniously as I possibly can.

Say aloud, if possible, filling in the person's name and/or relationship to you—e.g. "I release you, John David Jones, my father."

I release you, _____, my _____.
I release you with love, compassion and blessings.
I release you from the hooks of my desires, opinions and expectations.
I release you from the barbs of my judgments, thoughts and beliefs.
I release you to your higher self, your guides, and to God, however s/he may appear to you; I release you to your own highest good, your own karma and destiny, whatever that may look like on the level of form. I acknowledge

that I cannot know your soul's path, your highest good, and that your life and being are not mine to judge.

I ask my higher self, my guides and God to help me dissolve the mental structures of judgment or desire that I may have imposed upon you, or upon our connection, or upon myself in relation to our connection, and I ask for help in releasing the belief that anything that happened between us has harmed either one of us. I affirm that my deepest healing and my highest self-interest are served by relinquishing any belief, idea or concept that I was in any way "victimized" by you, and allowing the deeper truth to enter and be known and felt by every level of my being.

I affirm that both my soul and yours are fully capable of learning and growing from any experience, no matter how difficult it may appear on the human plane. I acknowledge that I can only do my own learning, not yours; to that end, I ask for help from the higher realms in using all of my experiences, including all of my experiences with and in relation to you, in the service of my soul's evolution and my highest good.

I ask for help from all of the compassionate universal forces in understanding and fully experiencing the truth that everything that occurred between us, everything each of us did, thought, felt and believed, can serve my highest good. I affirm the vast wisdom, the magnificent creativity, the enormous loving power of my own soul, and ask for its help in embodying these intentions and prayers.

And as part and parcel of my releasing you, I ask that all of my energy which you might now be holding—any energy I gave to you, any energy you took from me—be returned to me now. I ask for help from my higher self, my guides and God in retrieving this energy, and ask that its return strengthen and serve me in my growth and healing. I also ask that any energies of yours which I might have taken, or which you might have given me, be returned to you now, that they may strengthen and serve you in your own growth and healing. I ask for help in restoring full, complete energetic integrity in relation to you in this way, and I send blessings that you may restore your own full, complete energetic integrity in relation to me.

I also ask for help in healing my heart, freeing it from any wounds or confusions it holds in relation to you. If anger, rage, fury, shock, hurt, grief and other emotions arise in my being as I work with these prayers and intentions, I ask that all of the compassionate wise forces and powers help these emotions to run their energetic course in my body and be transformed or released, while also helping me to remain fully present and connected to myself.

Finally, I ask for help in purifying the quality of the love I feel for you now. May that love be so illuminated that any strains of bitterness, regret, withholding or judgment simply burn off, so that the love that remains is so pure, bright and shining that simply feeling it brings healing to my heart. And, as I feel the full extent of the deepest, widest, purest love I ever felt for you, may I also receive help in directing that same love toward myself.

Prayer for Returning and Retrieving Energies

Note: you may use this prayer to return energies to, and retrieve energies from, a specific person—or, you can use it more generically, simply asking that all energies that belong to others be returned to them, and that all your own energy come back to you, no matter where it is or who may be holding it.

I ask that any energies which rightfully belong to _____, which I may currently hold in my own energy field, be returned to him/her/them now. I affirm my willingness to release these energies, and ask for help in returning them to their rightful place, so that they may further _____'s continued evolution. And I ask that any energies which rightfully belong to me, which _____ may currently be holding, or which anyone else may be holding, be returned to me now. I affirm my willingness to receive these energies, to joyfully accept and incorporate them back into my own being, to accept whatever new gifts and challenges they may bring me, and to allow myself to become fuller, stronger, larger, clearer and more powerful as my energies return to me.

Finally, I ask for help in accepting my own fullness and strength, my largeness and clarity, and more fully inhabiting these characteristics for the good of the world, and for my own highest good. May I use this largeness and clarity now to forgive myself for whatever harm I may have caused, including any harm I have caused to myself; may I forgive _____ and all others for harm they have caused me, or harm they have caused themselves. And, as I feel my power and strength increasing, may I move beyond the perception of harm; may I become able to recognize that even my most difficult and painful experiences with _____ took place as part of a trajectory of growth and love that I can come to trust, even though when it is too vast for me to see. May this understanding help me move beyond the need to forgive at all; may I open to the truth that forgiveness is not needed, because nothing is, was, or could ever be wrong.

May I celebrate myself and all that I am in this process of restoring my energetic integrity, and the energetic integrity of others. May I celebrate all that I know and have become through the circumstances of my life. May I fully and completely inhabit, claim and honor my life, with gratitude and with love.

⟳ *Prayer for Forgiveness and for Awareness*

I ask for the healing currents of forgiveness to wash through my being on every level, physical, mental, emotional and spiritual, particularly in relation to _____ [name of person and/or circumstance]. I ask that these currents bring opening, loosening, warmth and ease to any places which may remain cramped or closed inside of me. Guides, larger self or God, please help me to fully and completely forgive both _____ and myself for any and all mistakes we may appear to have made, even as you help me to remember that on the highest level, no mistakes exist.

I ask for help in glimpsing that larger tapestry in which I can better see all that I experience as "mistakes" as a necessary and even beautiful part of the larger design. I ask forgiveness for all of the ways I may appear, on the human level, to have caused harm, and ask for help in forgiving all the ways in which _____ may appear to have caused me harm. I affirm my deep regret for the human pain and confusion _____ and I have caused to ourselves and one another, even as I affirm that on the level of the soul, we have committed no harm, and no harm has been or could ever be done to either one of us, so that on the level of ultimate truth, there is therefore no need for forgiveness.

I affirm both my human self, which does need to grant and receive forgiveness, and my larger self, which dwells in a place of such wholeness, love, compassion and wisdom that forgiveness is rendered unnecessary. I acknowledge that on the higher levels of the universe, in the vast multidimensional tapestry, all that exists is already in balance and in harmony; yet I also affirm my willingness and intention to do my part, on the human level, to serve that balance and harmony with all the levels of my being, by aligning all of my thoughts, feelings, words and actions more and more fully with the currents and energies of love—which leads naturally and inevitably to soul-healing forgiveness, and also to the beautiful state of awareness that lies beyond forgiveness, in which I know myself to be one with all others, and with life.

Prayer for Becoming Able to Receive

I declare my intention to value, honor, nourish and attend to myself, and I ask all the compassionate larger forces to help me feel, know and recognize that self-care is an essential part of my purpose on earth. Please help me to feel, on every level of my being, the truth that my own heart, spirit, mind and body are completely worthy of receiving their full complement of life support. Please help me to know, with every cell of my body and every fiber of my being, that it is right for me to be fed; it is deeply right and in alignment for me to get, receive, and allow myself to have, what *I* want and need.

Please help me to recognize and release the misconception that I must go without, in order that others may have what they want and need. I affirm and take into myself on every level the truth that it is right for me to receive what I need, and it is fully within my role and purpose on earth for me to receive what I need. In fact, it is an essential part of my role and purpose that I honor and attend to myself and my own needs, not only alone but within all my relationships, both personal and business.

I affirm that I do not have to choose between others and myself. Please help me to know that I can give to others, help and love others, and still receive, whether from them or from other sources, exactly what I myself need. Please help me to remain in contact with the truth that it is right for me to honor myself in this way, and to expect, ask for and receive the honoring of the universe in this way. I declare, I affirm, and I remember that it is deeply right and in harmonious alignment with the universe for me to receive what I most want and need. I ask that this truth penetrate, saturate, infuse me and transform me on every level of my being, strengthening me to fulfill my inner design, to play the roles most harmonious to my being, throughout my human life. I acknowledge that I can only do what I came here to do—can only live from the fullest parts of myself—when I am feeding and nourishing that self, and also allowing that self to be fully nourished by other sources, physical and non-physical, human and non-human. Please help me know, sense, remember and feel that whatever help I need *is* available to me, and that I do deserve to receive it—and please help me become receptive to whatever help and nourishment come to me, even when they come in forms I did not expect, or fail to come in forms I expected or hoped for. Please help me to receive, and to flourish in and from that receiving.

꩜ *Prayer to Serve As a Vessel of Light*

I affirm my intention to bring joy to myself and to the world by serving as a conduit and a vessel for light, peace and love. I ask for help in more fully embodying these energies of light, peace and love, knowing their truths and accepting their brightness on all of the levels of my being: physical, mental, emotional and spiritual.

I ask to become more fully and powerfully aware of the blessings of light I am already receiving in every aspect of my physical being, in each and every one of my cells, my bones, my muscles and my organs, and in every circumstance in my physical life. And I ask that this recognition infuse my mental and emotional functions with light, so that all of my thoughts, beliefs and feelings can be transformed and illuminated, and can serve more and more fully as vessels of light.

I ask for help in continuing to grow in my ability to access, hold and radiate light, even and especially in the darkest corners of my own being, and of the world. I acknowledge that in order to carry light into places of darkness, I must be willing to travel into such places, and I affirm my willingness to do so. I know that in order to serve as a bearer of light I must be willing to see everything, both inside and outside myself, and flinch from nothing, and I affirm my willingness to see all that I am given to see. I ask for help in removing the distortions in my vision, so that I can see more clearly. And I ask for life's help in bearing all that I see in ways which do not wound or burden me, but only increase my commitment to holding light.

I also ask for help in working with all the knots, tangles, confusions, hurt or distortions that I encounter, both within and outside of myself, which would impede or weaken my ability to hold light. I ask the light within me to clarify my obscurations, release the misconceptions and errors in my thinking, and heal my emotional being.

I ask for help in opening myself more and more fully to receive the light and the love of the universe, so that I may also spread this light forward in all of my interactions and relationships, in every encounter with others, no matter how casual, as well as in my closest relationships, including, of course, my relationship with myself.

I affirm the power of all of my actions, including my mental actions, my thoughts, to carry light or to obscure light, and I ask for help, day by day and moment by moment, in choosing those thoughts as well as those actions that carry and serve the light. I affirm my desire, my wish, and my intention to use all of my actions to help myself and the world move closer to states of peace, love, harmony and well-being. I also ask for help in recognizing all of those places where my energies, actions and thoughts depart from this goal, and open myself to receive help in correcting those places in my being that are insufficiently aligned with light, so that I can more fully and completely serve as a vessel and a vehicle for light.

I affirm that as I take in more light from the universe, I will also have more light to bring to others, and as I bring more light to others, my ability and willingness to take in more of the light which surrounds me will increase exponentially, like the widening of a riverbank as more and more water flows through it.

I affirm my gratitude for the opportunity to be of service on this beautiful and troubled earth at this time in history. I affirm my intention to embrace all facets of life on this earth, to turn my head and my heart away from nothing. I ask for help in embracing this earth and this life exactly as they are, in saying Yes to life in all of its varied manifestations, no matter how distressing they may appear to me.

I affirm my gratitude for all of the help I have received already, from every person with whom I have ever interacted—from family, friends, partners, teachers, co-workers, and those whom I did not know. I affirm and acknowledge the help I have received from works of art and writing and music, from the beauty of nature and the wonder of animal life, as well as from my larger self and from the universe, and I ask for help in continuing to receive even more blessings, wisdom and teachings from all that I encounter, both within myself and outside of myself. And I ask for help in recognizing and making use of even and especially those blessings and teachings which come in difficult disguises, which are painful and difficult to bear, those which I long to reject or shun, and those which I wished with all my heart never to receive. I ask for help in recognizing and receiving the light at the core of these experiences and feelings, as well, so that I can make use of them, so that they can work with me and within me to transform my experience, increase my commitment, and serve as a vessel and vehicle for ever greater amounts of light.

And I ask for help in remembering this commitment more and more fully and completely as I go about my daily life, so that it can inform even my automatic and reflexive reactions and responses, infusing them with willingness to see what is there to be seen, bear what is there to be borne, and learn from all that I can. I thank the light and all the forces of light for working with, in and through me in these ways, for allowing me to consciously participate in the joyful enlightenment of the human plane.

Prayer for Embodiment

I declare that I wish, decide, desire and intend to bring my entire soul, all of the energies of my spirit, and all of the light I can access, into my physical body. I affirm that my physical body is the vehicle I have been given for use on this earth, and I ask for help in fully embracing and celebrating it, bringing all of myself to it, and housing myself joyfully within it. I ask for help in accepting all of the gifts and blessings, as well as all of the responsibilities and challenges inherent in having a physical form. I ask for help in learning all of the lessons and bringing myself fully to all of the opportunities my body brings me, in health and in illness, in ecstasy and in pain.

I also ask for help in loving the exact and specific nature of my own body in every one of its particular contours and forms, its abilities and limitations, and I ask for courage, grace and humility so that I can more fully receive the teachings my body offers me about damage and healing, about limits and the need for rest, balance, attentiveness, respect and gentleness.

I thank life and the universe for the opportunity to be here in a sensate human body, to touch the things of this earth, and be touched by them. I ask for help in remembering the blessings of my astonishing fortune—all of the nights when I have had a warm, dry place to sleep; all of the times when I have been hungry and had food available to me; all of the times and ways in which my physical body has worked well enough to allow me to see, hear, smell, taste or touch so many of the wonders available on earth and in physical life.

Above all, I ask for help in embracing the sacred vulnerability of embodiment, and affirm my embodiment as a teaching which can help me more fully understand and embrace all other embodied beings. I affirm my intention, my desire and my willingness to join the physical and non-physical aspects of my being in sacred partnership, so that my spirit can learn from, give to, and receive the gifts of my body, while my body is held within the larger, unbounded knowing and love of my spirit.

⟳ Prayer For Alignment

I ask for help in accepting, knowing, remembering and trusting that the tapestry of existence is far larger than I can see, and that greater designs are at work. Yet I also request help in continuing to find sense, meaning and purpose wherever I can, in whatever ways will serve my continued growth, healing and expansion, and in whatever ways will help me to carry more light.

Please, guides, help me to surrender the belief that I can ever know what should happen, and to loosen the grip of my desire for any particular outcome. I choose to remember that I will never know the end result of my actions, that my sphere of influence is limited to myself and to my intentions. I accept that others may believe I have caused them harm even when my intention was only to serve truth and light, and I reaffirm my commitment to serving only truth and light, while praying for peace to enter both the hearts of any who might believe I have harmed them, and my own heart.

I also ask for help in seeing clearly any areas of my life, my thoughts and my emotions where I am deluding myself, where I am thinking or feeling or acting in error, where I have hidden agendas or impure motives. I ask for help in surrendering, releasing, dissolving or healing any parts of me that do or might wish to cause harm to any other, for any reason.

I ask for integrity, for help in aligning all the forces of my own being more fully toward light, love and truth. I commit myself to the work of this alignment, and at the same time ask for help in accepting every circumstance and condition of my life exactly as it is, and every person I encounter, exactly as he or she is—or rather, exactly as he or she appears to be, from my limited vantage point of the moment. I acknowledge that each person has her or his own path, destiny, karma, higher self, and guides, and I release each person on his or her own recognizance, to his or her own forces of light and learning. I ask that the light I carry may serve as a candle to illuminate the journey of others, if they allow it to; but I also ask for help in fully accepting those circumstances in which, on a human level, it appears that I can do nothing.

I ask for help in glimpsing the greater order of things, the larger designs of the tapestry, whenever I am able to; and I also ask for help in remembering that there *is* a greater order, even at those times when I am unable to see it. I ask for help in beholding and loving and accepting this world exactly as it is, or as it appears to be, even as I work to hold more light and bring more light onto the human plane. May I do all that I do in a spirit of love, peace, acceptance, and gratitude for the light and harmony which are already present on earth; may I join in partnership with those forces, that I may both fulfill my inner design and play my part in the harmonious unfolding of human evolution.

Prayer for Mealtimes

I give thanks for my miraculous body: for my tongue and the exquisite taste buds which line it, which allow me to savor my food; for my saliva, which helps my body begin to break down my food in order to make use of it; for my nose and its ability to smell my food; for my teeth, which allow me to chew my food so that it can pass from my mouth to my stomach. And I give thanks, also, for all of the miraculous workings of my digestive system, for its ability to make use of what will nourish me, and for its ability to release what I do not need and cannot use. I thank all of the organs of my body for their participation in this elegant, intricate system which is operating within me at all times, every moment and hour and day of my life, even without my conscious awareness. And I affirm that by choosing to become more conscious of it, I am able to more fully appreciate and celebrate the miraculous wisdom and constant effort of my body.

Now, as I take in nourishment, I honor my human life, my physical being, and all of the forces, factors and phenomena which came together to create it, including my parents, grandparents and all of my other physical ancestors. I thank all those who worked to make it possible for this food to be here before me, those who planted and harvested it, those who helped it come into my hands, and those who prepared it. I thank the earth itself for its role in bringing this food into being; I thank the sun, wind, rain, insects and other creatures who contributed their efforts to the creation of this food, and as I eat, I ask for help in remembering and honoring my part in the vast chain of life. May I always know how fully and continuously I am supported by life, and may I also play my part in fully and continuously supporting others. May this food nourish me and strengthen me, that I may use that strength gratefully, and in service to life.

❂ *Prayer For Self-Acceptance and Self-Love*

I ask for help in fully and completely loving and accepting myself, exactly as I am in this moment. May I remember that as I become more able to fully love and accept myself, I grow closer and closer to seeing with the eyes of God, or the eyes of those universal forces which are most wise and most compassionate.

As I work to more fully accept myself, I also ask for help in fully accepting all others with whom I come into contact—in seeing and encompassing both their wisdom and limitations, their beauty and their frailties, along with my own. In this way may I recognize the truth that others and I are one. May my growing self-love spill over and help me love others; may the love I feel for others tip back toward me again, filling my own heart. And as I bathe in this healing spring of love and acceptance, may my heart grow deep and large enough to encompass even those others who are in this moment unable to see, love or accept me. May I see, love and accept *them,* and in so doing bring more light to their hearts, and also more light to my own.

I ask for help in remembering the truth that by allowing the currents of love and acceptance to flow freely through my being, I am contributing to the larger flow of harmony and peace among all of humankind. May I accept the work of loving myself as a sacred task; may I honor life as I honor myself, and serve all others by serving, loving and accepting myself in ever deeper, wider and more profound ways.

I affirm that it is completely possible and necessary to *both* fully love and accept myself exactly as I am, and to recognize all of my wounds, errors, limitations and distortions as they exist in this moment—while also remembering that all that is currently unhealed within me may be healed. I ask for help in opening myself to the vision and perception of life and the universe, which behold me exactly as I am: never denying my flaws or errors, never judging or blaming me for them, and also never believing that those flaws or errors are what I am.

As I love and accept myself more fully, may I also develop the capacity to see myself more clearly. May I see every aspect of myself, including my flaws, with eyes of compassion—and in that sight, may I find, develop, cultivate and strengthen the inner and outer resources that will help me transform whatever in me is in need of transformation. And even as I pursue this growth and transformation, I also ask for help in relinquishing any notion or idea or image of myself as flawed, defective, insufficient, wrong or inadequate in any way. I affirm my unique wholeness at this moment, regardless of internal or external conditions—while also affirming that part of my wondrous wholeness, adequacy, sufficiency and perfection is my ability to grow and change. I ask for help in growing and changing, moment by moment, in every way that serves my highest intentions.

I give thanks for the challenging and miraculous gift of my will, and I ask for help in continually using my will in alignment with my highest good, and with the larger tapestry, even when I do not know what that requires. I ask for help in aligning my will with that of the Divine, with all that I can recognize as most truly loving, peaceful, life-affirming and light-filled, both inside and outside of myself—and, in the course of that alignment, developing and experiencing complete self-acceptance and a deep, nourishing, restful and harmonious state of love for myself.

Prayer For Drinking Tea

As I drink my tea, I affirm my gratitude for all that went into the making of the cup, the vessel which I now bring to my lips; the development of the ceramic or plastic or metal or glass, the refinement of the material, the creation of the factory, the workers who worked in the factory, and all the processes and circumstances and efforts by which this cup came to be in my hands.

And I thank, also, the people who discovered the tea bush, *camellia sinensis*, and who learned over years to harvest the tea leaves and dry them, and those who owned and worked at the tea plantation where this tea came from, and those who developed the mechanisms to ship this tea to the country and city I live in, and who created and worked in the store that sold it to me.

I thank my mouth for being able to experience the sensation of this warm tea filling it, and my taste buds for tasting the specific and exact flavor of this tea, and my throat for providing a vehicle through which this tea enters my body, and the miraculous properties of both my body and this tea, which allow me to make use of the antioxidant properties of the tea in such a way that my health benefits.

And I thank life for creating me in this fashion, and creating my world in this fashion, so that I can sit here on a chair and sip warm tea and enjoy it, and recognize the miracles present in this moment, and be grateful for them.

Prayer For Times When Those I Love Are Suffering

When there is suffering among people I love, I give thanks for the ability of my ears to hear pain, the ability of my eyes to witness pain, the ability of my mouth and lips to speak in response, and the ability of my heart to contract and expand in response, knowing that all of these functions connect me more fully to the human experience, and therefore to myself. I thank life for allowing me to touch the nature of suffering.

And as I witness or listen to the pain of others, I ask for help in recognizing where and how it mirrors, and incites, and teaches me about my own pain. As I observe what may appear to me to be the blindness or weakness or limitations of others, I ask for help in seeing how it echoes my own, and in fully and completely loving myself, even with that blindness or weakness or those limitations; and I ask that this self-love translate into an increased ability to love others, exactly as they are in this moment.

I ask for help in doing whatever I can to alleviate the suffering of others, in a manner fully respectful both of my own path and theirs. I ask to be shown the wisest and most compassionate responses I can make, and I ask also for the ability, willingness and courage to make them. I ask for help in expanding my spirit, so that I may have the generosity to extend myself wherever I can be of service, wherever I can bring more light into a circumstance, quarrel, or difficulty. And I also ask for help in recognizing those times when the most loving action I can take is to compassionately withdraw from the circumstance, releasing the person or people involved with love and respect, trusting in their own higher selves and destinies to bring them to light, love and learning, however that may occur, and also releasing myself from responsibility for the choices and trajectories of others.

And if, as I listen to those who are suffering, it seems to me that there is a villain or wrongdoer, I ask for help in opening my heart toward that person, or people, or institution. I ask for help in recognizing how even those actions which may seem to me unjust or cruel or terrible stem from aspects of the human experience that live within me, too; and I ask for help in embracing the difficult gift of that humanness, and bringing light to the darkened places of my own being, and the beings of others, from which such actions come.

I also ask for help in being able to see the larger picture, in which what initially appeared to be "villains" and "victims" may grow more complex.

I ask for help in embracing that complexity, and recognizing it, too, as the human condition. I ask for help in expanding my spirit so greatly that it no longer finds "villains" or "victims" in any circumstance, but is always able to glimpse that larger picture.

And if I experience pain or anguish at the suffering of others, I ask for help in allowing light to completely surround that pain or anguish, suffusing it with light, until it transforms into a radiant emanation of compassion. May the radiance of that compassion fill me, soothe, nourish and heal me, and then spill out from me to help others heal and be nourished, too.

Prayer For Times of Suffering Among People I Do Not Know

When there is suffering in the world around me, among people or groups I do not personally know, I ask for help in activating the same inner recesses of understanding and compassion that move in me in response to the suffering of those whom I most dearly love.

I also ask for help in moving beyond those parts of my being that are conditioned to blame, judge, and find fault, so that I may move more fully into those parts of my being which see with a larger vision, which do not flinch from beholding suffering, but witness suffering in ways that bring illumination. I ask for help in remaining open and alive to the pain in the world, resisting the tendency to feel overwhelmed or to become numb, while also remaining connected to sources of inner and outer light which help me to bear my deep awareness and responsiveness to others' pain. I ask for help in shedding the tendency toward despair, and I affirm my intention to dwell in hope, and to embody hope.

May the suffering in the larger world serve me by touching and impacting me, exposing deeper and deeper regions of my being, and may the light then enter me more fully, healing all that has been thus exposed. And may I also serve the suffering by growing larger to contain this light; may I become able to extend my compassion and love to all the places, people and circumstances where such energies are needed in this world.

ꙮ Prayer For Times of Physical Injury or Pain

When my physical body experiences pain or disability, I ask for help in accepting whatever comes—with grace, and with the willingness to be deeply present with my own experience and to learn from it. I affirm that when I am deeply present with my own experience in this way, no experience, no matter how painful, is ever in vain. And I affirm my ability and willingness to make use of every experience, no matter how painful, in the service of my highest intentions.

I ask that this experience of injury or pain help me to deepen my compassion for the suffering of others, and also help me to connect more fully with the joy of others. I ask for help in deeply remembering that the joy of other beings can also infuse me with joy, even when my personal physical experience is difficult.

When any part of my body hurts or is injured, I thank that part of my body for communicating its vulnerability to me. I thank it for all of the work it has performed when it was not injured, or when it was less injured, which I may previously have taken for granted. I gratefully acknowledge its importance to the whole of my body and my life, and I pray for its well-being as I would pray for the well-being of anything or anyone that I love.

At the same time, I affirm the vibrancy and ingenuity of all of the other parts of my body; I thank them for whatever ways they may be compensating for the injured part, and I thank the whole of my body, its elegant and intricate systems which continuously support my life.

I also ask for help in learning whatever I can learn from this time of pain, fear and inconvenience. I affirm that there are lessons for me in the act of gracefully requesting and graciously accepting the assistance of others. I ask for help in dissolving, clearing or healing any aspect of my being which makes it difficult for me to request or receive that help. I affirm my need of help as an honorable aspect of the interdependence that I share with all other beings, and affirm my intention to fully receive and appreciatively take in any gesture made by another person to help me in my time of need, no matter how big or small it may appear to me. I also affirm that ultimately all assistance comes from life and from the universe, and I ask to remain alert to all of the many ways in which that assistance may come.

I ask for help in learning all there is for me to learn during this difficult time. May I become able to gracefully accept even those ways and times in which others do *not* come forward to help me, or in which I am unable to perceive their help and support. I ask for help in seeing the gifts both in what I do, and what I do not receive from others. I ask for help in releasing any sense of myself as a victim or martyr, and in taking full and joyful responsibility for myself, even when I am injured or sick, and even as I ask for, open to, and receive the support of other human beings, and of life itself.

May I connect more deeply and intimately with myself through this challenging experience. May I come to know more about my own patterns of thought, feeling and response, about my body, its needs, sensations, and forms of communication; about my relationship to others, and about my relationship to life itself. I ask for help in accepting this experience exactly as it is, and finding within it whatever gifts of insight and healing it can offer me; and I also ask for help in working toward my own healing, and toward the greater wholeness and integration of my body, mind, spirit and heart.

Prayer For Times When I Feel Lonely

When I feel lonely, I give thanks for the keenly alive heart within me that yearns for intimate contact with others. I acknowledge this yearning as an essential and precious part of my spirit, just as the physical sensation of hunger is necessary and precious to my physical survival.

I ask for help in recognizing all of the gifts that come to me through aloneness, and even through the experience of loneliness. I ask for help in receiving these gifts and the growth which can come about in my heart, mind and spirit during this lonely time.

And I also ask for help in allowing, opening to, finding and experiencing meaningful contact with other beings, and with life itself. I ask for help in recognizing all of the meaningful contact which may already be present in my life, which I may not have fully appreciated. I ask for help in widening the lens with which I view meaningful contact, and noticing all of those areas in my life which are already filled with contact—including contact with an animal or animals I call pets; contact with wild animals who live in my vicinity; contact with trees or plants or bushes or flowers that live nearby; and all of the daily contacts I have with other human beings, no matter how small they may appear, and no matter in what contexts they may come—the person who brings my mail or pours my coffee, the drivers in each other car on the street, the people who hurry past me without seeing me, the people in need, who ask me for money. I ask for help in opening my heart and all of my inner sensors so that I can more fully breathe in the nourishment of contact from each and every one of these various sources.

I also ask for help in recognizing my breath itself as a source of nourishing contact. I affirm that my breath is always with me, regardless of inner or outer circumstances; my breath is always able to willing to enter me deeply, then rise to the surface again, showing me that I, too, can dare to travel deeply into myself, knowing that I will always be able to emerge again at my own surface. I ask for help in recognizing, celebrating and learning from all the miraculous properties of my breath, including its ability to continually extract exactly what I need from the outer environment, and continually release what I do not need, what no longer serves me, into the environment again. I thank my breath for its steadiness, constancy and faithfulness in working with me and within me in this way, thousands of times each day, every day of my life. I ask for help in becoming more conscious of my breath, of all of the many gifts and teachings it offers me, all of the companionship and contact it provides to me, knowing that as I feel more and more fully in contact with my breath, I can enter a state of greater receptivity in which human contact, too, can come to me more easily, and enter me more fully, allowing me to participate more completely and more joyfully in the stream of life.

I also ask for help in accepting and welcoming whatever human contact is with me now, even when it takes forms that do not fit my expectations or desires. I ask for help in seeing and receiving whatever gifts are present in every encounter I have with other human beings, and also in all of my encounters with myself. I ask for help in opening my heart more fully, deeply and widely, so that all I experience can resonate more deeply within me, expanding my capacity to experience meaning, connection and love.

Please help me, guides, larger self and God, to recognize and dissolve those structures within my own being, those thoughts and emotions, which hinder me from finding and experiencing meaningful contact with others. Please help me take in and be nourished by such contact, wherever and however it occurs. And please help me, always, to feel *your* presence, to know that you are always with me, and to be strengthened and opened and comforted by your love.

Prayer For Times When I Believe I am Right

When I am believe that I am right, I humbly ask for help in remembering the limits of my own knowledge, awareness, wisdom and perspective. I affirm that there are many parts of the picture I cannot see, and much that I do not and cannot know. I ask for help in softening and opening, becoming less certain, and turning over the full force of my opinions to powers far larger than my personal self. I ask for help in trusting those larger and greater powers of the universe, knowing that events will continue to unfold according to some larger design beyond my comprehension. I ask for help in approaching the present circumstance, and all circumstances, with greater love, wisdom, discernment, patience and humility, so that I can be a vessel of light in whatever transpires, however it may appear on the physical plane.

I also ask for help in remembering what Rumi called "that field beyond wrong and right," remembering that ultimately what matters most is not whether I am "right," but whether I am able to hold peace, love and light in my heart—regardless of inner or outer circumstances, and what anyone else may say, think, do, feel or believe.

I ask that my sense of my own "rightness" be surrounded and infused by light, in order that its self-satisfied or self-protective coating may dissolve and be replaced, instead, by a profound internal certainty of my own merit, my deep intrinsic worth and value—and also a profound certainty of the intrinsic merit, worth and value of all other beings, especially those with whom I may disagree.

Prayer For Times of Strong Desire

When I feel a strong desire, I ask for help in holding the powerful current of my own wanting with grace, balance and love—love that extends both within, touching the deepest recesses of my own being, and without, to touch all that I experience as existing outside of me. I ask for help in remembering that the tapestry of my life is far larger than my current awareness, and that therefore, I cannot truly know what will be best for me, or even what will bring me most happiness. I cannot know what I will experience or learn if what I desire comes to pass, nor where I may be led if what I desire does not occur.

Therefore, I ask for help in remembering that receiving what I currently desire may not actually bring me the happiness I seek, and that that happiness, or perhaps rewards that are even greater, may come to me from unexpected sources or unimagined directions. I ask for help in trusting the universe and the largest aspects of my own consciousness to bring me that which will best serve my highest intentions, and I ask my guides, larger self and God to help me fully and completely accept whatever comes to me, whether or not it resembles what I believe I desire. Ultimately, I ask for help in trusting life itself, and trusting myself to find my own place within the vast and generous body of life.

⟲ *Prayer for Times of Despair*

When I feel angry at God, when the world looks to me like a random, cruel and unjust place, I ask for help in enlarging my vision, in seeing beyond the boundaries and limits of what I currently see. I ask for help in remembering that the tapestry of reality is far greater and more dimensional than I can perceive, and that therefore I cannot ever truly know what can or should or must occur. When things occur that seem to me to be wrong, painful, unbearable or tragic, I ask for help from the larger compassionate forces, that they may bring comfort and tenderness to my aching heart. And I ask that, as they comfort my heart, they also expand my range of vision, helping me to see further and more deeply, to glimpse the larger picture unfolding, or at least remember with certainty that there *is* a larger picture.

I ask for help in trusting God, trusting the benevolent forces in the universe, trusting my own evolutionary process, and the evolutionary processes of all those others with whom I share the planet Earth. May we together find ways to serve in each others' fullest unfolding, and in the full unfolding of human destiny; may we each play the parts our spirits are most suited to playing; may we experience connection, gratitude and light; may we be strengthened and nourished, comforted and inspired on this difficult yet beautiful human journey.

I acknowledge that life is a difficult and unwieldy gift, and I honor those parts of me that struggle with or even wish to reject that gift, but I also ask for help from the higher realms, that those parts of me may receive the healing they need. I ask for help in embracing my life, my physical human life. I affirm my willingness and desire and choice to say *Yes* to this life, just as it is, with all its conditions, all its apparent curses and blessings. I ask for help in remembering that I cannot truly know which events are curses, and which are blessings. I ask for help in redirecting the strong current of my will, which so often moves toward judgment and rejection, so that it may move instead toward understanding, acceptance and embrace, both of my own particular life in this moment, and also the larger life. I ask the higher forces to help me heal my despair, and enliven the core of hope within each of my cells. Please help open me to small glimmers of contact and connection, whatever their source.

May I notice the tree outside the window, or the tired face of the person in front of me in line, or the comfort of driving in my car, or the food available to me. May I notice that there are people in this world who know my name, who smile at me, even if our contact is brief. May I notice that I too know the names of others, and can smile at them, and can hold them in my heart. May I remember always that I am held—that all of us are held—within the larger heart of life itself.

Books, Teachers and Other Resources

Campbell, Joseph—*The Soul's Code* and other books

Castenada, Carlos—*Journey to Ixtlan: The Lessons of Don Juan; The Way of the Yaqui*

Chödrön, Pema—*When Things Fall Apart* and other books

Conner, Janet—*Writing Down Your Soul*

Forrest, Steven—Spiritual astrologer; ForrestAstrology.com

Goleman, Tara Bennett—*Emotional Alchemy: How the Mind Can Heal the Heart*

Gucciardi, Isa—Founder of the Foundation of the Sacred Stream, which offers a wide variety of shamanic workshops; www.SacredStream.org

Hanh, Thich Naht—*The Heart of the Buddha's Teaching* and other books

Harner, Michael—*The Way of the Shaman* and other books; founder of the Foundation for Shamanic Studies, which offers a wide variety of shamanic workshops; www.shamanism.org

Hoffman, Jennifer—Channel for Archangel Uriel; www.UrielHeals.com

Ingerman, Sandra—*Soul Retrieval, How to Heal Toxic Thoughts;* teacher of soul retrieval and other shamanic practices; www.SandraIngerman.com

Ingerman, Sandra and Wesselman, Hank—*Awakening to the Spirit World*

Jung, C.G.—*Memories, Dreams and Reflections*

Katie, Byron—*Loving What Is: Four Questions that can Change Your Life*

Kornfield, Jack—*A Path with Heart: A Guide through the Perils and Promises of Spiritual Life*

Lyon, Bret—Teacher of practices to heal shame; www.HealingShame.com

Madden, Kristen—*The Book of Shamanic Healing*

McGinnis, Ann—Founder of Wildheart Enterprises Life & Career Coaching; excellent, highly intuitive coach; see www.Wildheart-Enterprises.com

Meiche, Michele—Host of the Blog Talk Radio show *Awakenings*

Mitchell, Edgar—Founder of the Institute of Noetic Sciences

Moore, Thomas—*Soul Mates* and other books

Pathwork, The—www.Pathwork.org: lectures channeled by Eva Pierrakos, all available without cost online, and also available in various books, including *The Pathwork of Transformation*

Roberts, Jane—*Seth Speaks* and other books

Saly, Judith—*Creating Union: The Pathwork of Relationship*

Salzberg, Sharon—*Faith: Trusting Your Own Deepest Experience*

Tallard Johnson, Julie—*The Wheel of Initiation: Practices for Releasing Your Inner Light;* JulieTallardJohnson.com

Temple-Thurston, Leslie—*The Marriage of Spirit;* Founder of Corelight, "An international non-profit dedicated to the awakening of the global heart;" www.CoreLight.org

Thesenga, Susan—*The Undefended Self: Living the Pathwork*

Thomaides, Kelli—"More Will Be Revealed," www.TaoPractice.org

Tolle, Eckhart—*A New Earth, The Power of Now*

Torbett, Nichola—Founder of Seminary of the Street and Recovery from the Dominant Culture; www.seminaryofthestreet.org

Vajta, Stacy—Founder of Expanded Pathways, a resource for energy healing; see www.ExpandedPathways.com

Ware, Bronnie—*The Top Five Regrets of the Dying*

Weiser Cornell, Ann—*The Radical Acceptance of Everything;* originator of Inner Relationship Focusing, www.FocusingResources.com

Williamson, Marianne—*A Return to Love* and other books

Zeta, D.L.—Channel; see www.CelestialVision.org

Made in the USA
Coppell, TX
04 December 2020

42974800R00206